Dave Robinson #89

Roger Author

Lori Keck
chapter 16

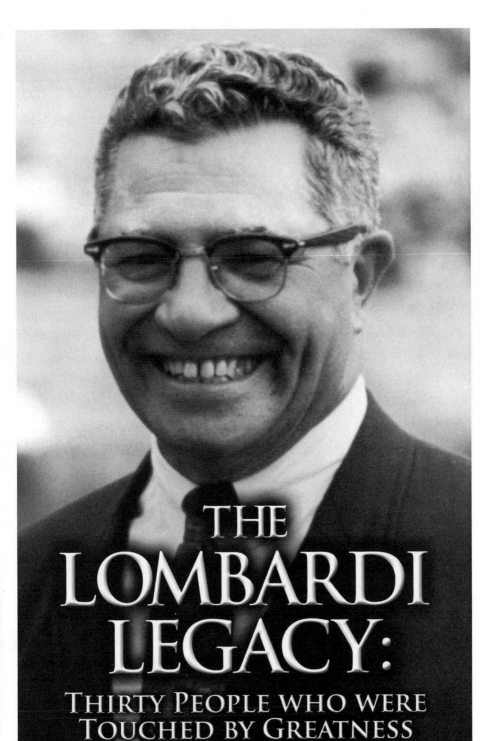

# THE LOMBARDI LEGACY:

## THIRTY PEOPLE WHO WERE TOUCHED BY GREATNESS

### DAVE ROBINSON & ROYCE BOYLES

©2009 Royce Boyles

Publisher: Goose Creek Publishers, Inc.
4227 Vermont Avenue
Louisville, KY 40211
502-384-5109

For sales, signings and personal appearances please contact:
Royce Boyles
608-524-9699
royceb99@msn.com
www.TheLombardiLegacy.com

Cover photo: Vernon J. Biever, copyright.
Book and Cover design by Bobby Durham.

ISBN:  Trade Casebound 1-59633-021-X  $24.95

# TABLE OF CONTENTS

# DEDICATION

*To my parents, Leslie and Mary Robinson, for their guidance and direction; and to my wife, Elaine, for being a true partner and teammate in life. (Dave Robinson)*

*With love, respect and gratitude to my parents, Frank and Stella Boyles. (Royce Boyles)*

# ACKNOWLEDGEMENTS

# THE LOMBARDI LEGACY

Without the support of two remarkable women, Stella Boyles and Lori Keck, it is difficult to envision our project reaching completion. Please accept our love and appreciation.

Each person who agreed to be a part of this book will be extra special to us forever. Thank you and God bless you.

We would like to thank Tom Murphy and the staff of the Green Packers Hall of Fame, Art Daley, legendary Green Bay Press-Gazette writer and originator of the Green Bay Packer Year Book, Dana Caffey, Tom Brown and his Rookie League, and Buckets for Hunger. David Zimmerman's direction put us on a clear track to the finish. Beyond description, former Packer Publicity Director Chuck Lane has been insightful, supportive and emblematic of Vince Lombardi.

We were privileged to receive rare, personal pictures from several people who are acknowledged on the photo pages. Dianne Koeppler was especially kind supplying very rare photos of two best friends; Vince Lombardi and Jack Koeppler. The great Vernon Biever and Pete Mozina from the Gallery of Sports Art were most helpful and cooperative supplying photographs.

A sincere "thank you" to Scott DeLaruelle for his tireless work and genuine encouragement. His buddies Scott Feilstead and Randy Milepske were most helpful regarding audio and video portions of the The Lombardi Legacy.

A very special group of men, Duane Frey, Joe Nelson and John Spalding. These gentlemen are real men.

Boyd Dowler supplied a refreshing perspective in his usual efficient, dependable fashion. Thanks 86.

# THE LOMBARDI LEGACY

By writing our afterword, Packer President Emeritus Bob Harlan, once again, stepped from the shadow of Mr. Lombardi to cast one of his own and embrace the team's great tradition.

To one of Vince Lombardi's biggest admirers, Baseball Commissioner Allan H. "Bud" Selig, we extend our appreciation and best wishes as he serves as guardian of our great game of baseball.

The graduating class of 1966, Lincoln High School, Wisconsin Rapids, Wisconsin was a continual source of inspiration and dedication. To all of them; Sully, Pauline, Ebby, Jake, Mr. "C," Barb, Mary Jo, Mike, Jenny, Dan, Harry, Bob, Karleen, and the list goes on. Also, Scott Keating a friend and hero.

Keeping an eye on the home front, allowing time to travel, and to secure interviews was made possible by Jane Beran; thank you.

Special thoughts were continually with Lucille, Ray, Bob, Kent, Dale, Debbie, Tom, Tammy, and the boys and Ray A.

# FOREWARD
## BY BOYD DOWLER

# THE LOMBARDI LEGACY

This is a book that needed to be written for football fans to read. Vince Lombardi did things as general manager of the Green Bay Packers that were incredible. Many of his greatest accomplishments were invisible to those outside the organization.

I was a rookie the year Vince came to Green Bay, so 1959 found me in the right place at the right time. I was one of nine Packers to play all nine years in Green Bay while Vince Lombardi was head coach and general manager. Additionally, I was there in 1968, when Vince was general manager after turning the head coaching job over to Phil Bengtson.

During my forty years working in the National Football League, I worked with and for eight pro football organizations. When I consider the bosses, head coaches, general managers, even owners that I've been associated with, no one influenced people's lives like Vince. For instance, there was a broader influence from Vince Lombardi than there was from George Allen and that's not a knock on George. Vince was that special. He had real insight into the person individually and the collective whole. He was able to separate the individual from the team and yet motivate not only on an individual basis, but on a team basis. There wasn't any other person I've been around who was able to do that.

I was part of something very special, the NFL's first dynasty of the modern era. Our team winning five World Championships in seven seasons and three in a row has not been equaled. In the long history of the National Football League, no team has ever won three consecutive world Championship games. We did that in 1965, '66 and '67. It kind of irritates me that it is seldom mentioned we won three in a row. We won three titles in a row before they called it the Super Bowl and nobody ever seems to remember that. It doesn't matter that the Super Bowl hadn't been invented, it was still the last game of the year and it was still the World's Championship. That unprecedented and unequaled accomplishment is mostly lost on pro football fans. If the Super Bowl would have started one year earlier, if we would have won the first three

# FOREWARD

Super Bowls, our three consecutive championships would be more obvious.

General Manager Vince Lombardi turned the Packers into a model franchise for the National Football League and in the process became a figure of national prominence. Most, if not all of us who were there, did not know the scope of his impact regarding non-football issues. This book, *The Lombardi Legacy*, reveals new dimensions of the depth and width of his fairness and humanity.

Good things happened for my wife Pat and I while we were in Green Bay. Our kids were born there and we made a lot of really good friends and the team won. Pat and I were married in January of 1961. We won the first championship that year, so she claimed she was the reason we won right away. Her first year as a Packer wife was '61, which meant we were champions the first two years we were married. I loved the Green Bay fans, I thought they were wonderful and they were a tremendous influence on my life.

My former teammate, Dave Robinson and author Royce Boyles have combined to compile a truly unique, refreshing look at Vince Lombardi. I was amazed to read something new about him in each chapter. *The Lombardi Legacy* has new, funny, touching stories about the great man and those close to him. Dave and Royce present Lombardi as he has seldom been seen; standing for racial equality, negotiating contracts, interacting with families, standing down the Packer executive committee, standing up to an NFL commissioner, anguishing as general manager, all of this and more awaits the reader.

The Packer Dynasty of the 1960's was due, in large part to, legendary Head Coach Vince Lombardi. General Manager Vince Lombardi played a huge role as well. In magnificent trades, he got Willie Davis and Henry Jordan from the great Paul Brown. He switched players from offense to defense, from position to position, he was a much better general manager than has been recognized. During his first three years, he acquired four future Pro Football Hall of Famers. Ironically, Lombardi was an offensive coach and those four, Henry Jordan, Willie Wood, Willie Davis, and Herb Adderley played defense.

# THE LOMBARDI LEGACY

Three of them were moved from offense. Vince Lombardi was a team player.

We started the '59 season with three wins and all of a sudden our eyes opened up and we realized if we would do what he was asking, or demanding of us, we would win. He was consistent with that; it wasn't much different in 1959 as it was after we won in '61. It wasn't cute and clever; it was just tough, hard nosed football.

Vince and Marie Lombardi valued the contributions made by Packer families and rewarded them. My wife Pat and I appreciated the Lombardi's respect for our family. It's not as if there was a real social closeness with Vince, he didn't hang out, and we didn't go to dinner with him and stuff like that. Although, I was at his house for Christmas Dinner once, that almost blew me away. He invited me, my wife, Paul Hornung, and Paul's mother in 1962. He came up to me in the locker room and said, "We want you to come over for Christmas Dinner." I foolishly said, "Well, I'll check with my wife." My answer should have been, "That's just fine, I look forward to it." I was kind of shocked; quite frankly, it wasn't something that struck me as, "Boy, this is something I really want to do." That was in '62 and we were all pretty young, but it was a comfortable occasion and we all did well that day. Marie was very good with the wives and families and my wife fit it well, so that made it all the better.

Dave and Royce give credit, long overdue, to Marie Lombardi. How can you not be moved as you read Olive Jordan Frey's account of Marie's support and compassion in Olive's times of need? Marie Lombardi was a team player.

Congratulations to Dave Robinson and Royce Boyles for a compelling new and revealing look at the great Vince Lombardi. I was one of the fortunate ones to be "Touched by Greatness."

**Boyd Dowler**
**Green Bay Packers, 1959-1969**

# INTRODUCTION

# The Lombardi Legacy

Vince Lombardi is generally considered the greatest football coach in the history of the National Football League; however, he was the Green Bay Packers' General Manager one year longer than he was their coach. His accomplishments as head coach overshadow the tremendous job he did as general manager. When he left the New York Giants as an assistant coach in 1959, and accepted the duel position of Head Coach and General Manager in Green Bay, it was with the understanding his power would be nearly limitless. He quickly set out to make sure that was understood by all.

He directed the once proud franchise out of the dark ages by building new offices next to the stadium, replacing cramped quarters in a downtown hotel and instilling a new culture of pride, discipline and winning. The team logo, that familiar and famous "G" on each side of the Packer helmet was designed and first used in 1961, as per his request. Players traveled wearing matching sport coats, slacks, shirts and ties. Lombardi set the standard for a professional image.

As general manager, he was concerned with everything from player procurement, team image, equipment approval, office decorum, ticket sales, equipment room organization, parking lot striping, grass growth, to toilet cleaning. You get the picture. Quickly he had the best team and the best parking lot stripers in the NFL. He demanded and achieved excellence in everything and possessed an unbelievable capacity to manage it all. His unprecedented success was accomplished without a hint of cheating or scandal. Lombardi did it better than anyone before or since, and he did it the right way.

His complete renovation of, and long-term impact on, the franchise was put into perspective by former Publicity Director Chuck Lane who pointed out, "there has not been an unsold ticket for a Green Bay Packer home game since Lombardi's first year." Seating capacity was increased almost two thousand per year during the Lombardi Dynasty.

Lombardi's teams won five World Championships in nine years. It took him just one season to convert the franchise worst (1-10-1) team of 1958, into a squad that went to the title game in his second year. His 1960 Packers missed winning the crown by eight yards in a showdown with the Eagles. He would never again lose a championship game.

In the next seven years, he won it all five times. Green Bay won championships in 1965, '66 and '67, including Super Bowls I and II. Only one other time in league history has a team won three straight, and that was the Packers of 1929, '30, and '31. Pro football was still in it's infancy as the Packers were founded roughly a decade earlier in 1919. Given these coaching accomplishments, it is little wonder his achievements as general manager have been overlooked.

Just as his coaching accomplishments eclipse the actions of general manager; his explosive and domineering image dwarfs his cerebral abilities. During the 1940's while employed at St. Celia High School, he taught three subjects, chemistry, physics, and Latin. That is a staggering array of skills which separated him from other guys with whistles around their necks.

In 1936, the NFL implemented the draft of college players in an attempt to insure competitive balance and parity. The team with the worst record got to pick the first player, the second worst selected second and so on. Therefore Lombardi's success as Coach penalized him as general manager. The more he won the later he drafted. He and his organization overcame the obstacles created by the head coach.

History has not been particularly kind to Lombardi regarding the job he did adding talent to his roster. Except for Ray Nitschke, every starting player on defense for the 1965-'67 championship run was acquired by Lombardi and his personnel department. On the defensive line, it was Willie Davis (trade), Ron Kostelnik (draft), Henry Jordan (trade), and Lionel Aldridge (draft). He added Dave Robinson (draft) and Lee Roy Caffey (trade) to go with Nitschke to assemble the sixth best group of linebackers in NFL history. All of the defensive backs, Herb Adderley (draft), Bob Jeter (draft),

# THE LOMBARDI LEGACY

Willie Wood (free agent), Tom Brown (draft), and Doug Hart (free agent) who received significant playing time, were obtained by Lombardi. Equally impressive, he was an offensive coach, but his astute eye for talent built one of football's best defenses in recent times. No general manager has won three consecutive NFL championships in the modern era except for Lombardi. It is the goal of our book to bring attention to his remarkable achievements.

The content of our publication is highly reliant on direct quotes from many who, at one time, or another and for years at a time, were locked in orbit around Lombardi and his Green Bay dynasty. We selected 30 people who encountered him in various roles and dimensions, therefore, offering a unique look at this immensely talented and successful man as a general manager and human being. It stands to reason only very special people would measure up to his perfectionist standards, thrive in the environment and cherish the experience. A fascinating woman in her own right, Marie Lombardi had an active role in unifying all members of the organization, but especially the Packer women and she is respectfully recognized in several chapters.

Our subtitle, "Touched by Greatness," was originally chosen to depict a linear cause and effect relationship. Lombardi touched others with his greatness and made a lasting impact on them. It has become abundantly clear the dynamic was circular; the greatness of those around him complemented him as well.

The concept of synergism means one plus one equals something more than two. In Lombardi math that means him plus this one, that one and that one equals five World Championships, and a business that ran as smooth as a sewing machine. The huge collection of talent combined with a dedication to excellence, driven by a leader who would settle for nothing less, made the Packers a model organization to be envied and copied by other NFL franchises, perhaps by all American sports franchises.

The NFL benefited immensely from Lombardi's dominance of the

# INTRODUCTION

1960's. It was he who was the face of the game as the league experienced meteoric growth in its popularity. His Green Bay Packers propelled the game to the forefront of American sports.

We have tried to avoid repetition of many of the well known, but often told stories surrounding this great man. We hope we have portrayed a picture of the total transformation he performed on the organization he controlled for 10 years. Much of that change came directly from decisions he made as general manager. Today, the surviving members of the Lombardi Packer era are a wonderfully unique reflection of him. As a group, they are good citizens, good mothers and fathers, grandparents, friends and neighbors. Because they won so much for so long, they stayed together long enough to become a family over the years and decades. Black and white, offense and defense, their connections are a continuing product of one man's will to make sure all had the chance to fairly compete and win.

In the history of the National Football League, there may never have been a more important figure than Vince Lombardi in regards to advancement for minorities. Among his accomplishments, co-author Dave Robinson was the first starting black linebacker in the league's modern era. Stereotypically blacks were viewed as too dumb to play the position. Dave, who graduated from Penn State with a 3.2 grade point average and a degree in civil engineering, played linebacker well enough to make the NFL 1960's All Decade Team. Dear stereotype, rest in peace.

Lombardi stood up to powerful Commissioner Pete Rozelle when Rozelle wanted to stop a black Green Bay player from marrying outside his race. It is detailed in Vicki Aldridge Nelson's chapter. One of the reasons he won so much was directly the result of the quality black players he acquired, and the fact he treated them like individuals. One of his first personnel moves was to acquire a black defensive back, Emlen Tunnell, from the New York Giants. Tunnell's football accomplishments earned him induction into the Pro Football Hall of Fame. He was a better person than he was a player. It was

# The Lombardi Legacy

a true stroke of genius to put a veteran black player, who knew the coach, in the locker room. Lombardi had the foresight to realize high quality football players who happened to be black were part of a successful future and he helped usher it in. All of this occurred in the late 1950's and '60's when our nation was mired in a disgraceful, prolonged racial struggle. Yet Lombardi pulled it off without a hitch.

As you read, may you find much new and important information about this iconic American figure who has not left the national consciousness some 40 years after his death. To merely view Vincent Thomas Lombardi as the greatest football coach of all time, as significant as that is, would be to sell him woefully short. It is our hope to shed light on his magnificent accomplishments as a human being and general manager. After reading just a single chapter, it is our hope you never view him the same again.

Dave Robinson

Royce Boyles

# Chapter 1
# Gary Knafelc:

*"Coach Lombardi was the best thing
that ever happened to me."*

# THE LOMBARDI LEGACY

It is fair to say Gary Knafelc (Kuh-NAF-ul) was the first Green Bay Packer to realize he could be a more complete player and person because of the influence of Vince Lombardi. At 6' 4" and just 220 pounds, he was quite small for tight end, but to his credit, became the first Packer to play the key position in Lombardi's Power Sweep.

Out of the University of Colorado, Gary was drafted number two by the Chicago Cardinals in 1954 before signing with Green Bay as a free agent that same year. The dismal Pack won just 18 times in those five years before Lombardi's arrival.

Gary had some nice years on those Packer teams, including a 40-reception, eight-touchdown season in 1955. On City Stadium Dedication Day in 1957, his touchdown reception sealed a 21-17 win over the Chicago Bears. Green Bay's former number 84 caught the last pass in old East Stadium and the winning toss in the new one. Following the win, Green Bay fans carried Knafelc off the field, making him the only Packer player ever to be so honored. The likeable receiver became a critical component in the transformation to World Champions. Following nine years in Green Bay, he concluded his playing career with a one year stint in San Francisco with the 49'ers.

At the invitation of Lombardi and with a love for the Packers, Gary served as public address announcer for Green Bay home games for 40 years beginning in 1964. Inducted into the Packer Hall of Fame in 1976, Gary and his wife Emily have made Green Bay home since 1954.

As sorry as the Packers were when Lombardi took over, it was even worse in '54 as Gary Knafelc began his pro career. "When I got to the Packers we had nothing. We were at the East High School; our locker room was under the stadium. We had metal mesh lockers with the wooden seat and wire on the side. When we went to get our equipment, we walked outside of the stadium and there was a shed made out of wire and the shoulder pads were lying on the dirt floor. I looked at them and said, 'We had better ones in high school.' I called my dad and had him send me the shoulder pads I wore in the

# GARY KNAFELC

All Star game; I wore those for three years. We didn't have anything. When Coach Lombardi came we had already moved into the other stadium." Gary refers to City Stadium, later named Lambeau Field.

Knafelc's humor adds to the fascination and authenticity of his recollection of the dog days of the Packers and subsequent resurgence during Lombardi's regime. He recalls his first encounter with Vince Lombardi, laughingly he states, "The first time I met him, I was at a hockey game. Vern Lewellen was the business manager at that time, and he walked over and said, "I want you to meet Coach Lombardi and Marie." – they were at the hockey game; I wasn't aware they were there. I went over and met him. The first thing that happened, Marie said to Coach Lombardi, "Doesn't he remind you of Frank Gifford?" and I said, 'Well, I hope I can play as well as Frank did,' you know, polishing the apple a little bit. He looked at me and said, "I want to see you tomorrow morning in my office at nine o'clock."

"Yes, sir." So I went to his office the next day, walked in the door, and he says, "How much do you weigh?" I was a wide receiver for five years. "Two-twenty"--I lied.

"You're going to play tight end for me."

I looked at him and said, "Coach, I haven't hit anybody in five years."

"Where would you like to go?"

"You just found yourself a tight end."

"That was my first meeting, so I knew immediately if he could make a tight end out of me, he *was* a miracle man."

Knafelc was in the first full team meeting with Lombardi and witnessed the unthinkable. In front of the entire squad, having never coached a game in Green Bay, the first year coach ordered Dominic Olejniczak, Packer President out of the room.

Gary explains, "When he came here, he was in charge of the Green Bay Packers—which meant he was in charge of every *phase* of the Green Bay Packers, and no one ever questioned his authority. So when anyone walked

3

into his meeting, while he was talking to his players, they were intruding, and for him, that was unacceptable. Olejniczak and Art Daley of the Green Bay Press-Gazette walked in one time —just opened the door and walked right in—he stopped our meeting, turned around and said, "Get out. Don't you *ever* come into my group when I'm talking to my men." They never came back again."

A total upgrade for the team was part of Lombardi's prescription to change his new team's culture as Gary describes, "We stayed in better hotels, but travel was the big one. We always played the last two games on the West Coast (Rams and 49'ers) and took a train out of Chicago; it took us three days to get there. We didn't fly, we stayed in lousy hotels. When we did fly, there was a box lunch in your seat. When we went down to Winston-Salem (preseason), we flew in two DC-3's and split the ball club up according to weight and position, so if one plane went down, we could still play. I mean, that's how bad it was."

The lynch pin of Lombardi's philosophy was team. No one, no matter how good, was going to run the show or overshadow the team. Two time All-Pro wide receiver Billy Howton was the first to be eliminated for the sake of team unity and Lombardi's rule.

According to Knafelc, "Well, Billy was probably the best player we had. By no stretch of the imagination he was a great receiver. And he was the self-proclaimed leader of our ball club. He and I were roommates for our first couple years. So the day after I had my meeting with Coach Lombardi, Billy called me and said, "*Vince* called me and wants me to fly in and have lunch with him."

I told him, "Billy, first of all, I sure wouldn't call him Vince—I had a meeting with him yesterday and he's a no-nonsense guy."

"No, Vince wants me to discuss what we have to do to win."

"I'm going to tell you again, Bill, go in there and be very cautious. Listen, don't talk."

4

# GARY KNAFELC

"Pick me up at the airport, I'll go down and have lunch with Vince and then I'll stick around and take you and Emily out for dinner."

"Fine." I picked him up, took him down, dropped him off at the office. My wife had something for me to do, so I went to Prange's department store. I got home—I couldn't have been gone more than a half hour—and my wife Emily says, "Bill wants you to pick him up." I said, "I just dropped him off." She said, "He's got to go back to Dallas."

I drove down – he was standing outside on the curb. I picked him up, I asked, "How'd your meeting go?"

"Everything was fine, really good, I gotta go back."

"I thought we were going to have dinner."

"No, I gotta go back to Dallas."

He never said another word. I don't know what happened in the meeting. Next day, he was traded to Cleveland. So by doing that one thing, we all knew if he was our best player, Lombardi was giving us all a message, "You're going to win my way, or you're not going to be around." I'm sure Billy walked in and said, "Hi Vince, how are you doin'," and, boy, boom—he's gone."

Gary saw and felt a new culture emerging as Lombardi exerted his influence in all facets of the organization. He had to negotiate a contract one-on-one with 'Vince.' Knaflec asked, "With Coach Lombardi? I always get a kick out of that, all the guys talk about 'Vince.' No one ever called him 'Vince.' Well, his first year, in 1959, I had to go to him and negotiate a contract. Well, you didn't negotiate with Coach Lombardi, so I was very concerned—I found every stat I could possibly find, and I thought the most impressive—I had one more blocking award than Forrest Gregg. I had led the team in receptions. I forgot how many touchdowns I had, I had that written down. I led the team in third-down receptions, for first downs. I thought that was very important, I had that all down. And I led the team in percentage of passes thrown to and caught. I had my wife type it up and I walked in. He was acting like he was on the phone, I don't know if he was or

5

not, and he looked at me and said, "Sit down." I'm sittin' there, sweating like mad. He looked at me and I said, "Coach, I don't want to have a problem. I'd just like to have you read this," I laid it very softly in front of him. He looked at it, just glanced at it grabbed it and crumpled it up and threw it in the wastebasket.

"Gary, all you played was offense."

"I didn't know what to say. What do you want me to do, lead the band at halftime or sell popcorn? What do you want me to do? "

"He looked at me and said, "I'll let you know in a week." I got up. I could hardly wait. I was so happy to be invited back to training camp. It was wonderful the way it happened, I didn't get a chance to tell him what kind of a raise I wanted—and I was just asking for two thousand dollars. I got four, so I was pretty happy about that."

For the affable Knafelc, dealing with Lombardi did not get easier, "Not with me. I didn't even want to be in the room with him. When I saw him coming, I crossed the street. I was deathly afraid of the guy, because he had your life in his hands at all times, you know. He treated me better after I stopped playing ball."

There was a one year break in Gary's long-term relationship with Green Bay and again, Lombardi's emphasis on "team" was central to the issue. Knafelc said, "Well, we had a little difficulty my last year in 1963. I had to play 10 years to get in my five years in the National Football League pension plan." The initial agreement between the league and players took effect in 1959, after Knafelc had been in the league five years. "So Coach Lombardi called me in and said, "I'd like you to stay in shape,"—he had traded Ron Kramer and we had Marv Fleming coming and I was the only other tight end. He said, "I want you to stay in shape and coach Marv Fleming." I said, "Well, will you guarantee I get into three games, because of three games, I had my full year." He blew up and said, "I've given you an opportunity. I have to know by Monday." That was a Friday. So I was talking it over with my wife. I got a phone call on Saturday from San Francisco, saying they heard I was on the waiver wires and I was going to retire. I said, "No, that's not true." Dick Voris was our line coach two or three years previously. He was with the Forty-Niners and said, "Would you come out here?"

"Will you guarantee I get in three games?"

"I'll guarantee you'll start." He said, "We'll trade for you." I said, "Don't trade for me—if I come in Monday and tell Coach Lombardi, he's gonna cut me." Which he did. So I went out there and started every game, played the whole year, and retired with my 10 year pension."

After the season finale, Green Bay at San Francisco, Gary needed transportation back to Green Bay and wanted to hitch a ride on the Packer charter, but did not want to ask Lombardi directly. Knafelc says, "I went to Bart Starr who was my former roommate, and said, "Do you think I can fly back with the team?"

"Well, why don't you call Coach Lombardi?"

"No, I'll call Marie." I call Marie and Marie said, "Why don't you talk to coach?"

"No, *you* talk to Coach." So she called back and said, "Sure, you can fly back with the team." On the way back, Lombardi asked me, "Are you really going to retire?"

"Yes I am." I said.

"Well, would you like to do the announcing?" I said, "Fine."

Gary's transition from player to Packer public address announcer was not completely seamless as he explains, "Well, when Coach Lombardi came to Green Bay, he came with one purpose—and that was to change the whole organization, and to acknowledge the great tradition of the Green Bay Packers. He was a great believer in tradition. And that's the first thing he emphasized when he came here—about the great tradition we had and how we were letting that tradition down. He wanted to be involved in every single facet of the Green Bay Packers, how the grass grew, how the toilets were cleaned. Everything was going to be top-notch, first-class. If you travel first-class, you play first-class. The first game we had was the intra-squad game. Coach Lombardi was upstairs in the press box 'cause he's the head coach. The offensive coach took care of the offense. The defensive coach took care of the defense. Public relations director Tom Miller was sitting there in the booth right next to me, I'm on the PA. Young Vince (Junior) is my spotter, because I didn't know the new guys. The very first play was a pitch-out to Paul Hornung. I thought I was going to be clever with my public address ability, so I said, "And Peerless Pa," and I didn't even get 'Paul' out and the metal folding chair hit the back of the corrugated wall. Coach Lombardi came around the corner with that great big index finger hitting me in the back of the ear, and said, "That'll be enough of that s_ _ _." And from then on, "Ball's on the 20—five to go."

History has not given Vince Lombardi credit for his masterful managing of race relations during a troubled time in America. Without fanfare, he met the issue head on. The landscape was rich with racial land mines in the 1950's and '60's, but there was not a hint of difficulty during his watch. Without incident, he drafted and traded for black football players, in ratios as high as or higher than any team in the league. Again, he was not going to let an issue undermine team unity or keep him from getting excellent players regardless of color. Knafelc recalls, "Before Coach Lombardi came, we would go to Winston Salem for two weeks, we'd play the Redskins (preseason) and then play the St. Louis Cardinals. We stayed at the Oaks Motel and at that time, there was segregation, so the blacks could not stay with us. And maybe it was hard to believe this, but the blacks could hardly wait to get down there because they stayed by themselves. They had a ball. So when Coach Lombardi came in, we went down there one year and, in fact, that was the year we used to go to the Holiday Inn for our meals and meetings, and the black players weren't supposed to eat with us. Coach Lombardi did a very intelligent thing. When he came from the Giants, he brought (veteran defensive back) Emlen

Tunnell with him. Emlen Tunnell was a leader; not only of all the whites on the Giants team, but all the blacks. Coach Lombardi knew we were going to have a lot more blacks in, so he brought Emlen Tunnell in to kind of help them along the way. Emlen was not only a great football player, but a great human being. He knew the right buttons to push on everybody. He never offended anybody, but he was such a high-caliber guy, everybody looked up to him: black, white, pink or purple. Whatever you want to say, he was just a great individual. He would be in charge of them, so we brought him in the back door of the Holiday Inn to eat, and a guy from the hotel says, "You can't do that." Somebody told that guy, "Either he eats with us or your repair bills will be quite extensive. He said, "Are you serious?" He said, "We're serious." And from then on, they ate with us at all of our meetings.

"The next year, we went to the Army camp. We all stayed at Fort Bragg because we could all be together. Lombardi was going to have none of that nonsense. I think I can say without hesitation out of the group of players we had, I don't think we ever had a problem with the blacks and the whites. And I'm not saying that to be above anything else. It's bad to say, no it isn't bad for an adult to say, there was so much love in that ball club, but I don't care if the guy was pink, if he played, produced and helped our ball club, he was our man. You played, but not for you. You played not to make the man next to you ashamed of you. That's what Coach Lombardi taught you. Because of his military background, if you were in a fox hole, who would you want next to you? Someone you can count on. When you're playing football, it's the same thing. Each man must protect the other, or the whole play falls apart; I don't care if its offense or defense. You start thinking about 'me' instead of 'we', you'll never win."

Unequivocally, the Lombardi lessons have been indelibly etched on Gary Knafelc. "Coach Lombardi was the best thing that ever happened to me. He not only changed my ability as a football player, but made me so ashamed of myself for not having played better the five years previously. He taught you what you could do if you applied his fundamentals, and his philosophy of giving everything you have, every play. Before that, I caught the ball, jumped out of bounds, and combed my hair. I thought that was the way to play. His carry-over and his football tactics apply to your family, your business-- everything you do. I have yet to be late for a meeting at any event I've ever had in my life. I'm always on Lombardi time to this current day. If you've got to be there at eight o'clock, I'm there at seven forty-five. Those are the kind of things that came about by having Coach Lombardi, his attitude, his feelings toward everybody, his friends, and relationships. The guys that played under Coach Lombardi are the luckiest football players in the National Football League. We are closer today than we were when we played, because the things he taught us are more important now than they even were then; that's why we're tied closer together now.

"The best thing he ever did for me was when he made me a tight end. That changed my whole life. As a wide receiver, I enjoyed the game, made a lot of touchdowns, I had a lot of fun, but I never really played the game, fully. It taught me you could do a lot more with what you had. Of all the things he taught me, that was the greatest. And whenever he gave you a compliment, that was something you treasured all your life. But that was enough to keep you going through all the adversity you had. We were afraid of Coach Lombardi because we saw him everyday, whereas, our opponents, saw him at the most was twice a year—you could handle that. I'll never forget after a practice, we had one-on-one the first time, and Bart Starr and I were walking back to our room at St. Norbert's. Coach Lombardi was following us outside in the evening, and I looked back to Bart, I said, "He's coming behind us," so we even crossed the street and he kept on coming and I thought, "Oh, my goodness, he's going to cut me." He walked up to the side of us and just looked at me and said, "You had some good blocks today," and kept on walking. I think my reaction to him was, "Fear does wonderful things, Coach." But that one time carried me through the entire season."

# GARY KNAFELC

Possibly the most poignant moment in all of our interviews for *The Lombardi Legacy* occurred when Gary Knafelc was asked what he would say if he could talk to Lombardi today. "Wow, that's a tough one. I would think, if I could see him today, I don't think I'd say a word. I think I'd just hug him. (Chokes up). I'm sorry."

More powerful than words, Gary fought tears and swallowed emotions as he attempted to explain his appreciation for the most powerful person to touch his life. After a minute of collecting thoughts and emotions, thinking about his aging teammates and their frequent alumni gatherings, his words described Lombardi's presence in his life these many years later. "As you mentioned before, what would I do if I saw him today? It's that same thing – it comes back. Every time you see these guys, you see Coach Lombardi. It's in their eyes, it's in their action, it's in the way they think, in the way they move, the way they talk to each other – it's all there."

And in their hearts and in their very souls.

# CHAPTER 2
# PAUL HORNUNG:

*"It was almost sickening how perfect he was."*

# THE LOMBARDI LEGACY

Paul Hornung was Green Bay's bonus pick in 1957, the first player taken in the draft. His initial contract was fifteen thousand dollars with an additional three thousand bonus. The University of Notre Dame Heisman Trophy winner was destined for a bad team.

As a football player he could pass, kick, run, catch and block. One of the biggest problems was deciding where to play him. When he got to Green Bay his versatile talent confused an inept coaching staff that could not decide what to do with him. Frustrated with the bumbling Packer staff, he nearly packed it in to return home and sell real estate.

Hornung was a bonafide glamour boy who had it all. A native of Louisville, Kentucky, he resembled a Kentucky Derby champion in every imaginable way except one; as was once said of the great Secretariat, a Derby winner is famous, wealthy, handsome, strong and fast, but his sex life needs to wait.

When the Green Bay Packers emerged as a dominate football power in the 1960's, many young boys in Wisconsin wanted to be like Paul Hornung. Older boys and men *really* wanted to be like him. Most women of all ages fawned over him while a slightly smaller number stood in line. Number 5 did his best to keep the line moving.

In 1960, he scored a record shattering 176 points in 12 games for an average of 14.66 per game. His record for average number of points per game has not been touched for 39 years. Green Bay's "Golden Boy" was selected league MVP in 1961. National Football League Commissioner Pete Rozelle suspended Hornung for the 1963 season when it was learned he bet on Packer games. Paul had a somewhat star-crossed career, but a memorable one that earned him entrance into both the Pro Football and Packer Halls of Fame.

Many players with great talent, including Paul Hornung were wasting away before Lombardi's arrival: "The guys that were there in Green Bay a couple years before were all waiting to have a *good coach*. We hadn't been coached well at all. When Lombardi came, he established his authority immediately. He established a winning attitude; he wanted you to start thinking about winning. I remember him telling me, "You better come back to training camp in shape, because it's gonna be very, very tough on you if you're not in shape, in fact I want you to come back early." He made me come back up there early to start working out with Boyd Dowler and a few other guys."

Lombardi no more than arrived in Green Bay when Hornung saw the new general manager begin swinging deals, "Nobody ever writes about it and I think it's kind of stupid, he made the best trade in the history of the Green Bay Packers, he robbed Cleveland. He traded Billy Howton, a great friend and a great, great player and what we got out of Cleveland was the nucleus of our defense." In three separate trades with Paul Brown, he got three defensive linemen who anchored the front four. "We got Willie Davis who was a Hall of Famer, we got Henry Jordan who was a Hall of Famer, Bill Quinlan as a throw in. " It was Howton for Bill Quinlan plus running back Lew Carpenter, a fifth round choice for Jordan and A.D. Williams for Davis. Paul summarizes the trades, "I mean, he absolutely robbed Paul Brown. Billy Howton went over there and became the first president of the players association, but he only played a year. Lew Carpenter was a throw in, Lew played for five years Quinlan played four years, of course the other two played 10 years."

It was Lombardi's evaluation of Hornung and subsequent use of him that made all the difference. As an offensive assistant coach with the New York Giants, Lombardi had a versatile running back in Frank Gifford who was very similar to Hornung. Paul's face lit up like a kid when at age 74, he talked about the guy who salvaged his career, "He was the reason I made it in professional football, I wouldn't have made it without him. It just so happened his offense was perfect for me. The sweep, the option pass, I knew he came from the New York Giants and I talked to Gifford a couple times on the phone and he said, "I bet you're *really* gonna like what you got now. You're gonna have a guy who's gonna get on your ass, he's gonna make a football player out of you or you're gonna be working in business some where."

"Let me tell you how astute he was. The same year they drafted me, down low in the draft was an incidental choice and it was Jim Morse. Jim Morse was the captain of my Notre Dame team and he played two years in Canada and now he's coming back. He was negotiating whether he was going to play, or not for Lombardi. Of course I loved him, Jimmy and I were real close, but Vince said a few things to Morse that changed his life. First of all, he said, "Jimmy, you shouldn't be playing pro football." He said, "Look, let's be honest, your not fast enough and it looks like your gonna have to play defensive back or safety and you're a good athlete and might make this team, but you've got too much on the ball. You gotta get started in business." That businessman is worth over a hundred million dollars today. He just bought a G-5, the largest private airplane in the world, coming out next year. A 'G-whatever in the hell' it is. He has been very successful; he started the outlet malls all over America. Right away, right after sitting down talking with Jim Morse, Lombardi knew what to tell him and it was right on. That's how sharp he was, he made great decisions."

The mental part of the game was constantly stressed by Green Bay's head man, preparation, concentration and no mistakes were hallmarks of his philosophy. Mostly we hear about Lombardi teaching others, but Paul tells how Chicago Bear legend Papa Bear George Halas took Lombardi to school one Sunday afternoon. "We were playing in Chicago and both teams' locker rooms were up in the north end of the stadium. We were side-by-side and only the equipment room separated the two teams. As he would do every game, after the warm up, Coach would meet with the quarterbacks and go over the game plan. There came a knock on the door of the equipment room which was in between the two locker rooms." Gerald "Dad" Braisher was the Packer's equipment manager, and as Hornung relates, "Dad opened up the door and it was George Halas.

Of course, George knew Dad, and said, "Dad, I need to talk with Lombardi, it's very important."

Dad said, "OK coach, just a minute."

Dad, who was well aware not to disturb Vince at this time, had to knock on the door. Vince hollered, "Who is it, what do you want?" that type thing and Dad stuck his head in the door and said, (whispering) "Coach Halas is at the door in the equipment room. Coach Halas wants to see ya, it's an emergency."

Dad follows Vince through the room to meet Halas, so he's privy to this, Halas took one look at Lombardi and said, "Vince, you better have your team ready because we're gonna kick your ass." Vince looked at him; he didn't know what to do, he was flabbergasted which is exactly what Halas had in mind. Halas turned around and left and Vince stood there looking at Dad as if to say, "What the f____ was that all about?" So, now the game goes on, we win the game, but Vince understood what he did. Halas had him thinking the whole game, "What the f____?" He admitted it, "After that I realized Halas had me thinking all day long why he came in there and did that. I know now why he did it, because I wasn't even thinking about the game half the time, I'm trying to figure out the psychology of it." He learned a big lesson that day. Of course, Vince *loved* Halas, he realized Halas is the greatest name in the history of the game and the father of the game."

It was arch rival Papa Bear Halas of the hated Bears, who complemented Hornung in a unique fashion that made Paul realize he had made it as an NFL running back. Paul was flattered, "He called me a son-of-a-bitch. I knew I made it when he called me that. That's the best thing he could have told me. He cussed everybody out; I knew I had made it when he called me that."

As opposite as Hornung and Lombardi were, they clicked and Paul knows why, "I'll tell you what really made it; it seemed the bigger the game the better the game I had." Paul was one of the players who saw and felt the rough times in Green Bay before the turn around under Lombardi. The club compiled a dreadful 4-19-1 record in Hornung's first two years. Players avoided the public during those times, not because they would be overwhelmed with autograph seekers, but because the fans were sick of losing and let the players know it. Hornung tells what it was like, "Of course I was criticized my first couple years, I wasn't the only one, shit, they were all over Bart. I remember Max McGee and I wouldn't go to the parties, the team would stay in the locker room and have a party on Sunday night so they wouldn't have to go out in public. Well that was bullshit, that wasn't me, it wasn't Max. I don't care if you win or lose, we're gonna go out and have a nice steak dinner somewhere and enjoy our selves. We went to the Piccadilly, of course I loved the Piccadilly. Max did too. We had some great times out there. Of course we were losing our first couple years. Look who our coaches were for heaven's sake, we couldn't win with the guys who were there the first couple years. The fans would say, "Why pay eight dollars for a ticket to watch the Packers play when for nothing you could go to the Piccadilly on Sunday night and watch Hornung and McGee sing and dance." So, when Lombardi came in, he knew about all that and put a couple of those places off limits immediately, which was the places Max and I hung around, which was all right, we went there any way. I've been breaking rules all my life."

Paul's testing and breaking rules served a real purpose for Lombardi and Pete Rozelle. All the Packer players knew Lombardi had a special feeling for Hornung, so it provided the former high school teacher with an opportunity to deliver a lesson to the entire team; if Lombardi would fine Paul, he'd do it to anybody. Contrary to what some have thought, the Old Man did not secretly return the money to Hornung after making his point, "He would fine us five hundred or a thousand, he kept the money. See, we had a party fund, at the end of the year we'd have one big party and all the fine money that was collected during the year paid for the party."

# PAUL HORNUNG

One of the intriguing aspects of Hornung is his pursuit of a good time in spite of potential hazards, the largest of which was Lombardi. Paul knew how to play him, "I remember once in LA, we beat the Rams, Max and I had two pretty girls; I had a limo around front and we were gonna go pick up the girls, I said, 'Wait a minute, let me get a case of champagne.' Max said, "Oh shit, you can't get a case of champagne." I said, 'Bullshit, we pay for it why can't we get a case of champagne?' I went right up in front of Lombardi, picked the case of champagne up and carried it out, right in front of him, put it in the car. He didn't say a word, didn't say a word. That's how much he liked to win."

Some players, like defensive end Willie Davis, would get called up to Lombardi's office just to talk. Willie cherishes some of those conversations, many times void of an agenda, just talking about life, the team, civil rights, who knows what. It is then reasonable to conclude that Lombardi's surrogate son, Hornung, would get called up for some light chit chat, "No he never would, he was always calling me into the office to bitch at me and Max too. A couple times Max went out and got caught and I wasn't with him. Lombardi couldn't understand that. Max snuck out one year, *every night* for the whole training camp; never missed. He was in love with pro golfer Doug Sanders' ex-wife; he got married later on during the year. It might have been the year we went to the first Super Bowl. Anyway, Max snuck out *every single night* in training camp." That did not sit well with Hornung, "I was jealous as hell."

Real jealousy could have crept into the Packer backfield when Donny Anderson and Jim Grabowski signed big money contracts while the AFL and NFL were battling for talent. Paul Hornung and Jimmy Taylor manned the running back positions in Green Bay from before Lombardi arrived. From time-to-time, Tom Moore and Elijah Pitts filled in capably, but for the most part, it was numbers 5 and 31 lining up behind Bart Starr delivering the leagues most productive ground game. The two Packer backs won the league's MVP award in back to back years, Paul in 1961, and Jimmy in '62.

# THE LOMBARDI LEGACY

To this day, Paul has a very good relationship with the tandem of Anderson and Grabowski and there was never a problem, "Oh, no, not at all. It was Taylor. Taylor was really adamant against it. He was pissed they got…….. he was really pissed that Donny and Grabowski got all the money. He didn't understand, he didn't understand much anyway, but he could never fathom, and he was probably right in a lot of ways that those two were getting six figures and we were making, you know, seventy, eighty thousand dollars a year, which was a lot. Of course, I was always making so much outside of football that I didn't really bitch about what I was paid, I didn't care if Donny Anderson got a hundred thousand dollars, that was all right with me I was doing fine off the field. But, Jimmy wasn't. Jimmy couldn't take Grabowski making seventy five-thousand dollars, and he shouldn't have been, but that's the way it was."

Hornung was in the eye of the NFL's biggest storm in 1963 when it was learned, he and Detroit Lions defensive tackle Alex Karras had bet on games involving their teams. By comparison, baseball had been rocked by the Black Sox betting scandal in 1919, different, but still it involved players betting on the outcome of games. Baseball established the office of Commissioner as a direct result of the 1919 "fix" of the World Series. The NFL had a commissioner in place in 1963 in the person of Alvin Pete Rozelle and he was not going to allow the hint of gambling to infect the legitimacy and explosive growth of pro football. Both Hornung and Karras were All-Pro, popular players who were vital to their clubs, but Rozelle dropped the hammer by suspending both, indefinitely.

With strong lobbying by the Packer coach and general manager, both Hornung and Karras were reinstated after missing the entire 1963 season. Similar to Lombardi fining his biggest star to make a point, Rozelle could not have delivered a clearer message when he sat the two players out for an entire season. To his credit, Hornung saw the issues for what they were and is extraordinarily candid about what was going on at the time. He says, "I wrote Rozelle a nice letter and said, 'Look, I have no animosity toward you. You had to make a decision, you did it.' I knew there were a lot of guys betting, we had a couple guys on the Packers bet along with me, what the shit.

"I remember when I was a rookie; I was trying to get a bet on, we were gonna play the Colts. I hadn't bet at all and we were going to Baltimore. We were 13 point underdogs. We had played Baltimore earlier in the year to a dead stand still in Milwaukee, and I'm thinking, 'Geez, we're not making any money, we're out of the league championship chase, our record demonstrated it, we were not gonna go to the playoffs. I remember (Jack) said, "What's the spread?"

"Thirteen points."

"F___, they ain't gonna beat us by thirteen points, are you kiddin'?"

"Do you wanna bet?"

"What do you mean?"

"Well, I got a friend of mine in Chicago he'll make a bet for us. What do you want to bet?

(Herman) said, "What are you gonna bet?"

I told him, "I'll, bet five hundred."

(Herman) said, "I'll bet five hundred."

(Jack) said, "Oh shit, let's bet a thousand."

Paul said, "I don't know what it was, but it was at least five hundred. So I called up and couldn't get a hold of the guy, couldn't get the bet up.

"So, Baltimore kicked off, Al Carmichael fumbles the opening kickoff, they get it on the five yard line. One play later, seven to nothing—Baltimore. Baltimore kicks off again to Al Carmichael—fumbles the kickoff. It's fourteen to nothing, we haven't played a minute yet. (Jack, Herman and Hornung) are standing on the sidelines laughing our asses off, because we're gonna get killed it looks like, which we did. I think we got beat fifty-something to ten and we saved all that money."

# THE LOMBARDI LEGACY

Final score was Baltimore 56 Green Bay 0. At that time the Colts ran a horse and rider around the field after every Baltimore score, during the week following the game, the horse died, presumably from exhaustion.

Of Lombardi, Hornung says, "If I had to pick one guy that was instrumental *in my life*, in my entire life, it would be him because I looked up to him; I respected him and he was so right in the things that he did. It was almost sickening how perfect he was. He never left anything to chance, he wanted everything covered. He would have been a great president of Ford Motor Company, he would have been a great president of a bank, whatever he would have liked to have done in his life he would have been successful because he motivated. He motivated every son-of-a-bitch that came around him. He was the man for his time. There is always someone in every professional sport who stands out, who becomes *the* man. Lombardi became that, he was that man."

# CHAPTER 3
# JESSE WHITTENTON:

*"He definitely wasn't a sand bagger."*

# THE LOMBARDI LEGACY

There were some very good players on the early Lombardi teams who only played at the beginning of the dynasty. The original defensive secondary was pretty darn good. It became great in later years and overshadowed the first group. An All-Pro cornerback from Texas Western (Texas El Paso) named Jesse Whittenton was part of a group of defensive backs known as The Katzenjammer Kids. How perfect to have a Texan named Jesse out on the corner trying to steal things from other folks. There has always been something about the name Jesse Whittenton that sounds daring, untamed and renegade. He is one of the most likable thieves you could ever meet and pulled off a great heist in 1961. Wearing number 47, Jesse was a starter when the team won it's first two World Championships under Lombardi in '61 and '62. He participated in three Pro Bowls and the Packer Hall of Fame inducted the native of Big Springs, Texas in 1976.

Whittenton was one of many outstanding players acquired for Green Bay by Jack Vainisi, who served as "player personnel director" before the title was developed. In fact, the Packer Hall of Fame refers to Vainisi as a "talent scout" who served from 1950, until his death in 1960. Twenty, of the 36 players on the 1959 roster are in the Packer Hall and Vainisi had a hand in getting most of them.

Jesse's Green Bay career began in 1958, a year before Lombardi arrived and he retired following his All-Pro '64 campaign in order to tend to his golf business. These days, at age 75, he takes off his cowboy boots to slip into golf spikes about twice a week. In his prime, Jesse was the best golfer to ever play for the Packers. He was good enough to compete on the PGA Senior Tour and win his sectional two times allowing him to make expenses which he views as "a hell of an accomplishment."

Besides starring in the NFL he owned a popular restaurant and watering hole in Green Bay called King's X; he bought a golf course outside of El Paso and sponsored a young golfer on the PGA tour by the name of Lee Trevino. It was not boring to be Jesse Whittenton, or be around him.

# JESSE WHITTENTON

Unlike today, college players had little contact with pro teams in 1954, so Jesse Whittenton had no idea what would happen regarding a pro career: "I don't remember ever even talking to anybody, I was out on the golf course and they came out from the clubhouse and said I had a long distance phone call from Los Angeles. It was Eddie Cotell who was the scout for the Rams. He just asked me if I'd be interested in playing for the Los Angeles Rams, I said, "Sure." So they drafted me, there was no romancing, no nothing. I went out there and played two years with 'em. I made the starting lineup my first year, got traded to the Bears, played one exhibition season then came up to Green Bay. My first contract was seventy five-hundred dollars, sixty-five hundred base and a thousand dollar bonus if I made the starting lineup."

Throughout the league, Green Bay was viewed as the pits and Jesse recalls what he was told in LA and Chicago, "Both of 'em said if you didn't hustle or do good they would trade you to Green Bay and nobody wanted to go to Green Bay. As a matter of fact, I got sick when I was with the Bears. I was in the hospital and they couldn't find out what was wrong. The only way I could stay with the Bears was to go on injured reserve and be out for the whole year. Bears Coach George Halas told me Detroit and Green Bay was interested, in fact they needed me right away. I owed him sixteen hundred dollars because I got an advance to get to training camp. He said, "I'll tell what I'll do, I'll call that square." The Packers gave me another fifteen hundred dollars to sign with them, so I figured I made three thousand bucks, so I went up to Green Bay.

"The coach at that time was Ray "Scooter" McLean and he was just "one of the guys." When we were on the road, we'd get poker games goin' and he was just one of the guys. So we had no discipline whatsoever. When Vince came in, he laid down the law, we would do it his way, it was either his way or hit the highway, one way or the other. I think that's the real key, he let us know whose boss.

"He put it to us like this, Max McGee, Paul Hornung, (running back)

25

# THE LOMBARDI LEGACY

Howie Ferguson and myself showed up a day before training camp was to start. We played golf and we went out on the town. The next day the meeting was eight or nine o'clock and Packer President Dominic Olejniczak introduced our new General Manager and Head Coach Vince Lombardi. He got up and said, "Gentlemen, glad to see you all here......." then he said, "Mister McGee, Mister Hornung, Mister Whittenton, Mister Ferguson, that'll cost you two hundred and fifty bucks; each one of ya." Howie Ferguson said, "For what?" He said, "For missing curfew."

Howie said, "Curfew doesn't start until tonight."

Vince said, "Mister, your curfew started when you brought your luggage into the dormitory. If any of you don't like it, let me know what team you'd like to be traded to and I'll try my damnedest to get you there." Ferguson did not play in the NFL in 1959, but resurfaced with the Los Angeles (later San Diego) Chargers of the AFL in 1960. A new world order had come to Green Bay.

Like anyone else, Lombardi had his favorites, but according to Jesse it didn't really show or affect the way things were run. "He treated everybody the same which was a big plus. I played under Sid Gilman with the Los Angeles Rams and George Halas with the Chicago Bears. Boy they really showed their favoritism. I think the way Vince ran it, with no favorites, drew the guys closer together."

Lombardi liked Whittenton a lot and offered unusually high praise in his book *Run to Daylight*, when he said his cornerback was, "as close to being a perfect defensive back as anyone in the league." Jesse's preparation was impeccable and he teamed with fellow Texans Hank Gremminger and Johnny Symank to give the Packers a strong group of defensive backs. Emlen Tunnell played safety to round out the group until his retirement when he was replaced by Willie Wood. In some parts those three Texans were not to be trusted. Their position coach, Norb Hecker, dubbed them "The Katzenjammer Kids" as Whittenton explains, "Between Symank and I we were always putting that analgesic balm (similar to Icy Hot) in guys jock straps before they'd come to practice and just aggravatin' people. Somebody would be sitting on their head gear and we would go up there and yank it out from underneath them. Like The Katzenjammer Kids, always aggravatin' people." Jesse knew Lombardi ruled the roost, but still had fun, "I looked up to him, but I still did the same old stuff I always did."

Contract negotiations were not jovial times for Jesse, "There was no negotiation. He said, "I'm gonna offer you this." I think my largest contract was $29,000.00, it was his offer and he'd ask, "Do you want it or not?" The negotiation would last about 30 minutes, not long at all. I was scared to death of him; I wanted to get out of there."

In June of 1959, Lombardi made a huge personnel move that impacted the team's locker room and psyche more than can be measured. He swung a deal with the New York Giants for a black defensive back named Emlen Tunnell who had compiled a Hall of Fame career. He was a man of tremendous character and a leader of men whose best days as a player were clearly behind him. The general manager acquired Tunnell to help set the tone and change a losing culture in Green Bay; it worked wonderfully. Whittenton says, "That's how it was, I don't know that he ever played too much, but you knew he was there. Emlen really taught me a lot and Willie Wood too; he was very knowledgeable of the game." Emlen Tunnell, who was with the Giants during some of Lombardi's time as an assistant, let the Packer players know the new coach was dead serious, showed them how a true professional carried himself and let black players know it was OK to play in Siberia. Psychologist Lombardi was a man at work in the year of '59.

Whittenton's famous theft occurred at Milwaukee County Stadium against the New York Giants in 1961's game twelve. With the Giants leading 17-13 in the fourth quarter, big fullback Alex Webster got loose on about a twenty yard run and Jesse went for the ball rather than the tackle. Around the Giants 30 yard line, the Packer cornerback simply took the ball out of

# THE LOMBARDI LEGACY

Webster's arm. Green Bay scored shortly thereafter in an important win over Lombardi's former team. On the Packer sideline Green Bay's Coach told Whittenton, "It looked like a hand off; it looked like you were playing on the same team." It was a lot easier than it looked according to the thief, "It looked like I was gambling, but I really wasn't. I swear to God, I knew the ball was in my arms." The same two teams met in the NFL Championship game about a month later as Green Bay drubbed New York 37-0 to secure title number one in Lombardi's Dynasty.

Not surprisingly, Lombardi was well aware of his players off field activities, so when Jesse was considering buying a bar and restaurant in 1962, he sought his boss's approval, "Oh God yeah, he asked me the terms and everything, he said, "Good terms, you should be able to make it go." He said, "But I guess you know you can't get behind the bar and work that bar." I said, "Yeah I understand." I could go into it and eat, sit down just like anybody else, but I couldn't work." So the King's X was born and became a hot spot in Green Bay during those years. Along with the property, Jesse inherited an attractive bartender named Jackie Forchett who drew the attention of a certain wild linebacker; Ray Nitschke. Of his former teammate Whittenton says, "I could just see the problems it was gonna cause, because Vince had his hands full with him also. You get a few drinks in him and I'll tell you he was…" Nitschke was an ornery drunk who carved out a reputation for busting up beer joints and some of the people in them. Be sure to read the chapter on Lori Keck later in this book for an account of Lombardi's reaction to one of his drinking episodes.

By the way, Ray and Jackie Nitschke became model citizens.

Even though Jesse owned King's X for just four years, he reflects with mixed emotions, "I sold it in '65, worst thing I could have done. I went into the golf business and that was pretty nice, but I sure miss Green Bay."

Jesse and his cousin Donny tried to stay alert for business opportunities outside of football and a golf course development near El Paso drew Donny's

# JESSE WHITTENTON

interest. The club needed a pro and an injection of personality, Jesse happened to be Class "A" on both counts. Cousin Donny convinced the developer to sell the property under remarkable conditions as Jesse relates, "Nothing down, nothing a month and free water for eight years. At first, I turned them down."

The final nudge to leave football and buy the course occurred at Oneida Golf and Country Club outside of Green Bay after Lombardi witnessed an eye popping round by his All-Pro cornerback. Jesse recalls, "On Men's Day I drew Vince as a partner and shot 66. He said, "You're in the wrong business." I said, "I been meaning to talk to you, but I didn't know how to go about it." I told him about the deal I was offered to buy the course he said, "You got a good two or three years left in you, I was gonna move you to safety, but you'd be a damn fool to turn that down." So that's how I got in the golf business. I went down there; we got the golf course, hired Lee Trevino and then sponsored him on the tour in '67." When Trevino was hired, he was a long way from the superstar touring pro he would become. According to Jesse, "I hired him as range boy more or less, because we didn't have any money. He needed a place to work under a Class "A" pro and I was a Class "A" and he wanted to get out on the tour. I gave him thirty bucks a week; he opened the pro shop, ran the pro shop, picked up range balls until noon and then practiced all the rest of the day." Whittenton secured a ten thousand dollar loan in '67 that launched Trevino's trip to golf stardom by putting him on tour.

Jesse ended his nine year career by retiring after the '64 season then concentrated on this golf course. Two years later, in the winter of '66, Lombardi wanted out of Wisconsin's weather and onto Whittenton's golf course for a little while. Jesse offers great insight into Vince Lombardi the man as he relates this story, "He called me and said, "What's the weather like down there?" I said, "We get a little snow but it's usually warm enough by noon to play. You might have to wear a rain suit or something like that.""

# THE LOMBARDI LEGACY

He said, "Work up a golf match where you and I play Coach Bobby Dobbs (Texas Western) and your cousin Donny." Bobby Dobbs and Vince coached together under Earl (Red) Blaik at Army. I arranged it and it snowed that morning at about three or four o'clock. He called me at six o'clock and said, "What is this s____ on the ground?" I said, "It's just a little snow flurry for where you're from."

"Will we be able to play?"

"Certainly."

"Don't call it off, we'll have it."

"He was the type of guy that every club or golf pro would like to have as a member; he definitely wasn't a sand bagger. He would never post a bad score; he would only post a good score. When he was my partner, I think he was about an 18 to 20 handicap and he couldn't play to a 30. I got in his dog house because Donny and Dobbs beat us on the golf course. He was competitive. He concentrated and everybody went by the rules, he knew that rule book backwards and forwards."

Following his round of golf the great Vince Lombardi took time to talk with the locals about his former cornerback. Jesse said, "He sat there in our restaurant and talked to our farmers and ranchers for *an hour and a half.* We had two sports writers there, and after we were done I said, "I don't believe this, you wouldn't even let them guys in our locker room up there in Green Bay." He said, "It's different, you don't work for me now." He was a big cheese for the cancer deal then and that's what finally got him." Ironically, Lombardi served as Chairman of the Wisconsin State Cancer Fund long before the disease claimed his life.

Today Jesse lives in Las Cruces, New Mexico and is a 75 year old package of mischief who gets a great kick out of reliving his days of high jinx. His eyes sparkle, his mind is sharp and quick with a knack for the unexpected. When asked what he would say to Lombardi if he could talk to him, Whittenton said, "I'd tell him to post all of your scores."

# JESSE WHITTENTON

There has always been something about that name: Jesse Whittenton.

# CHAPTER 4
# BOYD DOWLER:

*"It became easy if you understood what it was you were supposed to do."*

# THE LOMBARDI LEGACY

Another of Lombardi's multi-talented, physically gifted players, Boyd Dowler was a college quarterback at Colorado who led the Buffalos in passing, receiving and interceptions. YES, the quarterback led his team in receiving. Even at 6'5" and 225 pounds and had speed. He ran 9.9 in the hundred yard dash and 14.2 in high hurdles.

He led the Packers in receiving in 1959, '61, '62, '63, '64, '65, and '67. Being the team's leading receiver in '61 was particularly impressive because he was serving National Guard duty at Fort Lewis, Washington during the Berlin Crisis. Dowler was a weekend warrior in the National Football League. Selected in the third round of the 1958 draft, for the '59 season, Boyd was part of a draft class that did not put a single player in the Pro Football Hall of Fame. That's the entire draft for all teams. He played eleven years for Green Bay from 1959 through 1969, was inducted into the Packer Hall of Fame in 1978 and is a member of the NFL's All Decade Team of the 1960's.

Boyd is one of nine players to be on all nine of Lombardi's Packer teams, one of 12 to be on all five World Championship squads and one of only two who played every game for Vince Lombardi. Forrest Gregg was the other. Somewhat lost in the vast array of Packer star players, Boyd was a big time performer in big time games.

John Maxymuk, in his wonderful book, *"Packers by the Numbers"* offered an astute assessment of number 86, "Lanky Boyd Dowler never got enough recognition in Lombardi's run-oriented offense, but he caught 448 passes for a 15.4 yard average and 40 touchdowns in his 11 years in Green Bay. He was deadly in title games, catching touchdown passes in 1961, 1966, two in the Ice Bowl, and one in Super Bowl II."

When he retired as a Packer, Boyd was the team's second all time leading receiver having caught just 41 passes less than career leader Don Hutson and 104 more than third place Max McGee. He compiled those receiving numbers on powerful running teams that had depth, balance and enough wins and championships to qualify as the first modern day NFL dynasty.

# BOYD DOWLER

After the Lombardi years, other Packer receivers caught more balls for more yards, but didn't win nearly as much. The list of better receivers than Boyd Dowler ever to play for the Packers is a very, very short one. For good measure he punted for a 43.3 yard average in 1962.

This bright, articulate, thoughtful man retired from the Packers after the 1969 season. He became receiver coach on George Allen's Rams staff in 1970 and came out of retirement in '71 to serve as player coach for Coach Allen in Washington of all places, the year after Vince Lombardi's death. He went on to serve as coach or scout for seven teams until 2007.

Scouting and evaluating college players in 1958 was a far cry from the near scientific process of the 21st century. Boyd Dowler explains how he was pursued by the pros while playing for the Colorado Buffalos.

"Pursued is an exaggeration, I heard from a couple of teams. I heard from the San Francisco 49'ers, I heard from the Calgary Stampeders who were of course, in Canada. Jim Finks was the general manager at the time and he called me told me I ought to come to Canada because I couldn't play quarterback in the NFL, "But you can play quarterback up here." And I said I wasn't really interested in that. I said I'd probably just stay with whoever drafts me in the NFL. The Packers didn't call me. I can't think of anybody but the 49'ers who did. On draft day, I was tsken with the 25th pick which led off the third round, there were only 12 teams picking. The Packers were picking first coming off of a one win season. The next pick was the 49'ers, of course they couldn't pick me, they picked my teammate from Colorado, a good friend."

It was the woeful Packers coming off a 1-10-1 season that wanted Dowler's services and he didn't mind, "I certainly didn't have any problem with that; I knew they weren't any good. My main thought was, "Maybe I can make the team." I checked to see who the receivers were, basically it was Billy Howton and Max McGee and I couldn't come up with anybody else. I thought, "Well, I might have a chance."

# THE LOMBARDI LEGACY

Boyd was one of many quality players added to Green Bay's roster by Jack Vainisi, an extremely important yet, obscure figure in Packer history. Vainisi stocked the cupboard with potentially great players who needed someone to bring out the greatness in them. That someone was an assistant coach with the New York Giants when the 1958 draft was conducted. Dowler explains, "The draft was held in the middle of December. I had been picked to play in the East-West Shrine All-Star Game in San Francisco and I had already been drafted. Most of the guys out there had been drafted already and that was during Christmas week and the NFL season wasn't even over. So I don't know whether they used Street & Smith Football magazine, threw darts at the board or whatever, but that's how they did it. It wasn't nearly as involved as it is now days. I think it might have been two of three days later before they ever called me on the phone. They said they would come to Denver and wanted me to sign a contract."

Dowler did not know where he was to play, offense or defense; he got his first indication when the former Giants' assistant and new Packer Head Coach Vince Lombardi called him to Green Bay. According to Boyd, "They flew me in for a sort of quarterback mini camp, I had been a quarterback in college and they called and said come in for four, maybe five days. It was in June. Bart Starr was there, they traded for Lamar McHan, and Joe Francis from Oregon State had been on the team. He was a good football player. The Packers drafted another quarterback (Randy Duncan) beside myself, we came in and for the first full day we sat in the meeting room with Vince up there going through the offense and everything throughout that day."

Boyd remembers it was a small meeting with a big aura, "Oh yeah, he was still scary. Nobody was interrupting him, there wasn't anybody laughing. No, no, there wasn't any of that going on. The next morning we did the same thing. I thought I was gonna be lining up at quarterback. I had no clue. He finally said, "Well, let's go out on the field and throw the ball around a little bit today." He said, "Dowla, you're a flanka," in that Brooklyn or New

# BOYD DOWLER

York accent of his. I said, "Fine." I kinda thought I'd have a better chance of making it as receiver. I'd caught a lot of passes in college, which is another story being a quarterback. I played pretty well in the East West Shrine game as a slot back and caught some passes.

We went out and threw the ball around that afternoon and I kicked the ball around something terrible, I dropped the ball, it was miserable. Came back the next day and I was a whole lot better, I wasn't scared. He said, "You're better off today, you relaxed a little bit." The day before, when I was kicking the ball around, he threw me some balls and said to watch the ball— typical stuff, like what my dad would have done."

Like most assistant coaches back then, Lombardi was anonymous outside his own team and family. Dowler didn't know him, "Not really and I didn't know about him. I knew he'd come from the New York Giants. The minute he walked in the room with us five guys sitting there and started talking at the black board I thought, *'This guy is not fooling around.'* You could just tell this is a no nonsense guy and his voice could scare ya. He was very direct, he told us exactly what he wanted us to do, he told us *exactly* how to do it. I liked that, there wasn't any joking around, wasn't any patting you on the back or this, that and the other thing. He was easy to understand, you knew exactly where he was coming from."

Regarding his initial contract, Boyd was signed by the great Jack Vainisi, not Lombardi, "No, he wasn't even hired when I signed the contract, because I signed the contract before the first of the 1959 year. The Packers prior season, 1958, wasn't even over yet. So he hadn't even been hired when I signed. One year, eight thousand dollars, no bonus.

"My second contract I negotiated with Lombardi, or he negotiated with me, or he told me what I was going to make. I went into his office and sat down; I had made Rookie of the Year and been the leading receiver on the team as a rookie. I sat down in his office, he said, "You're a good player, we want you here, you have a good future, we're gonna win, the board of

37

directors has told me that I can't give any more than ten per cent raises, but we're gonna give you a 25% raise. We'll give you a $10,000 contract." I signed the contract and that was the extent of the negotiation. I went from $8,000 to $10,000 and I was a starter already and led the team in receiving. It wasn't much of a contract. I'm not sure there weren't guys who were drafted after me that didn't sign for more than I did."

A contract with Lombardi was a sacred document, "He made it very clear to us that he didn't care who it was whether it was your wife, or your parents, or your roommate, *you do not tell*, especially your teammates, do not tell them what you're making. This is between you and the organization. I didn't discuss it much with anybody."

Lombardi saw individual bonuses as harmful to team unity and Dowler got the message loud, clear and early, "I started to punt. Max McGee and I did the punting for a period of three or four years. After I'd punted for a year, and had actually done pretty well, I went in to talk to him about a contract and I said, "How about giving me a couple extra thousand if I'd punt?"

He said, "I'm not doing that, you're a player, you're a football player, we're paying you to be a football player, so you'll do that." So I said, "Well, would you give a bonus for catching a certain number of passes or anything like that?"

He said, "No, 'cause then you'll be thinking about how many balls you're catching instead of winning games and that sort of thing." But, he said, "I'll tell you what I'll do, if we win eight games I'll give you two thousand dollars, if we win ten games I'll give you the same bonus and if we win the division, I'll give you the same bonus." And he said, "We'll probably do all three." Then he smiled. I said, "Fine." And we did all three. He didn't want anybody to get too far away from somebody else. When he had to compete with the AFL, for (Jim) Grabowski, (Donny) Anderson and (Gale) Gillingham, he knew he had to compete a little bit, he told me, "I'm giving these guys a little bit more money, but I *have to do it* to compete with the other league.

I'm trying to keep their base salary in line with you other guys. I'm giving 'em some pretty good bonuses in order to get 'em signed and I hope you understand that's the way it's gonna be." I don't know of too many guys who had any real problem with it, I know I didn't"

As far as dealing with Lombardi the general manager, Dowler says, "He was still very direct, he was still very honest. He sat behind a desk and he had a shirt and tie on, but he was not unreasonable. He wasn't unreasonable as a coach, he was demanding, but he wasn't unreasonable and he wasn't as a general manager. What he was able to do as a general manager was visualize and totally understand what each player was capable of doing all the way from what position he was capable of playing. He knew, he knew. He was gonna move me to wide receiver and he was pretty sure that if I did what he asked me to do I could be pretty good.

"He kept coming up with ways to put me in the game; this started in preseason. When I first got there they ran a three back offense, Hornung, Taylor and a guy by the name of Don McIlhenny. That's what Lombardi had done with the Giants. When we came to training camp in 1959, he started with the same system, three running backs, one tight end and one wide receiver, who was the starter, Max McGee. I got to training camp after the College All Star Game. I missed the first two weeks of practice. I looked pretty good right away and he wanted to work me in. He said, "We're gonna do three ends. Paul you're gonna be the halfback, Jimmy you're the fullback and that's the way it's gonna be. Dowler, you're gonna play wide side on the right. McGee, you're gonna be the split end on the left." We went six or seven years where that's all I ever did was run out of the huddle and line up wide to the right, Max would go wide to the left. Even the first preseason game, he shot me in the game quickly and I had a pretty good game. You know, you can tell in practice if they're working you or if they're ignoring you. It's not hard for a player to tell and I looked around. I looked at the situation and I thought, "If I can keep from screwin' up, and do what I'm supposed to do, and catch the ball, and things like that, I'll get to play." I wasn't sure I'd get to start, and I didn't for the first five games, but he put me in there. I dropped the first ball thrown to me in the Bear game.

"First league game, middle of the first quarter he threw me in the game, first play Lamar McHan was the quarterback. I go to the post, Erich Barnes was playing corner, came up and tried to cut block me down and I hurdled him, just jumped right straight over him and didn't miss a step, ran wide open down the middle of the field and dropped the ball. Would have been a touchdown, but I dropped the ball. That was my first play in an NFL regular season game and it took me a little while to get over it; I was a little bit like a deer in the headlights." At that point you'd expect one of Lombardi's classic, "What the hell's going on out there?" Boyd says, "No, he really said, "You'll be alright." He didn't yell at me, there were a couple of defensive players that did, but it wasn't Vince, no. He was pretty nice about it, he said, "You'll be OK, be alright." I got back in that game and actually helped. I think the first game I started and played all the time was the second Bear game in Wrigley Field. I did pretty well and I had a big year, the rest of the way I got hot." Boyd had a very solid first year with 32 receptions for 549 yards, four touchdowns and was selected NFL Rookie of the Year.

When General Manager Vince Lombardi started making player moves, he found a willing trading partner in Paul Brown of the Cleveland Browns. For several years, three of Green Bay's four defensive linemen were players acquired in deals with Cleveland. Boyd watched his general manager build a winner, "The guys from Cleveland were real helpers. Of course he'd already gotten Bill Quinlan, who played right defensive end. That first year he got Henry Jordan who had not really been a full time starter with the Browns. The Cleveland Browns and New York Giants were real rivals. They played each other twice a year and Vince knew the personnel of the Cleveland Browns. He knew about Henry Jordan, Bill Quinlan, and Willie Davis. He realized Cleveland had a lot of depth. Those guys weren't playing very much.

# BOYD DOWLER

He and Paul Brown communicated pretty well; I think Paul Brown liked Vince and respected him. He didn't have to play against those guys (twice a year once they were traded to Green Bay), because Paul Brown had always said about players, "If you screw up here, we'll send you to Siberia." Well, Green Bay was Siberia."

Lombardi and Paul Brown were cerebral men and wanted players with a degree of intelligence. Dowler believes Lombardi may have trusted he would get bright players from Brown, "I think that had something to do with it and when you mention bright ball players, he could not tolerate dull mental mistakes. You could miss a tackle, you could drop a pass, but don't be jumpin' off sides all the time, don't be making stupid out of bounds penalties, late hits and don't blow assignments. It drove him crazy, as it should have. When you look at our football team and you look at our line up, both on offense and defense, there aren't any dumb guys in there. I mean, guys were football smart and they were basically intelligent people. He just wasn't gonna have it any other way and you did not make mistakes. We went forever without jumping off sides. We didn't have illegal formations. Now days, how many times a game do you see linemen, pre snap penalties? They set up to pass block before the ball is snapped; you don't even get to run the play, you back up five yards and go back in the huddle, you don't even get to practice." When that happened in a Lombardi practice Dowler said he would go off, "Oh, he'd get after you bad. He'd start yellin'. He'd start yellin' and screamin'. He'd tell you, "You better clean it up."

Boyd made a very revealing comment when asked if games were easier than practice, "It was easier to deal with him 'cause he was on the sidelines and we were on the field. There were times when guys would turn around and say, "Shut up," and stuff you know. He didn't mettle much, he didn't call plays. We were on our own when we crossed that line and went out there and he was over on the sidelines. He was there to motivate, before the game he'd make his pregame talk and at half-time he'd make his half-time talk. We were kinda out there on our own, a lot of us played together a long time on offense and on defense too. We handled things pretty well.

"The worst day I can remember of preseason training camp was when we had to go down in the stadium and have what they called the intra squad game. There might be 50,000 people there. I remember one year where somebody, Jesse Whittenton or somebody intercepted a pass and ran it back for a touchdown and something else happened; time ran out and the defense was ahead. This was in our early years. He was up in the press box. He came down on the sidelines and he was worse than upset and he said, "OK, we're staying out here. You're gonna take the ball on the ten yard line and you're gonna drive it the length of the field for a touchdown and we'll stay out here until you do." We did. The defense might have helped us a little bit but it was not fun. The defense knew what we were doing.

"I ran routes everyday in practice against Herb Adderley forever. Herb's pretty good, he's a Hall of Fame corner and we got along good. We competed and we went after each other pretty good, but we'd laugh." He'd say, "Good pattern," or this or that. If I'd beat'em, he'd say, "What ya see?" We weren't fist fighting. We weren't doing things like that; no extra curricular stuff. I think we might have had two little 'dust ups' in the whole time I was with the Packers."

Boyd's description of his relationship with Adderley supplies a snap shot of Lombardi's philosophy, competitive, but not combative. They were competitors, but friends. Even though Boyd and Herb went at it hammer and tong in practice, in the bigger scheme they were working together to make the Green Bay Packers a better team. So it was offense and defense, black and white, with a lack of issues on and off the field. Dowler saw the influx of black players and the way Lombardi managed it, "He couldn't have handled it any better. I think my rookie year, which was his rookie year, we may have had four African American players. You're right about the lack of any issues because we did things together, we would go over to somebody's house and have a cocktail, or a couple beers, and then go to dinner together on Sunday night. There was a group of us that kinda hung out on Monday night together. The African American guys who lived in Green Bay, the town's people treated them real well. Vince himself said from the get-go, "We'll never have anything like that." He said, "You're not calling me, because I'm Italian, any of those names that they call Italians. There's to be no reference to race. We're all here; this is a family together as a team.

"We hung out together. It was a very good situation and we're still good friends. We became good friends, not just guys who played on the same team. Willie Davis was a captain and a good leader and the other guys were too. Another thing which was very smart on Coach Lombardi's part, he brought Emlen Tunnell in. He brought Emlen with him initially in 1959. He had been close with Emlen when they were on the Giants together. Emlen was so squared away and understood.

"We had Elijah Pitts and Marvin Fleming basically in the beginning, for most of the time. They were basically the only black players we had on offense. Elijah was mistake free and very, very involved in his mind, and his whole make up. He was not going to be the guy that made a mistake, because he said it reflected on him, and it would reflect on the other black guys. He could play halfback, you could shoot him in the game at fullback and always knew what to do. He never made an error; he never made a *mental error* for sure. That's how we were. I think when I came there were four African American guys on our team. I think by the time I left there must have been a dozen.

"We had four the first year and we had four black guys the second year and then gradually as the years went on, then Herb came up—Bob Jeter. All of them were very strong character people. They were all smart. They were all team guys and never a problem. And I think Vince had a lot to do with that. They were top caliber guys anyway. They'd have fit in on any team. I think Vince made sure of that before he brought them in. He didn't back off because a player was African American. I think he was more concerned with whether he felt if he could deal with the player, if he dealt with the issue, the team would deal with the issue. I think he felt comfortable enough and confident enough in his own leadership in the fact that he was the main influence on the Green Bay Packers. He wasn't afraid of it; he didn't recoil with the thought, "Oh no, no I don't want to get too many African Americans." I don't think that bothered him one bit 'cause he thought he was beyond that, above that and he would handle it and he did."

As general manager, Lombardi drafted several players who were skilled enough to play multiple positions then moved them to their best position. Dowler was one such type, but he also saw a couple more guys who were first tried at his flanker spot, then moved to cornerback. "We drafted Herb in the first round (for '61) and Herb came in and was actually my backup at wide receiver as a rookie. Jeter was my backup ('63) at wide receiver. Both Adderley and Jeter spent one year running at wide receiver before they put them on defense and they went out there and started right away. I really don't know what was behind playing them on offense at all." Both of them had been outstanding college offensive players. Yes, but they both played both ways. I played both ways, there was some suggestion when I came out of college that I would play safety, because I did play pass defense pretty well. I intercepted quite a few passes in college. I wasn't much of a tackler, mostly arm tackles. Herb and Jeter were tough guys, they'd tackle ya, they could cover and they could run. Basically, instinctively they fit. They had more of a defensive temperament than an offensive temperament. Lombardi realized that. He watched them a year and said they're going over on defense."

Head Coach Lombardi and General Manager Lombardi saw eye to eye. As an offensive coach, he could have horded talent for that side of the ball; however, General Manager Lombardi knew he needed his best players on the field, at their best positions. According to Dowler, he didn't need much help evaluating the talent, "No, no, he could tell, he could see what was going on.

# BOYD DOWLER

When they moved Adderley over on defense, I came back from running a route. I'd walk by him and say, 'He's really quick, he's a struggle, he's tough to beat." You know, we talked that way in practice, he was coaching the offense basically, we communicated. I didn't have a problem offering my opinion on something like that. Willie Wood was the same way. See, Willie Wood was a college quarterback at USC and he was also a real good defensive back. When they brought Willie in (1960), he played some at corner. Willie Wood was a good cover corner, didn't really have the real good blazing foot speed that Herb and Jeter had, but Willie could cover you. Willie was a very instinctive defensive player and he was so quick. They put him at safety full-time the next year and good Lord, one year he leads the league in interceptions and the next year he leads the league in punt returns. Vince knew the minute Willie came and started practicing what he had."

Adderley, Jeter and Wood were all shifted to the Green Bay secondary, but not Dowler. With his speed and 6'5" height he might have made an interesting safety. Lombardi made him a flanker and Boyd knows why, "I was an offensive player and had an offensive temperament. Those guys were better, they were really good tacklers and they liked the competitive part of defense as far as hitting people. I wasn't that interested. I wanted to catch passes and punt the ball and stuff like that."

There were no challenges to Lombardi's iron fisted control of the team. When Jim Taylor chose to play out his option in 1966, the locker room could have split if there would have been players who felt Taylor was needed to win three consecutive titles. Getting three championships in a row was extremely important to Lombardi. According to Boyd, the standoff between the head coach and Taylor did not split the team, "Not really, Ron Kramer did the same thing in 1964. For a different reason, but to your teammates you're playing out your option, the reasons are kind of immaterial. Jimmy basically thought he should be making more money and he was gonna bow his neck, dig in his heals, and that was what he was gonna do. Vince wasn't gonna bend either and they were both strong personalities. That's the way it worked out. That's the reason he drafted Jim Grabowski. There was never one of us who went in to see Vince, or thought about going in to Vince and saying, "Come on, you gotta get Jimmy signed." No. If that ever happened, if anybody ever did that, I didn't know anything about it."

The Berlin Wall Crisis complicated Green Bay's pursuit of the 1961 NFL Championship. The Soviet Union built a wall that physically divided the city of Berlin, Germany in half that escalated the Cold War to a critical point, and prompted a state of military readiness by the United States. Three Packers starters Boyd Dowler, Ray Nitschke and Paul Hornung were called up to the National Guard. Much publicity has been generated regarding efforts made on Hornung's behalf to get weekend passes so he could play, but like so much in Dowler's career there was not much fanfare about him getting time off to play. All of it was made easier by Boyd himself because he choose to become a good soldier and not flaunt his star status. He didn't miss a game. Boyd said, "Part of it had to do with the unit we were assigned to. Hornung was put down in Fort Riley, Kansas in some Army Reserve, or National Guard unit that wasn't from Wisconsin. I don't think Paul was real interested in being a soldier, I'm not sure he did everything he was asked to do so they didn't work with him.

"I happened to hit it just right, I was assigned to the 32nd Red Arrow Division Artillery Headquarters, with a general who owned a small local newspaper in Mosinee, Wisconsin. General Francis X. Schweinler, a good German guy. He took a personal interest in getting me back for games. I played the Sunday before Thanksgiving. Of course, we played the Detroit Lions every Thanksgiving. I was supposed to be on the base the prior Friday. I played against the Rams in Green Bay and my wife and I got on the airplane and flew to Seattle. I reported to the 32nd Division Artillery Headquarters two days late, Vince had been on the phone and taken care of that. The first person I talked to was the General. He said, "Do you want to play

Thursday?" This is Monday, I said, *"Yes sir."*

He said, "OK, you cooperate with us, we'll cooperate with you. Do what you're supposed to do. We'll make sure you make the games. After this week, you can have noon on Friday 'till Monday noon. You can go, wherever the Packers are playing—go."

"I played five games (that way) I believe. I went back on Thursday; we beat the Lions in Detroit. I got dressed and was ready to go for warm ups and everything like that. I asked Lombardi, "You want me to start?" He said, "Hell yes, what do you think I brought you back here for?"

Boyd said, "We didn't do anything in practice anyway, we only had two days." I said, "OK, I just thought I'd check and see if you wanted me to run out there."

"I had a pretty good game. From then on, I would get in to Green Bay on Friday evening then somebody would pick me up at the airport and give me the game plan. Any changes were pretty easy. We had a "fool around" practice on Saturday's usually, it wasn't very intense—go over stuff and go out and play. I didn't miss a single snap the rest of the year and I was in the Army all week.

"A Major at Fort Lewis with the 32nd Division had a couple of apartments. He asked, "Do you want an apartment, you need an apartment?" I said, "Yeah."

"I have two."

"Well, Ray needs one." Ray and his wife lived across the street. So, after duty, Ray and I would throw the ball around and run sometimes until dark. But, Ray got a little obnoxious to some of the people. He was in a supply unit, and I don't know if somebody told him what to do and he didn't want to do it. He missed a couple games, but I got there like clock work, it was really good. I met a lot of nice people, good Wisconsin people. It was a very, very positive experience. That was our first World Championship. We got two weeks leave for Christmas and played in the championship game. The score was 37-0 (win over the Giants). Everybody in the Army played good. Nitschke played good, Hornung played *great*, I caught a touchdown pass and had a good game. The three guys in the Army came back; we got to practice for a week and a half. The whole thing just fell into place like clock work. It was good."

Dowler had close working relationships with some of the greatest coaches of the modern era. After playing for Lombardi, he coached on the staffs of Head Coach George Allen and General Manager Paul Brown. All three had a high degree of autonomy in running their operations. Boyd sights similarities in the three men, "Very smart, all of them smart. Very smart, but with different personalities and each one went about their jobs in a little different way. They all stayed true to their personalities. George Allen didn't try to act like Vince Lombardi, of course, Vince Lombardi didn't try to act like Red Blaik who was his mentor so to speak, coming out of Army. George Allen was uniquely George Allen. They all three had one thing in common as football coaches, they knew personnel and they knew how to approach the game with offense, defense and special teams complementing one another. The great coaches all had a healthy respect for all three areas and were able to put it together. I think that is partially a coaching trait and a general manager trait. A lot of the things that those guys did in the general manager part of their jobs was to put together a roster.

"The first place I went was to the Los Angeles Rams and George Allen essentially played the same role with the Rams and with the Redskins." Boyd was on Allen's staff in '70, and then moved with him to Washington in '71. Long time Lombardi assistant Bill Austin, served as interim coach for the 1970 season following Coach Lombardi's death. Allen was subsequently fired in LA and hired by Washington. Boyd says, "George Allen had the same role with those two teams as Vince had with the Green Bay Packers. He was *the* coach, he ran the football team, and he was in charge of the decisions that were made if it had anything to do with football. Vince made them, so did George Allen. Then, I ended up after that with some other teams where things were different. They had to be different. The league evolved into a situation where it is today where it's almost impossible to be *the* coach and *the* general manager. It's just too much for one man to do, but at that time it wasn't and quite frankly, the most successful teams and the best run organizations were with a strong coach/general manager; Vince and George Allen. I was with the Cincinnati Bengals and Paul Brown was the general manager and he was still running the team. The coach, coached the football, he (Brown) ran the team. He was actually the one who drafted and cut the team roster, this and that. When Paul Brown was still living, I thought he had a well run organization. Some of the others, not as good. I don't need to go into detail, but I've been with eight teams. Of the eight teams, the first two were the best organizations and they had a coach/general manager. Vince was best at it. Vince was best at it because Vince motivated better than anybody. That's the difference; the motivational skill. You know I'm a little bit partial. I was with some teams that won other than the Packers, but you know when you play for Vince Lombardi, for nine years and win five World Championships, you would never get me to say anybody was any better, because they weren't in my mind."

Dowler was a player, coach, and scout in a career that spanned 50 years. In each of those jobs, who would he have wanted to work for? "I would like one Vince Lombardi to be the coach and I would want the other Vince Lombardi to be the general manager. Hopefully they could get along together. You know that's a tough question because times change, the league is different, you've got salary cap to worry about now days, you've got agents to worry about, you've got all kinds of things that happen. You *need* to have a general manager, but the two of them need to work together very well, and that's the secret. If they don't communicate well, if there's some sort of friction going on, if they have different agendas, if there's a personal agenda in place for either one of them instead of, 'let's get together here and see how many games we can win.' If it isn't that, it's like any other thing, the people need to come together, they need to be able to work together—common goal."

There could have be a sign over the entire Packer organization during the Lombardi years, "Dummies don't fit." Dowler's mental make up and pedigree made him a great fit for the Packer dynasty, and Lombardi was ideal for Boyd, "I was raised by a coach, my dad was a high school coach. I had two younger brothers who were both college scholarship athletes coming out of Cheyenne, Wyoming, High School. We were pretty much raised from a pretty good gene pool which produced pretty good athletes. It was taken for granted that we were gonna play. It was almost demanded at home that we were gonna be good, achieve, compete and all of those things that go into what Vince Lombardi was talking about. I went to college and had pretty good coaching. I always listened pretty well; I was raised that way. When I got to Green Bay, I knew this guy was not to be fooled around with. You had better come out everyday, you better be ready to perform, you better be able to work hard, you better be able to think and you better be able to *perform*. It's all based on 'can you make plays.' If you can make plays, do what you're supposed to do and did it on a consistent basis, I think that's what he did better than anybody and what he did for me from the beginning, every single day. It didn't matter if it was Tuesday or we had a week off and we were out on the practice field. It didn't matter, he wasn't gonna let up and you can't let up. Pretty soon everybody is in that same mode, you better not back up. That's why we were able to repeat. You know we repeated once in '61 and '62, should have won it in '63 and we *didn't*. It was a disappointment and then we won the three in a row. Lombardi did not allow us to play below our level of excellence, whatever it was, both individually and as a team. He *did not* allow it. He would drive us and that's what he had. Everyday is a new challenge, 'what have you done for me lately?' That's exactly how he was and I think you can teach it, I think you can demand it. People say and ask me, "Well, he wouldn't have been able to handle today's players." I just kind of chuckle, I say, 'Oh yes he would have, oh yes he would have.' And he would have done just fine and that's exactly how I feel about it. That's what he instilled upon me and I think most of my teammates in one fashion or another would say the same thing."

Boyd is a bright guy, so when he makes a statement about football, it deserves consideration. He once said, "Lombardi was easy to play for." He sees it like this, "If you had the ability, if you were good enough, you did not let him down. If you weren't a good player, you weren't gonna be there anyway. It became easy if you understood what it was you were supposed to do and went about doing it, you didn't have a lot of problems. Don't screw it up though, don't screw it up on a daily basis, definitely don't screw it up on a yearly basis. That's why you didn't see many of us guys having bad years. The only time a guy had a year that wasn't pretty much up to his level, which was our level, (the player) might have been dinged a little, might have been hurt a little, might have had a little something else going on. I had a year, our first Super Bowl year, I was dinged, I was nicked, I wasn't very healthy. I got started a little haywire, dropped a couple balls. I snapped out of it finally and had a pretty good game down in Dallas at the Championship game in 1966. I was not myself and he understood that and he didn't get on me much."

Retired now and living near Atlanta, Boyd has gratitude plastered all over him as he reflects on what he would say to his former head coach and general manager if given the chance. "Thanks, thanks and I can't say how fortunate, how blessed I was to have been drafted by somebody else (Vainisi) and come in to Green Bay, Wisconsin, the same year you did.

"How could it happen any better? That was the beginning of a special period of time in my life, about most everything. Both of my kids were born in Green Bay. How can anything be any better than to go to Green Bay at the very same time as Lombardi, start from the very ground up, work together with these people, and win five World Titles in seven years? I could have been drafted by the Washington Redskins or the Pittsburgh Steelers of those years and ended up kicking around and doing nothing; who knows. But it just happened, it was a fit and the fit began after I was drafted. They hired Vince Lombardi and he came to town. "Thanks. You didn't know about me and I didn't know about you, but it sure did work."

One of Dowler's regrets was he did not attend Lombardi's funeral, "*No, no*, and it upsets me. I'm upset at myself and I always have been, but I was also upset with George Allen. It was my first year coaching with the Rams. Of course Vince gets sick, it was 1970, we're in training camp and Vince dies. The next day, George called me into his office and says, "We need you here." He didn't even ask me if I wanted to go, he says, "We need you here, we'll send somebody to represent the club." I was within my first two or three weeks as a coach with a new boss and instead of saying, no, I'm going. I didn't, I waffled and I didn't go and I've been sorry about it ever since. That was the wrong thing to do, I should have said, 'Nope, I'm not representing the Rams anyway, I didn't play for the Rams when he was my coach, we were Packers.' I should have gone and I didn't do it. It was a bad deal. I resented George for that, I never told him. That was my first year away from Green Bay after 11 years. I should have flown to Green Bay and gotten on the plane with them and go to the funeral, but I didn't do it."

It is one of the very few things Boyd Dowler has to regret regarding his relationship with the Green Bay Packers.

# CHAPTER 5
## PAT COCHRAN:

*"Lombardi leaned over and kissed the coach instead of Marie."*

# THE LOMBARDI LEGACY

Red Cochran was a football man. For the most part he was a football player, coach, or scout from 1940 to 2004. Except for two years spent as a B-24 bomber pilot in World War II, he was involved with the game. At times Red's temperament was somewhat akin to the bombs he dropped. He played college ball at Wake Forest and had a three year career with the Chicago Cardinals from 1947 to '49 playing running back and cornerback. The Chicago Cardinals team record for punt return average (21 per attempt) is *still* held by John Thurman "Red" Cochran.

In a twist of irony, Ray "Scooter" McLean was fired as Packer head coach following the disastrous (1-10-1) season of 1958. The Detroit Lions terminated Red in order to make room for McLean on their coaching staff. Subsequently, Cochran was the first assistant hired by Vince Lombardi. In all, Red served the Packer organization for 42 years as a coach (1959-'66, 1971-'74) and scout (1975-2004). He gained Packer acclaim as backfield coach of three Hall of Fame players; Paul Hornung, Bart Starr and Jim Taylor.

The Packer Hall of Fame inducted Coach Cochran in 1997, six years before he passed away on September 5, 2004.

The Cochran's, like many Lombardi era Packers, chose the Green Bay area as home and raise their family of three children, Tracy, Cindy and Russell. Pat still lives in De Pere, Wisconsin, long time site of the Packer training camp dormitory at St. Norbert College and Red's 'lil Red Truck is still parked in the family garage

Red's wife of 48 years, Pat, is friendly, funny, blunt and brutally honest. She became a Packer player favorite with her hospitality and many of the guys stopped by the Cochran residence for a home cooked meal and trusted friendship. She is welcomed with open arms by players at alumni functions these many years later.

Because Lombardi fostered real stability within the Packer organization, many people stayed around for a long time during the dynasty and thus numerous significant relationships developed during those ten years. Pat and

# PAT COCHRAN

Marie Lombardi became close friends allowing Pat to gain intriguing insight into the formidable Mrs. Lombardi, some of which is shared in this chapter.

It was a precarious journey from Detroit to Green Bay for her family as Pat Cochran explains, "We met and married in Detroit—had one baby and the second one on the way. We had won a championship in 1957 in Detroit with George Wilson as the head coach, second year, we had a good year. We were buying a house and all of a sudden we got home and Red's mother said, "Go to the office—they've been calling you all day." He went over to the office, and was fired to make room for Scooter McLean. Red was looking for a job, and it was a very nervous time, because he had only been into pro coaching two years—he didn't have a resume. We got this phone call from a sports editor—somebody out east who had talked to Vince and knew Vince had gotten the Green Bay job. When he called us he said Lombardi wanted coaches who had played the game and that he was going to call Red. So boy, were we happy when the phone call came, because things weren't so good. You can't go out and look for a job in coaching--you really end up waiting for them to call you. You have to have a friend out there somewhere to push you a little bit, and this reporter did that for us. Vince and Marie were coming to Green Bay to look for a house, look around and get settled a little bit. Red met him at the airport. The plane was late, and Marie always told me, "I hoped that young man wouldn't be sitting in a bar, 'cause if he was sitting in a bar, and wasn't at that gate when Vince got off that plane, there wouldn't have been a job." Red was waiting there for him."

The meeting went well and the Cochran's had a shot at getting a job, "Vince said to Red, "Just don't do anything. I'll get back to you as soon as I can." It wasn't long and Red was the first assistant hired. Red came over in early winter."

Even though Red and Pat had experienced winter in Detroit, Green Bay's was tougher, "We had bought this house and the gentleman was going to a rest home, but he left some furniture, thank goodness, and there was a stove, and a little refrig—things I could use with two babies. So, we moved in there. Well, we got the snow cleared off for the movers, and we looked and we waited and we looked and we waited, the movers never came. And so that Sunday, I looked out, and here came this couple, both in camel hair coats and I said, 'Oh, my God, it's the 'Old Man.' He came in, he took one look around, and he said, "Marie, get 'em over for dinner tonight." That was very Lombardi. We just had a real nice family night with the Lombardi's. I didn't know 'em from Adam. It was good, Susan-his daughter, took my two little girls off my hands to let us visit, which was nice. Vincent Jr. was home. It was just a nice Sunday night dinner. I can still remember it—we had sauerkraut and ribs."

Moving to Green Bay was an adjustment enough. The winter of 1958-'59 was particularly snowy as Pat relates, "This is one of my fond memories of Vince—he had this little 'wiener dog,' I call it, and he took it out to go to bathroom. He came in just laughing, and said, "How's this dog gonna live here in all this snow?"--little stubby dog. And honest to Pete, my neighbors called us and invited us over for a cocktail one night, and they asked, "Do you have any children?" Tracy was two, and they couldn't see her—the snow banks were higher than she was—they didn't know we had any children. So winter was something else."

In order to get a fast start as new coaches, Red and defensive coordinator Phil Bengtson lived at the downtown YMCA in Green Bay as they looked for housing before moving their families. Pat explains how the two assistant coaches battled winter, "They had to walk down to the Packer offices and Red said, "What in the hell are we doin' in this place, Phil?" Phil said, "I don't know—we needed a job." Back then the Packer office was downtown."

Red was fortunate to land a pro job anywhere with only two years coaching experience, let alone on the staff of a guy who would be the game's greatest coach. Pat recalls Red's impression of his boss, "Well, number one, he said he thought he was the most organized man he'd ever been around.

He spent a lot of time with his assistant coaches, because it was going to be Vince's way. And so he spent a lot of time training them to do it his way, and it was a great thing for Red. They were a lot alike—they both blew off at the drop of a hat, then five minutes later, you'd never know they were mad. I think they had some difficult times, he certainly appreciated working for him, let me put it that way. Lots of times, he'd come home and he'd say, "(mmm, mmm)," because Vince was a male Italian, it was either gonna be his way or no way, and sometimes he just flew off the handle."

During games, Red was stationed in the press box to help with the play calling even though most of that was handled by Bart Starr. However, there were two times he left his elevated position during games to deliver some thoughts in person. Pat says, "It was a championship game, and I'm not sure which one—early in the '60s, and Bart was hurt a couple times, where Zeke Bratkowski had to come in, and he won the games, we're ahead in this game, we're gonna win this game, we know it. Red came down from up in the box and he said, "Coach, don't you think we ought to put Zeke in there and let him get a few reps here in this game?" Lombardi said, "Damnit, don't tell me what to do--Zeke, get in there!" The other time he came down, which was Super Bowl I, he didn't like what was being called."

Assistant coaches did not put in brutal hours throughout the entire year because Green Bay's head man tried to build in family time, "They were probably at the office by eight in the morning, but he came home every night for dinner—you could do that because of the size of the town—and here again, Vince thought, "Let's keep 'em happy, keep the wives happy--If you don't have a happy wife, you don't have a happy ballplayer, either." So we'd get an hour and a half for dinner and then they'd go back and stay— nine, ten, eleven o' clock, sometimes midnight, on Monday-Tuesday. Then Wednesday it tapered off and we had off Thursday 'family night,' which is what Vince named it. And then Friday, the scouting—there was one scout, Pat Peppler. So Red got on a plane, he had the south, so he flew to Atlanta every Friday."

Pat became one of the player's favorite people. Her straight forward, open demeanor was a welcomed personality for most of the guys, including those of color, "Well, first of all, the married ones couldn't find a place to live. The only black person up here was a shoeshine boy at the hotel downtown. And also, to go out to dinner, or any of that, it was very hard on them. I would say very hard on the black wives, it was extremely hard on them.

"Personally, I grew up in a little white town--one black family. Where I got to huggin' the Packer white guys; I'd hesitate hugging the black ones, but eventually, that went away, too.

"The towns people were kind of in awe of them, and as a sidelight, the girls really thought they were neat, and that became a little problem. Vince didn't want to stir up anything in the town, let's put it that way, because there was still that feeling."

Red Cochran ended his long football career as a Green Bay Packer scout having logged 52 years in the pros as a player, coach and scout. Forty-two of those with the Packer organization, and it all started with the meeting in Detroit's airport, "Red and I both said, 'We're sure glad he came our way.' It was a ball. I loved every minute of it. Everybody got along, or seemed to. I don't recall any trouble, or ballplayers getting mad at each other because one was gonna play and the other one wasn't. Vince somehow had a handle on that. If they didn't fall into how he wanted to, 'bye.' But if they were really good, he'd think twice before he 'bye'd' 'em.'" Salary wise, "We were in the teens. We never made more than $40,000 in his whole career. But it went further than it would today. Vince didn't make that much money. In fact, when he died, Marie was shocked that they had as much as they did--she didn't know. He got into some real estate deals—dorms down in Madison-- but they didn't have money either. They weren't paid well—he had to have a second job in New York when he was an assistant."

In Green Bay, the championship bonus money made a huge difference between just being able to raise a family on a regular salary and buying extra items, "Well, everything in this house. I can say I got my first freezer when we won the championship and that hutch, we furnished our house—none of us had anything."

As a couple, the Lombardi's had a relationship that worked for them, two strong willed people who trusted each other enough to clash. Pat explains, "Stormy, volatile, and they had an extremely good marriage. They lived with that. Now me, I had a hard time living with Red's screaming, 'cause he screamed, and they're (coaches) all out on the field and they're screaming all the time. I had a real hard time with that 'cause my father never did. Marie and Vince screamed at each other, and they were fine. And I mean, he was absolutely lost if she wasn't with him—she went to every game, she went on every trip and if the guys got a little noisy on the bus, she would also quiet 'em or she'd say, "OK Vince,"—she would kind of stick up for 'em, when Vince was down on 'em. She was always part of it.

"Marie helped women get settled, she came by to see if you were OK. She stopped by my house an awful lot of the time, 'cause I was on her way home." The topic of conversation inevitably turned to the center piece of their lives, "Football, football, because it was our life. And it was certainly hers, 'cause she was such a big part of it. She would say, "Well, he wasn't a happy coach last night," or things like that--she didn't go into it a lot."

Vince Lombardi's organizational skills and attention to detail amazed his colleagues these many years later, seldom would the minutest detail escape his exquisite eye in the office, film room, or practice field. On the home front, Pat relates an episode that shows his human side, "Well, Vince was a clothes horse, which most people don't know—so he probably had 20 suits or so in his closet. Marie told me this story; I guess he got up earlier than she—she was laying in bed. He's gettin' dressed to go somewhere; he went in the drawer and no handkerchiefs. And he's screaming at her, "Where in the hell are all these," so she gets out of bed and she goes in the closet and she starts pulling handkerchiefs out of the pockets of these suits-"Here's one." I can see it, "here's another one." Every once in a while, she screamed back at him, and I guess you'd have to if you lived with him."

According to Pat, the Lombardi's relationship had affection, but not necessarily tenderness, "Well, yes and no. He wasn't always fawning over her, or she fawning over him. Well, it had to be, because he couldn't be without her. But he'd scream, he'd yell at her in front of people, but you know, I never saw 'em hugging. He'd take her arm, help her on a plane. I'm sure they had it—in their own way-- you'll see some people always holding hands, or bumpin' shoulders or something. I didn't see that. But I knew that it was a very good marriage."

Former First Lady Nancy Reagan supplied the biggest and most trusted support for her husband, President Ronald Reagan; much like Marie did for her spouse. According to Pat, there were some similarities between the Reagan and Lombardi relationships, "I guess, in a way. I know she would be the go-between, between the players if she thought Vince was being too tough on a player, and the players liked her, because they knew she was the go-between, or she could calm him down or say, "Come on, Vinnie," or "This isn't right." I always thought of Nancy Reagan as she always looked up adoringly at Ronnie—that wasn't that kind of relationship—that relationship wasn't going on between them. It would be, "God damnit Marie, get up here." That's how they lived. But as I said, it was a good marriage, a very strong marriage.

"The preseason games—Lombardi always had a big buffet dinner over here at St. Norbert's. Beautiful food— shrimp and anything you would want, and all the wives were always invited to that. Thanksgiving, when we played Detroit—we all went to the Elk's and he had babysitters and movies and bowling—there was bowling downstairs for the kids, and this was a big family thing, and he just loved it. We all got dressed up and hoped that we won the game, because it always was a whole lot more fun if we won. It was not fun to be around Vince Lombardi if we lost. Sometimes, it wasn't fun to be around him when we won, if they didn't do what he thought they were up to doing."

Family unity and involvement were consistently promoted by Lombardi. Pat tells of a time when her son was to spend a night at training camp. "The boys could go over and spend the night with their dads, and so I took Russell over and waited for his dad to come get him. We were sitting in the car in front of the dining hall, where the players all ate and here comes— we called him 'The Happy Italian'—not to his face. I thought, 'Uh-oh.' He said, "Hey Russ, where's his suitcase?" And I said, 'In the back.' He just took Russell with him in there, they went in, and I thought, "Oh, Lord," because Russell wouldn't even eat a hot dog, he was such a picky eater, so I guess they got along. Red comes along and he said, "Where is Russell?" I said, 'He's in there with Vince.' So that was another side to Vince. He had a lot of sides, like we all do. When I told Marie this story, she said, "Wish he'd do that for his own children."

Complicated and unpredictable, Lombardi scared some people, but not all, "I wasn't intimidated. One time he hugged you and said, "Hi, honey." Then two or three times he'd walk by and didn't even know you were there. So, I had a hard time with people like that. I was never intimidated by him, 'cause I grew up with Italians, but that was just his way. Marie told a story— when he was either at Army or with the Giants. He had to commute and she'd take him down to the train-- (maybe it was the Giants)-- and then they picked up another coach. Somehow, or other, Lombardi leaned over and kissed the coach instead of Marie. I mean, his mind was on football, and that's how he was. But mine was the same way, just before training camp; they all get that glare in their eye. You could peck, peck, and peck at 'em and they don't even know you're around. But family wise, I don't think he was too good with his own family."

For Pat Cochran, life has moved on without Red and the Lombardi's, but the memories linger in their mind and in mementoes, "Well, my most precious thing, is I have a ring from the first 1961 championship. Red didn't like rings. He had big hands and big knuckles from playing football and he got a tie bar. When we won the first Super Bowl, we got a dinner ring. And both of those things I cherish very much, and Red just loved those rings.

"The Lombardi's were a part of my life--a good part of my life and as you know, when you get older, you do tend to go back. But things will just happen that remind you of things. One year, we got a beautiful silver tea set. I don't know what the year was—(looking across the room), that's where it sat for a long time. I donated it to the Hall of Fame; because my two girls aren't gonna clean silver. There were always things to remind you. I used to have that sitting around me."

The Cochran's were the first of the assistant coaches to be hired, were a part of the resurrection of Green Bay's Dynasty under Lombardi, but after the 1966 season, Red decided he wanted a change, "He just had it. First of all, Red was the backfield coach, which also included the quarterback at that time. Well, Vince was also an offensive coach, so they were in each other's pocket all the time and they were two volatile men, and to stay on top was a whole lot harder than getting there. Everybody's out for you. We won second place twice 1963 and '64 and boy, it wasn't going to happen again. There was a playoff bowl in Florida one year, and he said this was the end of that, he wasn't gonna be in any more of them damn playoff games. He was ornery. He was not a happy camper down in Florida. I don't think they ever had a screaming battle over it. I think Red one day just had it up to here (gestures up to top of her head) and he had to quit.

"There were some hard times, of course—it wasn't all roses—but, boy it was sure more roses than anything else. We traveled, we met celebrities. when we went to the first Super Bowl, we were the celebrities. There were movie stars out there hanging around, waiting to meet us. It was fun. It was just fun. I got to meet all the astronauts—they came to all these golf outings

(Lombardi Golf Classic) after Vince died, but you know, we were celebrities. We didn't think we were, but we were. One time, I was with Cherry Starr in Milwaukee, and Joe DiMaggio came in and sat down with us at the counter. Well, Red had a really good friend, Tommy Byrne, who was a pitcher for the Yankees at the time. Red could go in the Yankees locker room and Byrne said, "Don't go around Joe DiMaggio—he doesn't like that." But I got to meet him, and Red said, "You got to? You're kidding." I said, "No, he knew Cherry." But, you know, it was just fun."

The impact of Lombardi's cancer induced death hit Pat and Red with predictable force. "It was bad. We were in San Diego and Red was coaching a game. He couldn't get to the funeral and we always felt so bad. Red did not go, and I said Vince would've understood that because he had a game that week and just couldn't go."

Marie and Pat continued their friendship after the Lombardi's left Green Bay and the bond remained strong; "Yeah--went down to Florida. She had come back here for the Lombardi Golf Tournament. She'd come in for that and then I always saw her. We kind of hung out together, and she was just devastated. One time she said–her brother had cancer, her sister had cancer– she said, "I think I've got it." She was a smoker and was scared and she said, "Why don't you come down?" So I did. She was in Palm Beach at the time. Vince had a dream, he wanted to be an owner, and Marie always wanted to live in West Palm. All the salespeople knew her, she took me to her favorite restaurants, she belonged to a club, she had a beautiful apartment, right on the ocean, but all we did was talk about Vince. But she didn't have any friends. The Miami Dolphins were nice to her, and they invited her down to their games, so I drove her big Lincoln and we went to a game down there. She said she was always very hurt when the Packers came; they never contacted her when they played Miami—that was one of her hurts."

# CHAPTER 6
# BUD LEA:

*"It was like going to war with the Fifth Armored Division."*

# THE LOMBARDI LEGACY

Bud Lea was a hard nosed newspaper beat writer. The Milwaukee Sentinel needed additional sportswriters when the Boston Braves moved to Milwaukee in 1953, so Bud was hired out of Rochester, Minnesota. As a young reporter he was given the worst sports assignment on the paper, the moribund Green Bay Packers. Wisconsin's hot sports item was the Milwaukee Braves with Eddie Mathews, Hank Aaron and Warren Spahn. The Braves were perennial pennant contenders and the Packers were predictable losers. According to Bud, the University of Wisconsin, Marquette University and the Milwaukee Hawks of the NBA were all preferable assignments to the Packers. During his career, the Green Bay native rode the tide of worst assignment, to best, as the Packers exploded on the national scene under the whip of Vince Lombardi. Bud, in collaboration with Vernon and John Biever, authored *"Magnificent Seven, the Championship Games that Built the Lombardi Dynasty."* It's a terrific capsule of the five NFL title games plus the first two Super Bowls. It is highly recommended reading for Packer fans.

For 43 years, Lea covered Wisconsin sports for the Milwaukee Sentinel and served as Sports Editor from 1972- 1980. This esteemed newspaperman retired when the Milwaukee Sentinel and Milwaukee Journal merged in 1995. In recent years, he has been actively involved with the Milwaukee Braves Historical Association, preserving the legacy of Milwaukee's original major league baseball club. He is also a frequent contributor to Packer Plus, a weekly magazine published by the Journal Sentinel.

Bud Lea describes the Green Bay environment pre-Lombardi, "Well, before he got there, there were no rules. You did anything you wanted, talked to players any time you wanted to--no rules at all. And this guy from New York comes in, and suddenly everything is changed. Now there are rules. Lombardi said, 'If you want to cover my team in training camp, you gotta stay in St. Norbert College. I said, 'Why do I have to do that?'

"Those are the rules."

"So, that first training camp under Lombardi, I and other media guys, and the rookies, stayed in the second floor of Sensenbrenner Hall. And I couldn't stand it--I mean, the guy I roomed with from United Press in Milwaukee—snored, and I couldn't get any sleep. We went to the end of the hall and they just had a big bathroom, and you get these huge guys, and I'm a skinny little guy and my parents lived in Green Bay, why should I have to stay at St. Norbert in Sensenbrenner Hall? So, after two days, I just left. Still covered training camp, but Lombardi was so wrapped up--training his team—turning what he thought were a bunch of bums into something, he didn't even notice I was absent.

"We were all afraid of him. Scared to death. I think the Green Bay guys were at a *bigger* disadvantage because they were there at every single practice, and he disliked the media. I think he thought all of us were a bunch of PR guys; that we were there just to promote the Packers. Now in Milwaukee, it wasn't much better, but a little bit, because we're two hours away. I remember Lombardi's boss when he was at West Point was a guy named 'Ockie' Krueger. When Ockie retired at West Point and Lombardi got the job at Green Bay, he asked Lombardi, "What do you have?" Lombardi owed Krueger kind of a favor. And he says, "Well, we've got this, and this and this." He said "What other kind of jobs do you have at Green Bay?"

"Well, we've got a ticket office in Milwaukee."

"How far is Milwaukee from Green Bay?"

Lombardi said, "That's two hours."

"Krueger said he took it because he knew about Lombardi's hot temper and he didn't want to be around that Green Bay office, but being that far away, it was tolerable."

Bud Lea was a crusty reporter; he would not back off a story. If anyone in the Wisconsin press was going to take on Lombardi, it would probably have been Bud. So, did he? "Honest to God— you're talking about a championship team, so how many times are you really going to nail him?" Lea said, "I remember we had to go to this Five O' Clock Club. What the hell is a Five

# THE LOMBARDI LEGACY

O' Clock Club? When the Packers were out of town, you had to go up to Lombardi's suite and check in, and the rules at this Five O' Clock Club—all the media had to go there, along with all the assistant coaches. The rules were everything was off the record. What happened at this Five O' Clock Club? Well, the media, they hung all together and the coaches hung all together. We'd all have some drinks with the coach, and about five minutes to six, everyone cleared out—those are the rules. But I remember once, I think it was over in Cleveland, maybe I had too many scotches that night--but I said, 'OK, Coach, I'll put up with this under one condition.' He asked, "What's that?" I said, *'Don't lose.'*

He said, *"Mister, I don't intend to."* And he kept winning and winning and winning."

Every facet of the Packers was controlled by Lombardi. His capacity to observe, understand, and manage all issues is mind boggling. In the following account of a trip to the West Coast, Bud touches on Lombardi's attempted control of the commissioner, Packer Executive Board, the media, team and family.

Lea said, "I remember that first Super Bowl against the Kansas City Chiefs, the Packers went out a week before the game—there was a big argument on where they were going to stay." Lea recalls, "Lombardi always wanted to stay at Palo Alto. He didn't want to go and stay in Los Angeles, where the game was going to be held. He thought his players were getting too familiar with the starlets and all the celebrities there. So, he was going to take his team back to Palo Alto. The game was not selling and NFL Commissioner Pete Rozelle said, "You come to Los Angeles." They had a big fight, and they finally compromised. The Packers stayed up at Santa Barbara, which is 90 miles away from Los Angeles.

"That was one of the few times I asked Lombardi a favor. Instead of flying from Milwaukee to Los Angeles, then having to go all the way to Santa Barbara, I asked him if I could get on the Packer charter. The Milwaukee

Sentinel would pay for everything, but could I make sure I could get that lift. He said, "Let me think about it." I think it was the day before departure when he finally got back to me and said, "You can come with us, on one condition."

"What's that?"

"You don't talk to anybody."

I said, 'OK.' I get on the plane with the Packers, they're flying to California, and he would patrol the asile--go up and down. I'd be sitting with players, and every time he came by me, I'd look down like I'm not doing anything, but I continued to talk to players. About an hour out of Santa Barbara--there's a big scream, from the rear of the plane. The players were playing cards, they had their shoes off, and Lombardi's daughter Susan—she's kind of a chunky girl— wandered back there and accidentally stepped on Elijah Pitts' foot and he just screams like hell, and Lombardi comes running back there, "What the heck happened?" She said, "Daddy, I didn't see him." Pitts is holding his foot. Lombardi tells Susan to go back where she belongs. He goes by me and gives me that look—"One sentence of this gets in that paper--watch out." Well, it never got in the paper. As far as the executive committee, I think they were planning to go out to that first Super Bowl. Lombardi picked out his own hotel. When he heard of their plans, he said, "You're not staying here. Pick your own hotel." He ran the Packers. He was the only guy that ran them."

Lombardi was a difficult interview after a game, win or lose. Bud recalls an incident when an East Coast writer crossed the coach. "I remember one time at Milwaukee County Stadium, Lombardi had beaten the Rams, I think it was like 9 to 6, really low-scoring. Some guy came in from New Jersey and said, "Boy that wasn't too sterling." Lombardi said, "That was a golden performance." He got in an argument with this guy from the New Jersey paper and it got pretty heated. The guy kept asking Lombardi questions and Lombardi said, "You know what's wrong with you? You don't know a goddamn thing about football." And this writer from New Jersey said, "You know what's wrong with you Vince? You don't know a goddamn thing about journalism." Honest to God, it saved our day—we were just so happy that this guy could talk back to him. His name was Jerry Izenberg from the New Jersey Star Ledger, and I called him a few days later and I said, 'What happened? How are you going to resolve this with Lombardi?' He said, "Oh, heck, he called me a couple days later and said, "Aw, Jerry, you know—you know me, that's the way I am." But we didn't know Lombardi like that. Everyone was treading very softly when they were around Lombardi, because he was such a demanding personality you just did not second-guess."

As the 1969 Packers fell from the lofty heights of NFL superiority under new Head Coach Phil Bengtson, Lombardi anguished from a distance; he was very quiet as general manager. Lea said, "He picked his successor. Dominic Olejniczak didn't, nobody from the executive committee did. He picked his successor. Do you think he really wanted a very strong guy to follow him? Phil Bengtson was a hell of a defensive coach; he was not a head coach, and hell, the players took full advantage of the situation. That was a big change, but he never went down to practice, never would be in a position where he was going to second-guess Bengtson. But I remember going to Washington D.C., the Packers played the Redskins. There were signs in the stadium saying, "Bring back Lombardi--Coach the Redskins." The Redskins could give Vince something the Packers could never give him—part ownership of a team—because the Packers are owned by the fans."

Bud Lea is not easily impressed, he's been around thousands of athletes and coaches, but Lombardi holds a special place, "Of all the things I've covered in sports, from Olympics to major league baseball, to the NBA, to college football to major golf tournaments, to auto racing, nobody can compare with him. I never saw a leader like that. I remember going out to Yankee Stadium for that 1962 championship game against the New York Giants. At that time, the writers could get on the Packer team buses. I remember sitting in the first bus, and there's Vince Lombardi and Marie Lombardi, and it was like going to war with the Fifth Armored Division, and there was General Patton in the first seat. They were that confident."

# CHAPTER 7
# OLIVE JORDAN FREY:

*"Coach Lombardi asked him for a cigarette."*

# THE LOMBARDI LEGACY

General Manager Vince Lombardi made two significant trades with the great Paul Brown and by far, got the better end of both deals. Before the 1960 season, defensive end Willie Davis was acquired from Cleveland for A.D. Williams. A year earlier, Lombardi swapped a fourth round pick for defensive tackle Henry Jordan. The two former Browns anchored Green Bay's defensive line competing in six championship games, winning five world titles and earning entrance into the Pro Football Hall of Fame.

Lombardi placed a high priority on family involvement. In unprecedented fashion, he rewarded the wives with gifts of appreciation for their contribution to the team's success. Possibly equally as unique, Marie Lombardi cared for, and interacted with, Packer families. Olive Jordan, wife of Henry, serves as an example of the intricate role wives played during the Lombardi years. Henry and Olive had three children, Henry (Butch) Jr., Theresa and Suzanne. This bright, vibrant, funny, lovely lady combined with Henry to play an important role off the field to generate team unity.

Used little by the Cleveland Browns, Henry wore Green Bay's number 74 in the Pro Bowl in 1961, '62, '64, '65, '66, and '67. The Virginia native was inducted into the Pro Football Hall of Fame in 1995 and the Packer Hall in 1975.

Olive Jordan Frey explains the uncertainty she and Henry dealt with during their two years with the Cleveland Browns. "After every game he'd say, "Well, I'm probably gonna be traded," because on Monday or Tuesday, that's when they were gonna be traded. Then, the year that we were traded, 1959, he came home and said, "I think I'm gonna be traded," and we got a phone call and he was. He went down to the Brown's office and made them tell him to his face."

The nightmare began when the Jordan's became Green Bay Packers in September of 1959 while the team was holding a training camp ending session in Pewaukee, Wisconsin. Olive said, "We were told we had 24 hours to get there. I had the option to go home or stay with Henry. I wanted to stay, and he wanted me to, so we jumped into the car. It was 72 degrees when we left Cleveland. Heading up to Green Bay, Highway 41 then was just a two lane road, there were no lights, we didn't see anybody, it was cold. It was 32 degrees by the time we got to Pewaukee at three o'clock in the morning. Got to our room, no crib for the baby, I was ready to go home. Seriously, I was. I thought, 'This is it.' We're going home; this is Siberia, 'cause we didn't even know where it was. We had to get a map to find it. I didn't even unpack, went and had breakfast, saw the other ladies, sat back, fed my son, went back to the room and in he walks, happy as a clam. He used to call me momma, "Momma," he says, "We found a home." I thought, 'Oh boy.' So we did, we really did.

"In Cleveland, Paul Brown was a stickler for a lot of things. Where Vince Lombardi was strict in some ways, he was liberal in others. Paul Brown used to make the players take lessons on how to eat and how to act in public. If you were caught smoking…You *did not* smoke in public. When Henry got to practice and they were sitting around that first day, Coach Lombardi asked him for a cigarette, Henry said, "I'm home."

That first training camp in 1959 set the tone for a powerful Lombardi value; family. Olive recalls, "Oh, absolutely, that was the most important thing. He figured if the family wasn't happy then the players weren't happy, and if the players weren't happy, he couldn't get 100% out of them. So he wanted everything nice and quiet and happy at home. Henry didn't come home a lot, but we tried to see him everyday of course, because of the children. In those days you could go out and sit right out there and watch practice."

When Olive's world was rocked later that first year, a life-long appreciation for Marie Lombardi and the entire Packer family began in earnest. She recalls a life changing event, "In 1959, we were in Green Bay, and at three o'clock in the morning on November 13th, Friday the 13th, we got a phone call that my mother had been killed by a drunk driver. That was devastating. She was my best friend and I was just getting to know my mother as an adult. Henry felt terrible because he said, "I have to go play the game." Of course he called the coaches, it was three in the morning and he still called them. We get to the train station, because they were traveling to Milwaukee by train and everybody came up to me. Marie was one of the very kind ones. I sat in the car while Henry got on the train and she came up to the car and said how sorry she was and if there was anything she could do, let her know. Marie Lombardi was a wonderful woman and she was wonderful to me. I will always be eternally grateful for all the nice things she ever did for me. Whenever I was in the hospital, and I was, with two kids and kidney stones, she was there, she was there for everything.

"For some reason or other, I will always wonder why Marie was so affectionate to me, but she did tell me, quietly and not around anybody else that she admired how I handled my mother's passing. Because I didn't make a stink, I didn't interrupt a football game. I went home, had the funeral. I stayed at home and Henry came back and played his football game. So I did not disrupt the team, my life was disrupted but I did not disrupt the team." For several years, the sanctuary of the Jordan's household helped unify the team as Henry and Olive hosted many team gatherings. "We had a lot of fun. When the boys were winning so much, it was a little difficult to have a good time out in public. We would have everybody over to the house; everybody would go in the basement. A lot of times we were there 'till three, four, five in the morning. Monday was their day off, so this would be like a Sunday night. We just had a good time."

Precision was a hallmark of Lombardi's style, the players lived it and the wives learned it. According to Olive, "He was a great coach. You knew where you stood with him. What Henry liked about him, if practice was going to be from nine to ten, it was exactly from nine to ten. Lombardi had his own time. Henry liked everything about the way he organized everything. Everybody knew where they stood, they knew what was expected of them, they knew how they were to do things; he was a great teacher.

"We were all a little bit terrified of him to say the least. We didn't want to ever embarrass him. When he gave us our first mink stoles, somewhere there's a picture of him sitting with all the wives. He walked in nervous, sat down, had one picture taken. If we'd have been there with our eyes crossed and tongues hanging out or whatever, it wouldn't have made any difference. Coach Lombardi had his one picture and he was out of there.

"We, as wives, were not around him that much. Thanksgivings were wonderful. Everybody got together. He was an Italian and very family oriented, and to Coach Lombardi, the team was the family. His religion, his team in that order. His religion always came first, you know he went to mass everyday, never missed a day. Family was very important to him. He would walk around the room seeing everybody on Thanksgiving.

"We'd see him at practice; we would go down and see the guys. We'd walk back and sometimes Coach would walk with us and say, "Hi." But, you didn't have a conversation with him because we were twenty years old, twenty-one, twenty-two years old, we were scared to death. That was Coach Lombardi for heaven's sake. That was the one that was holding our future in his hands."

Boyd Dowler had a 40 year career in the NFL as a player, coach, and scout. He worked with some truly great coaches and general managers and believes Lombardi's ability to motivate people separated him from anyone else. The Packer Coach would appeal to people's pride, fear, logic, money, courage, but his most original motivational tool may have been pregnancy. One day at practice he noticed an enlarged Olive, "I was pregnant, he came up to me and patted my stomach and smiled and said, "Good." I couldn't figure out what that was all about and Henry said, "He loves it, because that's another mouth to feed, and I'm gonna have to work harder."

Henry liked, respected, and admired Vince Lombardi. However, there came a point when he had enough and was willing to pack it in. Olive is not certain of the year, but recalls the events, "Training camp ('65 or'66). They had a particular game during training camp and Coach Lombardi was on a tear. He was yelling at everybody and he brought up Henry's name just one too many times. Henry had it. Coach Lombardi said one too many times, "and if you don't like it, you can turn in your play book." So all of a sudden, at home in walks Henry. I said, 'What are you doing?'

"I'm quitting."

"What?"

"I've had it, I'm quitting. Coach said I could turn in my book, get traded if I want to and that's what I'm gonna do."

"Well, I guess everybody saw Henry leave and there was a buzz. I didn't know what to think. Coach Lombardi called him and Henry went to see him and took his book. Henry said, "Coach, you said "If anybody wanted to leave, they could. Here's your book." Coach Lombardi sat back and said, "Son, you're gonna die here."

"Henry Jordan had an IQ of 170, he was very smart, but he always gave this, "I'm an old Virginia boy." Country Bumpkin come to the city. He worked very hard, but he also thought about things, he was a very deep thinker. One thing that really hurt Henry was when Coach Lombardi said Henry had to be prodded. Henry Jordan never had to be prodded for anything. That was in Lombardi's first book, *Run To Daylight*. That really bothered Henry. Then of course, it was quoted again by Vince Junior that that's what Lombardi felt about Henry. I think after Coach Lombardi got to know Henry, he realized he didn't have to be prodded. But, he also knew Henry could take a lot of criticism; that he'd sit back and he would take a lot of criticism. I think Henry was a buffer. Henry was a punching bag for some of the other guys that couldn't take it. But at that point, on that hot day, after that meeting, that was it. Henry had enough. He didn't get mad, didn't yell, didn't scream, he just got up, got his play book, took his stuff and left. It was so out of character for Henry to do something like that; I think that's what had everybody just dumbfounded. I was stunned and I know the guys were. He pretty much let things roll off his back, but that didn't."

As defensive tackles go Jordan was small, even though the game programs listed him at 6'3 and 240 pounds. Olive sets the record straight, "What do *I know?* He was 6"1 ½' and 220 on a good day. He was the smallest defensive tackle in the league. The reason he was as good as he was, was because of his agility and his agility came from running and wrestling. He wrestled in college and high school and that helped him."

Another thing that was quite small according to Olive, the pay check, "Well let's see, in 1959, Henry made $7,000.00, and then it was $7,500.00, then it was $8,000.00 then it was $8,500.00. In '62 he jumped to $10,000.00. It was very slow coming; Coach Lombardi believed a hungry team is a team that will work very hard. It was not a highly paid team. Bart was paid well, but he was not paid like the other quarterbacks were. The large dollars starting coming when Grabowski and Anderson signed. The highest money Henry made at the very end of his career was $34,500.00; that was in 1969." That's pay for a five time World Champion, future NFL Hall of Fame defensive tackle."

Working in the off season was a must according to Olive, "He was a speaker, he sold Pella windows, sold insurance. When we moved to Green Bay permanently, there was more of the basketball and speaking. The basketball was fun for the guys. There was a Packer basketball team, anybody that was around in the off season formed a basketball team and they played basketball with the Kiwanis Club, or the police, or whoever had a team in a little town. The Packers would play them."

On top of the salaries and championship bonus money, the wives were given excellent gifts by Lombardi with each world title. Lombardi's acknowledgement of the wives contribution was much appreciated, "Oh, my. Oh, my. Well, you know, we got our first stole, we got a ring, a necklace, we got a silver tea service. It was great. And we also got a stereo or a TV, whichever we wanted, that was one of the first gifts. I think Coach Lombardi was very generous to the wives. At that point and time, I don't think another team had ever done anything like that."

As the wins and championships piled up, it must have been great to be a part of the Green Bay Packer family and reach celebrity status at such a young age. According to Olive, "You know what, I didn't even realize it. In the first five years, we moved 17 times I had three kids, two miscarriages, and a kidney stone. So I was very busy that first five years. Being a celebrity, I didn't think of it as that, I really, really, did not. In fact, the first time someone asked Henry for his autograph when I was with him, I was startled. I wasn't raised around anything like that, nor was anybody I know of. So, the first time that happens to you, you're stunned or startled. One thing, Henry was always happy to give an autograph because he felt it was an honor to be asked.

"Bringing up children, at that point in time, was a little difficult. But a very good friend of my dad's once said, "I feel sorry for that little boy because he's gotta walk in his father's foot steps." Henry and I decided that my son was gonna walk in his own shoes and not try to be in his dad's shoes. So we had a wake up call early on how to raise the kids, that this was dad's job, this was not anything special. Dad was special because he was dad, but not because of what he did. It was a job. My youngest daughter at the time thought people asked everybody's dad for their autograph and everybody rode around in a big car. She didn't know the difference and we tried to make it that way."

The Jordan's saw black players added to Green Bay's roster because they were with Lombardi from the beginning and most of those players were on defense. It was, according to Olive, handled very well, "One thing about Coach Lombardi, he was great, there was no color, everybody was green and gold for the Green Bay Packers. I felt sorry for them because I know when we first went up there in 1959; it was very difficult for anybody to find an apartment. Because the previous generation of Packers had been a little bit rowdy; a lot rowdy, nobody wanted to rent to them because their apartments were torn apart. So when the new faces came up, it was very difficult to find a place. I often thought to myself, it was difficult for us, what was it possibly like for those guys. I know a lot of the black wives did not want to come up and I didn't blame them. Green Bay was a very small town then, did not have a lot of color there. I know it was very difficult. My goodness, they couldn't even get hair cuts. They had to go into Milwaukee to get hair cuts. If they wanted to let off some steam, they couldn't do it in Green Bay. They had to do it in Milwaukee or Chicago. So I thought it was difficult for them."

Notable black defensive players added to the roster early in Henry Jordan's career included, Emlen Tunnell, 1959, Willie Wood, 1960, Willie Davis, 1960, Herb Adderley, 1961, Dave Robinson, Lionel Aldridge and Marv Fleming, 1963. It was a non-issue. Olive says, "They were work associates, they were ball players." How did the wives handle it? She says, "I don't know how to answer that, how do wives handle it? There was nothing to handle, they were teammates. I love Willie; I loved *both* Willies, (Davis and Wood). I loved all those guys; they were so good to me. Not only before, but after Henry's death they really showed their true colors of friendship, they truly did and have. I will always be very grateful to all of them for the kindness they've shown my family and I."

In order to avoid waking up one morning unemployed, Olive said they started planning for life after football. "Probably about two or three years before Henry retired. Henry had injured his back badly in Cleveland and had gone to a chiropractor and had it fixed. Then, he injured it again and we had gotten letters from people all over the world actually, people saying, "Why don't you go down to this clinic in Madison, why don't you go there and get your back fixed?" These letters were coming from not just people in Wisconsin; they were coming from all over. So Henry told the Old Man, "I am going down to the chiropractor." And the Old Man said, "Fine, but don't tell Doc (James) Nellen." He said, "And I'll pay for it." Henry went down, that was like three years before he retired. He got patched up by our good friend, Dr. Alex Cox. He kept Henry in shape long enough for Henry to play but then that last hit he had, I remember seeing it on TV and I thought, 'He is really hurt this time.' Following the game, he got off the plane, there were guards there, and I pushed past the guards and ran screaming because Henry couldn't walk, he got off that plane and he couldn't walk. I knew that was it. Henry got a job in Milwaukee with Summerfest. All I knew about Summerfest at that time was an Indian maiden had climbed up on top of a pole and taken her bra off. I said, 'Henry, what are you doing? Are you sure this is what you want to do?'

"Yea," he said, "John Kelly's a good guy; I think we can make this thing work." We went down to Oconomowoc, Wisconsin, which was a wonderful town and spent seven wonderful years there with Henry doing Summerfest." The event has been a roaring success and has grown into the world's largest music festival.

Henry Jordan was truly a humorous and entertaining man by design, a gifted banquet speaker and fun interview. Olive believes some of the jokes had special appeal to the Coach, "Oh, I'm sure. Listen, Coach Lombardi knew everything that was going on, everything any of those kids said, anything they did, he found out about it; don't know how. He was a typical parent that knew everything. Yea, Coach Lombardi knew that Henry said, "He treats us all the same, like dogs." Of course he knew that and loved it, loved it."

He was also funny in a way, not by design as Olive describes, "Henry had an extremely high tolerance for pain *on himself*. On someone he cared about, *he was worthless*, he was worthless. I was getting ready to deliver our third child and as I'm being wheeled on the gurney, I passed by and there's my children's father, big guy with his head between his legs and smelling salts under his nose. He could not handle pain, he was good when something happened, he was great, he could handle the incident, but he couldn't handle afterward; he crumbled.

"When Coach Lombardi was ill, we were driving by the hospital in Washington, D.C. and close enough that we could have stopped. We pulled up and Henry got out of the car, then and he came back. He said, "I can't do this, I cannot see that man laying in that bed; I can't do it." I was surprised and I think Henry regretted that he didn't. I really think he regretted it, but at that point he couldn't bring himself to see Coach that sick." Henry was part of the Packer entourage that went to St. Patrick's Cathedral for Lombardi's funeral. "Oh, absolutely, absolutely. All the men went, the women did not go. I remember seeing Henry's face as he was going on the bus to the airport to take off to go to the funeral. Not just his face, but everybody. I cried like a baby when I heard he died. I couldn't believe it; he was not big in stature, but he was a giant. That he had died, I couldn't believe it."

Rumors swirled that Vince Lombardi was dying, so his passing, while powerful, was not unexpected. Less than seven years later, the Packer family was stunned by the sudden and unexpected death of Henry Jordan. A massive heart attack claimed his life at age 42 following a workout at the Milwaukee Athletic Club. Eight years after retiring as a player, Henry became the first of the great Lombardi Packers to die.

February 21, 1977 seemed like another day for Olive, "It was surreal. I remember waving goodbye to Henry and the kids that morning. Then hearing about it and not believing. This doctor friend of ours came up the walk. I turned off the TV for some reason. My son was gonna play a basketball game and we were watching television and I turned it off right before the news. Dr. Chuck Brumitt comes up the walk, walks in the house and said, "It's over, it's over." I couldn't imagine what was over. It was like watching a movie and thinking to yourself, "Why don't they know what's going on?" He told me Henry had died. Henry had been running at the Milwaukee Athletic Club. Three cardiologists tried to work on him. They found him in the bathroom. They pulled him out of the bath and tried to revive him, couldn't revive him.

# THE LOMBARDI LEGACY

Somebody got on the phone and called Oconomowoc, to a doctor there, to come and tell me. It was already news before I knew about it, the press had gotten a hold of it and it was on the TV, on the radio, it was all over the place. But Lionel Aldridge (WTMJ television) did not believe it because he knew Henry's dad had been ill and he thought it was Henry's dad so he would not put it on the air."

The Packer family had celebrated as a team with the Jordan's and now they mourned, "Everybody was there at the funeral; everybody came down. Marie Lombardi was there, that blew me away that Marie came to the funeral. The first call I got was Bart, I said, 'Bart, how did you know?' He said, "I heard about it on the radio." I got calls, calls, calls, and calls. Ron Kostelnik was the first Packer there; he came racing down from Appleton and thought about things nobody else had thought about. "What about her insurance, is she gonna be OK financially, does she need any money?" That was Ron Kostelnik.

Lombardi had emphasized family throughout his term in Green Bay, but even he could not have known the results of his efforts. The outpouring of love and support given to Olive and her family in their extreme hour of need may have been the first visual indication of how large and enduring a team Lombardi had built. Olive has come to the conclusion that "team" is much more than a photo of a group of players; it includes the families. "Absolutely, absolutely. I'm sure winning had a lot to do with it, but the times had a lot to do with it and the town itself. The '60's were a turbulent era, but we were isolated in Green Bay, Wisconsin. Coach Lombardi was our coach and he ran a tight ship. In Cleveland, people lived on the west side, they lived on the east side. The offense didn't talk to the defense and the 'this' and the 'that.' They didn't have that in Green Bay, *everybody* got together, everybody was a team. We just became so close, other teams talk about being close, but I truly believe there's a uniqueness in that '60's team that Coach Lombardi had."

Following Henry's death, the relationship between Marie Lombardi and

# OLIVE JORDAN FREY

Olive remained intact as she continued with her life. "With my own mother being gone, Marie kind of took that spot in a little bit of a way. I respected everything she said. I met a very nice guy, Duane Frey, who has stuck with me now for almost 29 years, but when we started dating he knew that Marie Lombardi was in my life. In fact, I told him early on I said, 'I'm always gonna be Henry's widow, people are always going to remember I'm Henry's widow and it's going to be a challenge for you and if you can't handle this we gotta quit seeing each other right away.' It was not a problem for Duane, never has been. He's been very good about it. Anyway, I told Marie, "I'm engaged."

"Well I want to meet him."

So I told Duane, "Marie Lombardi wants to meet you." He was more nervous to meet Marie than my dad and my dad was quite an awesome guy to meet. But he wanted her approval, and she wanted to approve him. I wondered at the time if she hadn't liked him what my reaction would have been. I have no idea, I'm sure I would have married him anyway. Fortunately, it was never a question for anybody, she was crazy about him saying, "*And* if you don't want him, send him down to Florida, I'll take him."

Olive kept him and as you would expect, he is a high quality, high caliber man. When word came in 1995 that Henry had been chosen for induction into the Pro Football Hall of Fame, a potentially awkward situation was handled exquisitely, thanks in large part to Duane Frey. Olive said, "Well, you know Duane has always been his own man and he didn't want to participate in anything and my son said, "No, you go with mom, I'll take care of business, you take care of my mom." But, that phone call from the Hall of Fame, I cannot tell you my feeling that was one of the happiest days of my life. I had always thought Henry deserved to go in, but because he'd been gone for so long I figured everybody would forget. I think Dave Robinson had a lot to do with it, bringing his name up and putting it to the fore. Dave always said he didn't, but I'll never be convinced that Dave didn't have a hand in it. For my children and I, it was wonderful, it was absolutely one of the most wonderful things to happen and the Hall of Fame people are wonderful. There were so many people that made my husband, my children and I feel good. My husband was in a predicament, this was not his thing but he wanted to be there because I wanted him there, my children wanted him there. They made him feel very welcome; they still do when we go back."

Now living outside of Ft. Worth, Texas, Olive looks back on her life, one touched by the Lombardi's, "Wonderful memories, a life of fun. I think when you're going through something like this you don't realize the impact this whole thing is going to have on the rest of your life. I think I was very fortunate to have married somebody who got into the kind of business he did, to move to Green Bay, Wisconsin and to have had the relationship with Coach Lombardi and Marie Lombardi. I've been a very fortunate, a very lucky woman to have been able to participate in something like this."

With success some people lose contact with the basic important ingredients of life, not so with Olive, "I was taught respect when I was growing up, but I think the Lombardi's taught respect for other people, respectful of time that people give, respectful of your family, appreciate your family, appreciate what you've got. He was a great teacher. He really was."

Naturally, one wonders what if Olive could see her heroin, Marie Lombardi, "Oh, I would love it. I would love it. Give her a big hug, yeah, I'd be happy to see her. I'm gonna cry." Olive did cry. Her tears said more about her love for Marie Lombardi than any words could express. She added, "I can't talk about Marie. This is just hard." What Olive could comment on was accounts of Marie Lombardi's drinking, "I read that and *I was furious.* Coach Lombardi had a thing down in the locker room I'm told, 'What goes on here stays here.' If he'd thought anybody should know Marie had a drinking problem, he would have told them. I personally never saw it. I spent time with her. She could not attend our wedding. (Marie invited Olive and Duane to Florida after the wedding) I went down there and stayed a week with her. I never saw this, I never saw this. She and I were by ourselves, I never saw it. She had me come to the Lombardi Golf Open when Henry first died. I was with her all the time, I never saw it. I don't know where this came from and I don't care, but I think it was a cruel thing to say about someone who is deceased, to say something that nobody had ever said before and personally as I said, I never saw it, never saw it."

# CHAPTER 8
# JACK KOEPPLER:

*"I never remember him consulting with anybody."*

# THE LOMBARDI LEGACY

Jack Koeppler was among the first people in Green Bay who really got to know Vince Lombardi. The two apparently attended a business meeting at the same time and shortly thereafter became playing partners for a round of golf at Oneida Golf and Riding Club in 1959. It was the first of many hundreds of rounds they played together until 1970. According to Dianne Koeppler, Jack's wife of 37 years, her husband was Lombardi's closest friend. Golf, hunting, card playing, and socializing provided personal threads of contact for the two buddies.

Dianne disclosed a hilarious account of one of Jack's most embarrassing moments. He traveled with the team to many away games, including the first AFL-NFL World Championship Game (Super Bowl I) in Los Angeles. Lombardi asked his trusted friend to safely deliver the World Championship Game Trophy back to Green Bay. It was renamed the Vince Lombardi Trophy in 1971.

Jack put a "ding" in the trophy. Dianne said, "The Old Man wasn't going to come back with the team and gave it to Jack to take on the plane. When Jack was standing in the doorway of the plane, somebody called his name and he turned around and hit the trophy on the doorway. He was so embarrassed he wouldn't tell anybody, so then he set it down on a seat of the plane by Forrest Gregg. You name it, they blamed everybody for years. Nobody really knew for sure and it was Jack."

On the business side, Jack administered the Packer pension plan and provided insurance coverage on all the Packer players through his agency. Koeppler was elected to the Packer Board of Directors in 1975 and held the position until his death in May of 2009.

According to Jack Koeppler, the Packer organization was a shambles when Lombardi arrived, "Organization is the wrong word. It was not organized at all. One of the first things he said to me as we were chatting about how it was going to get it started, he said, "When they say who's who in this organization, *I'm who.*" There was never any doubt about that. That got all

# JACK KOEPPLER

over town. Those that heard it, believed it, and those that really didn't believe it wanted to believe it because we had been so bad for so long. He pretty much had his own agenda; where he wanted that thing to go. He didn't share an awful lot.

"He drafted a quarterback out of Nebraska, Dennis Claridge and he said, "This guy's gonna be great." He wouldn't send him down to the College All-Star charity game. He absolutely wouldn't send him down to work out with the All-Stars. He said, "I need him in camp." NFL Commissioner Pete Rozelle called him and said, "It's gonna cost a thousand dollars a day for every day, including today, that he's not down there." So then, he sent him down, but later on, he had to cut him, and I couldn't help but think, "What happened to that mystic man you had?" He said, "Throws the ball back up—every pass goes out here, it goes down this way, went backward. I can't break him of it—not gonna monkey with it."

Lombardi's coaching pedigree is well documented with his journey from St. Cecelia's, Fordham University, West Point and the New York Giants. According to Koeppler, Lombardi's administrative expertise and micro management style came from the military academy, "Red Blaik. I think he got that when he was at West Point. That's just a suggestion, that's my own observation, 'cause he was organized, everything was bang, bang, bang. I suspect that the military of West Point and Colonel Red Blaik got him started along that line. I never remember him consulting with anybody. Once he made a decision, it was done and we'd go on to the next page, next item, next item, straightforward."

Lombardi was color blind in two ways, his physical eyesight literally had that handicap, and his character was blessed with the same condition. His racial and ethnic tolerance was real, not just convenient for building his dynasty. Koeppler initially saw it in Lombardi's private life, "The first illustration I got of that was at the Oneida Golf & Riding Course. We had a lot of Indian (Native American) caddies, and when we would be out there in

91

the spring, before golf carts, prior to the kids getting out of school, we all had Indians caddy for us. But once the kids got out of school, the Indians were kind of ignored, but not with him, and pretty soon all of us that played with him. He said, "If they're good enough to caddy in the spring and the fall, they're good enough to caddy in the summer." And we would all have Indian caddies, and from time to time, when the Indians needed extra money—their wife or their youngster—would be back at the 18th green when we finished, and he was pretty generous with them."

Lombardi drove his teams to win, but according to Koeppler, his competitive nature was evident away from the office as well.

"All the time. He didn't want to lose. At New Orleans one year, we played and the best net score won, the other guy had to pay for the caddie. And I happened to beat him four days in a row, just barely, because he could play with his handicap. The fifth day we tied. So he said, "Flip a coin and I'll call it." I flipped it and he called heads, it came up tails. He says, "Can't win; can't win." You know, he didn't want to lose."

Marie Lombardi would teasingly yank her husband's chain periodically as she did one June 11th when Koeppler got to see the playful side of the relationship.

"Well I think she kept a pretty good handle on him. We got down in his basement one day in early June; we played golf that day, and we went down to have a cocktail in his bar room. There's a big picture of half a horse on the wall—"Oh," he said, "Christ, it's my birthday." She had put a horse's ass up there. But they seemed to get along all right.

"I think Maraniss' book, *When Pride Still Mattered*, touched on her drinking excessively. I never witnessed that. I witnessed after the games—the home games, we'd go out to Nancy's and have dinner, not that she wouldn't have a drink, but never witnessed what he touched on as desire for alcohol; never, never saw it."

Following games played in Green Bay, a group of friends would gather at Lombardi's, and Jack explains what went on, "Not a hell of a lot. Just general conversation and basically the game was never rehashed. Might be something about, "Next week we have to go to L.A." I think at that time, Green Bay went out and played two games on the West Coast late in the year, but nothing really."

For forty-seven years Jack carried a memento given to him by the Coach, "I've got the money clip he gave me after they beat the Giants on New Year's Eve here--they beat 'em 37-0. I happened to be in his office, maybe two, three weeks afterwards, and it was lying on his desk in a box. I said, "Man, that's a good-lookin' money clip."

"I don't use a money clip, do you want it?"

"Sure."

"The only thing that's ever been done with it was the caption came off it and I had to have it re-braised or something like that. My son, he and I have had a conversation about that, and it's going to him when my tenure is over." May 25, 2009 was Mr. Koeppler's last day with the prized possession.

Jack was one of the people who saw the former coach anguish in 1968, the year he was just general manager. It was miserable, "Oh, no question about it—gee, he didn't know what to do with himself. They went into training and we're on the golf course one day, and he says, "Man, what a blunder." I said, 'Well, why don't you tell Phil you're going to take it back?' He said, "I can't do that to him. I absolutely can't do that to him." Koeppler said, "But, some of us who knew him could have given him some advice."

*If* Jack Koeppler was correct, and *if* Lombardi's friends would have convinced the coach to take his time to make his retirement announcement, he may not have left Green Bay. "All we had to do is say to him, 'Coach, you don't have to make an announcement now (February 1969). Hell, wait to make the announcement. Make it in May, or June.' None of us were bright enough to figure that out at that time, and had we got him to delay making that decision, he'd have never retired. Because by the time they went to camp, he wanted to go." During the process of conducting interviews for *The Lombardi Legacy*, more than one Packer player said the team would probably have one another championship if Lombardi would have remained at the helm in 1968. That would have made four in a row. Packer fans can only wish it would have happened.

Lombardi had access politically, some of which was earned during his time as an assistant coach at West Point and Koeppler saw the mind and power at work.

"He could get things segregated in a manner where he would go from football to politics. When we went down and shook hands with President Kennedy down at the Jefferson-Jackson Day dinner, Kennedy chatted with him. I can't remember whether that was before or after the Hornung betting scandal, but I know he did call to get Hornung to come home for a game, and he didn't call the state assemblyman. Yeah, he was a unique guy. I think he might have been a little bigger than football. He was great in football; he was going a little past that."

By the time Lombardi retired as coach in 1968, he was a national, if not international superstar. During his rise, from an obscure coach to five time NFL champion, he did not change according to Koeppler.

"Not that I ever observed. For some reason we drove when we went to Hot Springs, Arkansas. I don't know why that was, but General Motors always gave him a car to run and we had gotten a late start out of Green Bay. On the freeways, there were restaurants that used to go across the freeway, in Chicago—Harvey's or something like that, and we stopped at one of those one night for a bite to eat. He could hardly get to eat, somebody was always coming over with a menu, "Can you sign this for me? Can you sign this? Can you…" 'Cause, he had a distinct look. When you saw him, you knew who he was. And after about the fifth or sixth one, I said, 'Jesus cripe Coach, does that bother you when you can't even finish your meal?' And he said, "Bother me more if nobody came over."

# JACK KOEPPLER

According to Jack Koeppler, Lombardi enjoyed being Lombardi, "Sure he did, sure he did. He loved it."

Koeppler saw Lombardi in 1970 as the cancer gnawed away at his life, but Jack thinks Lombardi did not see the ravages of the disease.

"While he knew it was over, he didn't really think it was over, you know. The deterioration was evident to all of us, I'm not so sure he saw the deterioration on a daily basis, so it didn't seem so drastic."

Jack was asked, if given the chance to spend a couple hours with Lombardi, would he tell him some things he didn't say when they were both alive?

"Well, I've never been one to dwell on something of that nature, but if you made it four hours, I'd say a golf game. We had a lot of fun. We played Dr. (E.S.) Brusky and Judge Robert Parins at North Shore Country club when he came back, the summer that he had gone to Washington. We always played two dollar Nassau, and as we walked down the first fairway, I said, 'Why don't we play an additional two dollar best ball?' I had the lowest handicap by quite a bit in the bunch. He said, "OK." So, when we got down near the first green and he said, "There's no way we can win that best ball, is there?" I said, 'You got that right.' The next day we played at Oneida with Ray Antil and Dr. Brusky. He and I were partners that day, and after we had all the bets made he said, "We'll play you guys the best ball, too." Then he said, "Quick learner." Not for the money, he just wanted to win. If you played marbles, he wanted to win."

# CHAPTER 9
# BART STARR:

*"I came to appreciate the bluntness."*

# THE LOMBARDI LEGACY

The following is a complete list of all the quarterbacks who have guided their teams to five National Football League World Championships:

1.) Bart Starr

2.) _____

An unlikely candidate to author a brilliant career as an NFL quarterback, Bart Starr defied the odds to become the one and only five time world champion starting quarterback. Not only was he a 17th round draft choice who had languished in Green Bay for three years before Vince Lombardi arrived, he was a sitting duck to be cut from the team due to circumstances. Most new coaches want their own guys, especially an offensive minded one like Lombardi who served as his own offensive coordinator and quarterback coach. How could a signal caller with an average arm who was unable to distinguish himself in three seasons be expected to even make the team with a new regime in place? The two worst franchises in the NFL in 1956 were the Chicago Cardinals and Green Bay Packers and it was on one of those teams that Bart was attempting to secure a professional career. Probably no team would have been interested in signing a back up quarterback from either the Packers or Cardinals in those days if they would have been released.

Then as now, Bart's wife Cherry was firmly with him in those uncertain times as he followed his dreams to the NFL. Bart describes her has "the greatest teammate I've ever had, we just celebrated our 55th wedding anniversary (2009). It's been the greatest happening in my life; I don't even know how to put it into appropriate words."

Starr's cerebral grasp of football details, insatiable appetite for knowledge, adherence to discipline and excellent leadership ability were an ideal package of skills waiting to be sculptured into greatness by Lombardi. Without the Great Coach, Bart could have been a mere footnote in Packer history.

If ever a player displayed the difference between a quarterback and a passer it was Bart Starr. He has been called "the leader of the Pack," field general, Mr. Quarterback, an extension of Lombardi on the field; whatever description is chosen to portray championship quarterback play, Bart Starr was precisely that. Green Bay's great wide receiver Boyd Dowler says, "When you look at the championship games, there was one consistent factor, number 15." As of the year 2009, Starr's famous uniform number is one of only five officially retired in the rich history of the Green Bay Packers.

When Lombardi arrived in 1959 there were players floundering on the Packer roster who would become Hall of Famers. Waiting for the new coach were Bart Starr, Jim Taylor, Paul Hornung, Forrest Gregg, Jim Ringo and Ray Nitschke. The great Jack Vainisi had stock piled others destined for the Packer Hall of Fame; Bob Skoronski, Boyd Dowler, Ron Kramer, Jerry Kramer, Jess Whittenton and Hank Gremminger to name a few. Vainisi is one of the greatest yet least publicized people in the history of the Green Bay Packers. Bart comments, "I couldn't agree more because he was the Director of Player Personnel and when you look at the people he scouted, recruited and recommended to the organization, it's very impressive. I am very indebted to him for enabling me to be in Green Bay because he was a close friend of the basketball coach at the University of Alabama, a gentleman named Johnny Dee. He and Dee knew each other at Notre Dame." By his own description, Starr had a "pitiful" final two years at the University of Alabama, "I was injured my junior year and my senior year we had a coaching change, he (new coach) hardly played us seniors, so I didn't have much of a resume at all. Coach Dee just continually leaned on Jack to give me an opportunity, or otherwise, I probably would not have been drafted at all."

When asked to describe his initial contract with Green Bay, Bart had to chuckle before saying, "Very, very light, it was a sixty-five hundred dollar contract. Coming out of college my wife and I were married and obviously we had some debt. The contract called for a one thousand dollar bonus for a total of seventy five hundred. I'm not certain, but I really think I may have had to pay back that thousand after making the team. So total, it was only sixty-five hundred that year."

# THE LOMBARDI LEGACY

The glamour of pro football waited, only problem was it awaited other players in other cities while in Green Bay the facilities were brutal, "That's a good description, brutal. When I arrived in Green Bay our facilities were over at East High School on the east side of the city and that's where we played. The facilities inside were almost laughable. I remember walking in the first time and thinking, "Oh my God." Our facilities in my high school, way back in high school were almost larger. It was just unbelievable; the training room was not much larger than triple the size of a normal size closet. That *was the training room* where you were taped and everything, it was unbelievably small."

In contrast to the meager facilities, it appeared to Starr the basic organization was functional, "Overall I thought it was good. The people in it were obviously very committed; you could sense their dedication. Everything was smaller, the offices were in downtown Green Bay but the people appeared to be quality."

From the time Bart saw Vince Lombardi in their initial team meeting, until he served as his pall bearer 12 years later, nothing ever matched the first impression, "I think the most meaningful thing he ever said to me was actually in his first meeting with us as a team when he came to Green Bay. He held what today would be likened to a mini camp session. It was in spring time and was primarily a class room session. He opened the meeting by thanking the Green Bay Packers for the opportunity; that immediately told us a great deal about the quality of this man. We were seated at some tables and he walked up to us and said, "Gentlemen, we are going to relentlessly chase perfection knowing full well we won't catch it because nothing is perfect. But we are going to *relentlessly*," and he really hammered the word, "we are going to *relentlessly* chase it because in the process we will catch excellence." He paused for a moment, he walked even closer to us, got right up in our faces and said, "I'm not remotely interested in being just good." Now that's how he opens the session. Wow. We didn't even need a chair to sit in, we were so crouched and poised and primed. We could have been there without a seat the rest of the day." That was the opening session and it continued for nine glorious years as Starr explains, "Those who did not want to or who were reluctant to follow his guidelines and understand his principles of how it was always team first, they weren't around very long."

With the possible exception of Marie Lombardi, no person in Green Bay spent more time with Vince Lombardi than Bart Starr. He saw General Manager Lombardi transform the organization, "I personally felt that he did an exceptional job. He was a fabulous leader. This man was rigidly prioritized; it was God, family and others and the Green Bay Packers fell under the word 'others' and I mean it, that's how he lived. If you were not in a football meeting, he didn't talk about football he talked about life. Whenever he was with someone you could see the total person, which was continually emphasized by him." Lombardi's former secretary, Lori Keck said his raw intelligence surprised her everyday; the same is true for Bart, "Oh it did, we were so impressed. This was a total person. I could never be patient enough to get to the next meeting just to hear him teach, and appreciate the depth of the knowledge of this man. It was very impressive."

A complete make over of the entire organization was firmly under Vince Lombardi's control and he managed all facets. He was the new custodian of the Packer image and was concerned about how players appearing in public would represent his Packers, "Yes, there were opportunities to appear at father-son banquets or functions like that, or business gatherings where there were going to be fans, smaller meetings where you had a chance to answer some questions. He encouraged us to do so if we desired; again he made some comments about some of the things we possibly should be focused on to make sure we cover those."

During his career, Bart had a stable group of wide receivers, notably Max McGee, Boyd Dowler and in 1965 Carroll Dale was added through a trade. But a couple of other guys with huge talent, Herb Adderley and Bob Jeter made their Packer debuts on offense. Bart saw his general manager shift the two gifted athletes to defense, "You appreciate what Coach Lombardi saw in them, that they would be better where he wanted to move them. It turned out to be a great decision."

Ever the student, Starr relished the experience of soaking up knowledge from his mentor, including when negotiating his contract and watching the general manager in action, "It was very impressive and obviously we did not have agents in those days, I'm glad I went through an experience because you had the opportunity to sit down and have eye-to-eye contact. I think it helped develop a very, very strong quality relationship." Bart spent countless hours in game preparation sessions with Coach Lombardi; however contract negotiations were not the same. Starr explains, "They are totally different, here we are talking about contracts and other things; you were there for a different reason. But I literally loved going to those meetings to see what his preparation was, how he organized it and how we worked our way through it."

As it became more apparent that he could play quarterback for the Packers, Bart and Cherry made a family decision to move from Birmingham, Alabama and make Green Bay their permanent residence. Family concerns received prominent consideration, "When Bart Jr. was about three or four years old, he was born in 1957, we wanted to go ahead and get him into a neighborhood where he could grow up, get into kindergarten, rather than moving back and forth. It was an excellent decision. We were in a great neighborhood, we lived relatively close to the stadium and it really worked out well for Bart Jr. because the school he attended was near us."

Being from the Deep South and a team leader, Bart played a key role regarding race relations with the Packers, "There was never, *never* any kind of issue surrounding that. One of the greatest experiences Cherry, I and our family had, was to invite the African American players, different ones, over to our home during the season at least once a month, sometimes twice a month for dinner. It was a joy to be able to spend that kind of time with them. There weren't a lot of places in Green Bay to dine, so we really enjoyed visiting with our teammates and sharing home cooked meals."

Bart learned from Lombardi, he dedicated himself to preparation for game day; he took his job seriously, was exceptionally focused and fortunately had a roommate on road trips who offered a change of pace. Bart explains, "In the nine years we knew Coach Lombardi, he was at mass every single morning at 7:00 am. Henry Jordan, who was a great teammate and roommate when we traveled, had a marvelous sense of humor. He said, "Why Hell, if you ever heard him chew our asses out, you'd know why he had to be at church every morning at 7:00 am." Coach Lombardi loved that when he heard Henry's response."

Today at age 75, Bart can be found traveling the country or working in his office at Starr Enterprises in Birmingham, Alabama on a daily basis. Since 1970 he has served as Chairman of the Vince Lombardi Golf Classic in Milwaukee in addition to his tireless efforts on behalf of Rawhide Boys Ranch near New London, Wisconsin. The Starr's have also been charitable to many organizations and causes that remain anonymous. Bart's active involvement is a combination of who he is and the influence of two significant men, "My father was a career military person and it's ironic because he was very, very similar in his approach to life as Coach Lombardi. As I reflected on it, I was thankful for meeting Coach Lombardi and working with him starting those first few days and growing up over a number of years. I continually reflected on how much of an impact my father had on me that I perhaps had not taken as seriously as I did after meeting Coach Lombardi. I think of him consistently because something will just pop up that gives you a quick reflection on being with Coach Lombardi for several years and the lessons learned and it's very, very powerful.

"I came to appreciate the bluntness' and unique talent Coach had for teaching and re-emphasizing and practice sessions. If you did something extremely well in practice, he'd say, "That's just what we're looking for." If you made a mistake he was quick and sharp to correct it, "Now wait a minute, we told you damn it, we *will not* do such and such." You came to appreciate his thoroughness."

If he could spend a day with Lombardi Bart says, "I think I would play golf with him and reflect on all the times we shared together because of the privilege of getting to know him well."

After taking the Washington Redskins job, the Great Coach returned to Green Bay in order to play golf with some of his buddies and reconnect with others. Lombardi was emotional; he could laugh, cry or explode instantly. A subtle but powerful event occurred in the Starr home during his vacation offering a hint of Vince Lombardi's looming health issue. Bart offers details of the visit, "He had heard that Cherry and I built a new home, he called and said, "I'm be in Green Bay in about three or four days, I understand you built a new home, I'd love to stop by and say hello to you." I said, 'Coach, we'd love it.' So he stops in and Cherry takes him on the cook's tour of the house. We come back and sit down in the den and he said, "Cherry you should be very proud, you've done a great job with this home." She said, "Well Coach, we owe all of this to you." Instantly he gets up from the sofa where he and I were sitting and starts across the room to give her a big hug. He's crying, he turns around and hugs me, then leaves and just walks out the front door. We believe to this day that he knew he had cancer."

Late in the summer Green Bay's great Lombardi lay in a Washington, D.C. hospital succumbing to the colon cancer that claimed his life. Starr made the hospital visit and describes his thoughts and feelings as he saw his mentor dying, "Obviously we were very emotional and teary eyed because when we saw him he was not good. In fact, he was saying very little and after just a few minutes Marie said, "I think we need to leave." So we did."

Bart's account of seeing his coach alive for the last time brought an unmistakable twinge of sadness to his distinctive Southern voice 39 years after the fact.

# CHAPTER 10
# RON KRAMER:

*"He was commander-in-chief and you did what the hell he told you to do."*

# THE LOMBARDI LEGACY

Ron Kramer was the Packer's number one draft choice in 1957. Military service and injuries in 1958 and '59 delayed his entrance into the NFL. Regarded by many as the best athlete ever produced by the state of Michigan, he was an ideal fit in Vince Lombardi's offense. His speed and athleticism combined with 6'3" height and 240 pound size, allowed him to revolutionize the tight end position from a blocking function to an offensive weapon. Before Kramer, NFL tight ends were basically third offensive tackles; Green Bay's menacing number 88 changed all of that.

He played seven years for the Packers and three with the Detroit Lions. General Manager Vince Lombardi accommodated Ron by trading him to Detroit in 1964. Ron's 170 receptions for 2,594 yards and 15 touchdowns, including two TDs in the '61 championship win over the Giants, earned him induction in the Packers Hall of Fame in 1975.

A unique man, Kramer not only marches to the beat of his own drum, the rest of us don't hear the beat, or see the drum. He has two quirky tactics; kissing people on the lips (female, male, cheerleaders, linebackers, CEO's, whatever) and talking with a Manhattan glass on his head. All tight ends are not blessed with such talent.

Lombardi has consistently been admired for his fairness and that character trait became extremely evident when World Championship bonus money was being distributed. Players voted to determine who received a full share, half share, etc. Ron Kramer explains Lombardi's involvement.

"Some of the guys were trying to vote out guys like Dad Braisher, who was our equipment manager. Lombardi went bonkers. He said, "We don't forget anybody." And everybody got a part in the championship. That was the most important thing to him, that everybody in the organization was part of the team, and that's what made him so successful, and they don't have that anymore. What has happened in football today is that we have taken a team sport and made it an individual sport; you only read about the stars. If you look at the ocean, you have those beautiful sailfish, then you have the sharks, then you have the bottom feeders. In our society, human beings are the same way. You have those guys who just are like beautiful sailfish out of the water, others are sharks—they're doing their job all the time; the other ones just clean up everything and make a good living at it. Called a janitor.

"Lombardi was all of 'em. He was all in one. He could play any part. He could associate with every single individual, because he grew up as a fairly poor individual in Brooklyn, and I think his father was a butcher. And how ironic this is-- his nickname when he was a kid was 'Butch' because that was my nickname. How wild it was—I was 'Butch' Kramer. My uncles and aunts--everybody called me 'Butch' all the time. I couldn't believe it when I read the story that his nickname was 'Butch' and I never knew that. I'd have been calling him 'Butch,' obviously. He'd probably whack me one but he couldn't hurt me, anyway."

When Ron returned from a year of military service he was not surprised to see how Lombardi operated, "No I wasn't, because I had experienced some of his teams that he coached--the one team is the military academy—Army. Red Blaik was the coach and Michigan played Army in 1954, '55 and '56 when I was in school. In 1954, when he was there, they just beat the devil out of us, I mean they were good. The offense was fantastic and then they had that little problem at the military academy. I think there were some testing or whatever they did, (*academic honor code scandal of 1951_Maraniss 120-134*) Vince Lombardi left and went to the New York Giants--immediately the Giants became World Champions in 1956. Then, in '59, he came to Green Bay after a 1-10-1 record in 1958, and the next year the Green Bay Packers were 7-5, I think we were in third place, second place, whatever it was. After that, he won championships. It was always a contender. Great organizer."

When Kramer got to meet Lombardi in Green Bay, it didn't take long to realize the new Coach and General Manager was a very special person, "First day you met him. First day he said, "Hello, I'm Vince Lombardi." Yikes. You were mesmerized by the way he looked straight into your face, just like

I'm looking at you right now, and boy, you could tell this guy was intense. He was ready to play then, and he gave that impression to everybody that ever came on his team. Everybody had to perform, because you see, we only had 34 players then. It wasn't like now, where you've got 50 players running around with their heads cut off. I mean, everybody had to know everybody's position. When we played in the first championship game in 1961 against the New York Giants, we had a problem—a really big problem, because Jerry Kramer got hurt. So he had to make switches with our offensive line and how we were going to play the Giants and who was going to play where, because we only had one extra guy and that was offensive tackle Norm Masters. So he said. "OK, fine, I'm going to move Forrest Gregg to guard because he played guard eight or nine years ago. I'm gonna put Norm Masters at right tackle and Bob Skoronski stay at left tackle." Everything else was the same. That's a big move, and he could make moves like that, and that was incredible."

Both on, and off the field, Green Bay's players were in need of an image transplant and Lombardi performed the surgery in both areas according to Kramer.

"Well, first of all he said, "If you're going to go into a restaurant or bar, sit at a table, don't sit at the bar." That was the first image. The second image is to always wear a jacket when you're on the road. And conduct yourself in an adult manner, and this is the way he felt, and this would give the cohesiveness to the whole team—the team would be as a team. Ironically enough, we are still that kind of team. We're now in our 70's and all the guys are the same—the Paul Hornungs, the Bart Starrs—the Jerry Kramers, David Robinson—every guy that comes in, they're just accepted. Like somebody asked, "Do you guys get together?" I said, 'Yeah, we get together, playing a lot of golf tournaments and different activities.' We had stars--everybody was a star on the team, even though some people got a little more notoriety. We had the best tackles—Forrest Gregg and Bob Skoronski and Norm Masters. Jerry Kramer, Fuzzy Thurston, Jim Ringo--my goodness, they were fantastic. Max

McGee and Boyd Dowler and myself were the ends--we weren't like, 'the lightning people,' but we never made mistakes. Nobody on that team made mistakes because he was so precise in the way he taught football as a way of life."

In Lombardi's offense, the tight end was critical to his power sweep; Kramer was the first legitimate offensive weapon to play the position as an accomplished receiver in addition to being a devastating blocker.

"Well yeah, I had an advantage over a lot of ends. I was fairly athletic, because I did play basketball; I was the third or fourth draft choice for the Detroit Pistons. I also ran track in college. I was a 6' 7" high jumper so athletically, I was very active, but I had some size. I weighed 250 pounds and I could run. I ran the low hurdles and high hurdles in state meets in high school. I didn't run in college, but I could run, I was only a tenth of a second or so off Boyd Dowler, so, I could also run. I was one of the gifted guys. As a matter of fact, Vince made the statement in his book; he said it was like having a twelfth man on the field, because I could handle defensive ends without double-teaming them."

Like having an extra man? That must have been worth some money in contract negotiations, "Well, we didn't negotiate very much. He wasn't a good negotiator. He said, "This is the way it's going to be and this is the way we're going to do it." Hey, we always won championships. He said, "You're going to get a bonus at the end of the year, I'm going to make you money." It wasn't the idea of the money. I was an executive in a steel company in my off-seasons, in Detroit, so I had another job. I had something to go to when I quit playing. Unfortunately, the steel company went out of business and I owned about 17 to 18 percent of it. It cost me a little bit of money, but it was a good lesson, because I was able to carry that through the rest of my life in business.

"He said to me in 1960, after the 1960 season, "You got a lot of talent and the position of tight end next year is yours, if you want it." I came back, and it was sort of surprising because when I came out of the service, I was sort of sickly, I was 210 pounds; I had some ulcers, I had a lot of things going on. Well, one night Paul Hornung and I went out—my wife and I and Paul had a date at the time. I'm sitting there and I'm sort of one of those blah guys. He said, "What the hell, Kramer? What the hell's wrong with you?" I said, 'You know, jeez, it's driving me crazy—mentally. I'm like what the hell am I going to do with this situation I'm in.' He said, "Sit down." He brought over a bottle of champagne and we sat and we drank that bottle of champagne, had dinner, we had drinks, we drank all night long. Then we went to the pizza parlor at two o' clock in the morning; it was after one of the games. The next day I got up, I felt pretty good. After that, I said, 'Aw, the hell with it, everything's OK.' Off I went. This is the kind of feeling we still have with each other here on the Green Bay Packer team. And they all have that same feeling."

Ron is a likeable beast with a flair for the unusual, so it fits he would get tagged with an unusual nickname. Lombardi was originally given credit for Kramer's nickname, "The Big Oaf." Ron clarifies, "We were playing against the Minnesota Vikings and their Head Coach Norm Van Brocklin had been talking to Vince on the phone. I had a good game the week before and I guess Van Brocklin said, "Are you gonna bring that that 'big oaf?' So that's what stuck with me - Oafie."

Ron's personal and professional life took a major turn in 1964, about mid point in Lombardi's reign. He put into practice Lombardi's well known priorities of God, family and the Green Bay Packers. He played out his option and returned to Michigan.

Ron said, "That was a decision I had to make in life, which was most important. My wife and I were having some marital problems, but more importantly my son had lost an eye in 1964 and my daughter had an asthmatic condition that was critical and trying to bring them to Green Bay—it just was very difficult for me and I was contemplating retiring, but I was able to play out my option and Vince said, "Look, I don't want to lose you, but if you're going to make that decision." He called me one time—just once—and he said, "You're still welcome here." I said, 'I know, Vince, but I gotta do what I gotta do.' He accommodated and said, "OK, fine." That was it. He gave me the opportunity to go back to Detroit and take care of what I had to do without having a big to-do about it. But you see; he got a first round draft choice. That's why Jim Grabowski of Illinois, at every team event, I see him—hugs me and kisses me, because he was on the team in '66, '67."

By the time Ron left for the Lions Lombardi had molded Green Bay into a finely tuned organization. Motown did not have a model to match. Ron explains.

"Well, Detroit was sort of reorganizing and Bill Ford just bought the team. They hired a guy as general manager and he didn't really particularly know much about the game. He hired a coach that Norm Van Brocklin had recommended to him, his name was Harry Gilmer. It was incredible; it was helter-skelter. Here's how bad it got. A guy named Joe Don Looney, if you recall, used to play football. Baltimore got rid of him, the Jets got rid of him—this team got rid of him, everybody got rid of him. Gilmer says (in a Southern drawl), "Boys, I'ma going tuh tell you something," he says, "Aah'm going tuh get this boy and I'ma going tuh make him a football player because he's got so much talent." Well, Joe Don Looney didn't do anything and we were playing a game and Gilmer says, "Joe Don, come over here." Joe Don comes over to him and he said, "Here, take this play in; it's a critical play." And Joe Don Looney looked at Harry Gilmer and he said, "Coach, Call Western Union—I'm not a delivery boy." And that's the kind of organization it was."

The people who surrounded Lombardi share an admirable trait; they carry themselves with an unmistakable basic confidence. Chicken or egg, did they have to be confident to survive him or did Lombardi instill it in them? Kramer says; "Don't be so complicated, my God, it wasn't so complicated.

# THE LOMBARDI LEGACY

He was the commander-in-chief and you did what the hell he told you to do. There was no chicken or egg. He didn't care about chickens and eggs man; he said, "Play football!"

Ron sees some things a little different than most, when asked a theoretical question, what would it be like to spend time with Lombardi now? He responded; "Well, the theoretical aspect of that is that we all spend time with him every single day, yet, he doesn't have to be here. He was the kind of guy that will stick with you the rest of your life. Same as my parents. You see, my parents were very instrumental in everything I did. They had an influence in my life. They're both dead, but they're still with me; as is Vince Lombardi. And if you see all the guys, whether it be Robinson or Hornung—or any of the guys—Starr—anybody, he's still with them. He still guides the guys. He put so much sense to what living was about; not only football, but living, that you can't get rid of him. He is like, on you all the time."

# CHAPTER 11
## JIM TAYLOR:

*"He was a very tough negotiator."*

# THE LOMBARDI LEGACY

Jim Taylor was loved by Packer fans during the Lombardi years. He was tough, rugged, fierce, punishing, durable, and just plain great. Most avid Packer backers cannot recite Jim's statistics, but can tell you how he played and how it felt to watch him. He was Ray Nitschke on offense.

As for his Packer career numbers: rushing yards, 8,207; rushing attempts, 1,811; touchdowns, 91; points, 546. Those are only part of the Jim Taylor legend. In 1962, he was Most Valuable Player in the National Football League. He led the league in rushing. For his entire career he handled the ball 2,173 times and fumbled just 34 times, (1.56 %). Jimmy scored the first rushing touchdown in Super Bowl history and the only touchdown in the '62 championship game against the New York Giants. He was beaten before, during and after the whistle in an epic battle played in brutal weather conditions at Yankee Stadium. Giant's middle linebacker Sam Huff said following the game, "(I) did everything I could to that son-of-a-bitch. Taylor isn't human. No human being could have taken the punishment he got today."

Jimmy's thoughts of the game; "No one knows until they are faced with it just how much pain they can endure, how much suffering, how much effort they have left. That's the way it was that day." He was loved by Packer fans because of the way he played. For example, running backs almost never get penalties for unnecessary roughness, but Taylor drew just such a flag for an aggressive stiff arm to a would-be St. Louis Cardinal tackler.

Jim was as tough off the field, as on. He saw big money come into the National Football League and it came through the door of the Green Bay Packers in the persons of Donny Anderson and Jim Grabowski. Jim Taylor, in the twilight of his brilliant career was determined to get some of the money and he needed to stand up to Vince Lombardi in order to cash in. Despite repeated and prolonged efforts by Lombardi to sign Jim, the great number 31 played out his option and ended his career with the expansion New Orleans Saints in 1967. Jimmy received a landmark contract from Saints' owner John

# JIM TAYLOR

Mecom Junior that provided long-term security in his home state.

This Louisiana man was born in Baton Rouge, attended high school and college at Louisiana State University in the same city. Today, Jim lives there with his wife Helen. Because so little has been written about Jimmy Taylor and his personal life, here's a glimpse into his early years and a very surprising aspect of his athletic talents.

"Well, I've got two other brothers. One younger and one older. I think my father passed away when I was around the age of 10, and so it's a matter of what some of my coaches there at Baton Rouge High and my athletics did for me. I think I looked to them and took a lot from those men that were my coaches and brought me along. I started to be very competitive at that early age. Turning to basketball in the ninth grade and being moved up to the varsity was a big jump. I was really maturing and growing up pretty swiftly to compete in basketball at Baton Rouge High School as a ninth grader. So I grew up pretty quick there. I was throwing newspapers, working and in sports, just a routine, year in and year out, and that's growing up."

Jimmy turned out to be one of the all-time greats in football, however, in his senior year in high school, he was best at another sport.

"Without a doubt, basketball, because I'd lettered three years prior to that. I only played a little bit of football and finally got into football my senior year. The new coach, Carl Harrison, went to the single-wing, and he put me in there to take the direct snap, the spinning and running, passing some, and extra points, field goal kicking. I was versatile and a pretty good athlete. They tried to utilize, maximize my ability and talents I had as a player. They put the ball in my hands to try to make plays and things. Then we went on into the basketball. We were state champs and I had quite a few scholarships in the basketball arena with the different colleges. Football, I sort of had some scholarship offers. I had quite a choice, and then I went and took LSU and decided to concentrate just on one sport, on football. I started to kind of like the contact. I was a pretty good athlete so I could convert to either one. I just went on and stuck with the football."

Taylor was scouted and evaluated by Jack Vainisi, a talent scout who stocked the Green Bay roster with future champions. Prior to the draft, direct contact between the team and Jimmy was:

"None. I didn't follow or didn't know that much about professional sports or even professional football, but I learned pretty quickly after I was the number two pick by the Green Bay Packers and the 15th player picked in the draft."

Times were so different in 1957, despite being selected very high in the draft, he was not notified with direct contact.

"I probably found out by the newspaper or radio, it might have been two or three days after the draft. At first I didn't know what team, or where Green Bay was. I think I signed a one year contract; it was a ninety-five hundred dollar contract and a thousand dollar bonus."

After ten games of a 12 game schedule in 1958, the Packers were sitting on one win; Head Coach Ray "Scooter" McLean decided to give the rookie fullback a chance to play in the last two regular season games at San Francisco and Los Angeles. Jim describes his late season success, "I gained over a hundred yards in both games on twenty some carries in each. I had been on special teams, so at that time I realized I had made a step in the direction of being a player." Not only did Jim perform well, more importantly, he put his skills on film for the next coach to study. Vince Lombardi was a movie fanatic; he spent hours watching film of his new Green Bay team and found his fullback in the 1958 Packer horror flicks.

Who knows what would have happened in 1959 if Jimmy hadn't been burned by hot grease in a household cooking accident mid-way in the season. It burned his hand and foot and according to Jim, "I missed four or five games in the middle of the season." Taylor's absence coincided with a Packer five game losing streak. In spite of the mid-season slump, Green Bay improved to an astonishing 7-5 in Lombardi's first year. The Pack may have

# JIM TAYLOR

had another win or two had Taylor been healthy for the season. He ended the year with just 120 carries. Taylor knew the dog days were ending and he was the Packers fullback:

"After I came back from my household accident, I was starting to get the ball and he depended on me to pick up those first downs. He saw I was getting acclamated to be able to run the football and to do some things in a very positive way and making some strong contributions to the offensive unit. We had Bart Starr throwing only 12, 15, 18 times a ball game, so we were more of a ball possession type of football team.

"Lombardi was very serious, and he'd been around and knew what he wanted to set up and how he wanted to approach things. He'd been with the New York Giants, a great organization with some other great coaches for a period of time. They had been successful, so he knew what he wanted to do with the Green Bay Packers. The two prior years, Hornung and Ron Kramer's team won two ballgames. The Packer team I was on my rookie year won one ballgame, so he was ready to set up a plan to play football and to get the players he wanted. He made some draft picks and different things, and we had an outstanding draft that year with Jack Vainisi in charge. Dan Currie was the number one pick; a center from Michigan State (linebacker with Green Bay) and then I was the number two pick, Ray Nitschke was the number three, Jerry Kramer was number four, and then we got some other picks in there later on. We got some others in trades. We just built and got some players, and Coach Lombardi knew exactly what he wanted to do and how he wanted to put together a winning football team." The new coach from New York was an unknown to Jimmy and his mates, "I knew nothing about him. I don't know that too many of the Packer players knew that he had been an assistant with the New York Giants. Most knew little to nothing about Lombardi."

Ultra competitive and one half of a collision looking for the other 50%, Jimmy does not believe he would have been quite as hard nosed without

# THE LOMBARDI LEGACY

Lombardi's influence and steadfast commitment to the running game:

"Probably not. He was the "we're gonna move the chains" and he knew what my expectations were of what kind of football player I was. He was gonna give me the ball and try and develop me as a running back I was to be the Packers' number one running back. He kept it simple, you knew the rules and what to expect, so it's a matter of you putting out and exerting yourself. This is what some people want, to be pushed and be disciplined, to be demanded and moving you to a higher level of your capabilities.

"After a short period of time, I started to develop and started to do some things that got some yardage. Bart Starr, with his quarterbacking, you knew he was just going to throw the short pass and we were going to control the ball, control the line of scrimmage, move the chains and put a good defense out there, with Ray Nitschke leading. Coach was structuring good, sound, solid football. Eliminating the fumbles and the interceptions, we got field position and just played good defense. That was his philosophy and we started to implement the pieces of the puzzle. It wasn't long before we were really playing good football and winning football games."

A Packer fan of the 60's I loved to watch Taylor and Nitschke, two no nonsense, tough players who liked contact, loved to play and played with disciplined abandon. They were perfect for Lombardi:

"Yeah, I tend to agree with you 100% because we tried to epitomize the toughness and unselfishness, Ray on defense and me on offense just trying to be the best players we could be."

Before Lombardi arrived, neither Taylor nor Nitschke knew how well Lombardi's brand of ball fit their styles:

"Well, you didn't necessarily know it, but we were just ready and willing to be there for whatever. We were both former fullbacks, he came from Illinois and he was a middle linebacker. I was a middle linebacker and running back at LSU. So we knew we were capable of moving to that next level and Lombardi, being the motivator and being the coach he was, established that very early when we got to Green Bay. So, it was just a matter of us developing and moving to those levels and performing with toughness in our work habits and giving us the results that were going to move us up. In '61 and '62, we went 13-1 and 12-2, so the proof's in the pudding. We're the type of individuals and players that, we don't need praise, we love to play the game, we love the contact, and this is our personalities—this is us. Deep down, we don't need all the frills and thrills and the publicity and all this, we just want to play the game. We just want to give you results, and we want to max out our potential and play the game at the high levels and see what happens; let's see what the outcome is. We're not lookin' for honors or awards or anything; we just want the end results for the Green Bay Packers, we were very dedicated to being team players."

The 1962 edition of the Packers was the best Lombardi team and Jimmy Taylor had his finest year. The great fullback was the league's MVP, won the rushing title which marked the only time in Jim Brown's career that he did not capture the honor. Green Bay won their second consecutive title and as Jim tells it, "I just happened to have been on that team and I was the fullback, the running back. I'm sure, God rest his soul, Ray Nitschke, if he was here, I think he would tell you the very same thing that I'm saying here with you now, we just really enjoyed being a part, to perform and to end up with the results we did."

Following the 1965 Championship win over the Cleveland Browns, Green Bay's running backs, Jim Taylor and Paul Hornung carried their coach off the field, so Jimmy's relationship with Lombardi was fine:

"Yeah, I felt like we had a good relationship, it was kinda like a father-son relationship. You're trying to do the best job you can do even though he's your boss and has hired you to be a running back for the Green Bay Packers. It's kind of a fine line, but it may hinge on being almost similar to some type of father-son relationship."

As it turned out, 1966 was Taylor's last year with the Packers and he could have gone through the motions and just played out the string, but in the Championship game against Dallas he risked ejection standing up for a teammate. Packer receiver Boyd Dowler caught a touchdown pass and was clearly in the end zone when Cowboy defensive back Mike Gaechter flipped him. Dowler suffered a shoulder injury on the play and Taylor went ballistic. Even though Jimmy knew he would probably be playing elsewhere the next year, he went after Gaechter: "I'm a competitor. I felt like it was a cheap shot on Boyd after the whistle, he was in the end zone, and I just felt very strongly it was uncalled for. You just gotta believe and take up for your teammates and stand up for what you feel is right and what you felt was not right. So it's a fine line, but, yeah, this was the championship game, I guess, in Dallas, and if we win that then we go on to the Super Bowl. We were gonna be playin' in the '66 Super Bowl Championship if we win that game." Bart Starr and others restrained Taylor saving him an ejection and Gaechter an ass kickin'.

Taylor was as tough at the negotiation table as he was on the field, he and Lombardi had at it:

"Vince was very straight foreword and that was when you got to go eyeball-to-eyeball. You got to state your position and he was very difficult to negotiate with, but I think he felt like he was fair and responsible in negotiating with a player on his football team."

From a player's point of view, they were at a disadvantage because they had little idea what other players were making and therefore, didn't know what the going rate was for a top player at a particular position. According to Jim, "You have no idea what the top three running backs in the National Football League salaries are. You have no idea, there's no exchange of information. So, it was a fine line of trying to determine what your value is.

"I think after the AFL was established, this moved the value of all players up, and they (Anderson and Grabowski) just happened to have been two running backs. I said, 'Well, this moves the value of *me* up, since I've been around six, seven, eight years,' All of a sudden this moved my value to an unbelievable level from what I'd been playing at and been paid for the past few years."

In 1965, Jimmy knew his career was nearing an end, Donny Anderson and Jim Grabowski had signed lucrative contracts during the height of the bidding war. The leagues had merged and the big money days were over. The way for Taylor to make some money was through free agency:

"I was still trying to be the football player I had been for years and years. I knew the salaries had increased with the other league coming into operation. I didn't have factual information about salaries of other running backs who joined the other league, but I knew they had improved and increased to some type of level, so I said to myself, 'I'm like a stock, did my stock go up?' Not necessarily on my ability, or productivity, but the stock of a running back moved to another level. I said, 'I need to look into this.' I had played out my option with the Green Bay Packers. At the termination of the first Super Bowl, I was a free agent and I could talk to any team. I talked to the Washington Redskins. I talked to the Kansas City Chiefs; I talked to other National Football League teams, plus AFL teams."

At that point, Jimmy contends he did not know for certain his home state of Louisiana would be awarded the New Orleans Saints franchise:

"That wasn't even in the picture. That was no issue."

Taylor did not immediately reject Lombardi's efforts to work out a contract:

"We had, I don't know, probably four or five serious confrontations in discussing contracts and me returning to the Green Bay Packers and we were really negotiating. I think Lombardi came down here to play golf down in Biloxi, and I think I went over and visited with him and we possibly had some negotiations at that point during the off-season time.

"He was a very tough negotiator. He would give you points or give you situations, he might say, "Well, you missed that blitz block there," and he'd bring up some points when you had maybe not as an outstanding game as you should have. There were high points and some low points and negotiating situations were very strong. I think he kind of felt I had a year or two left and for me to make a decision to go to the New Orleans Saints for the contractual agreement I worked out with them made sense. In essence, he had given me a good, substantial offer to stay with the Green Bay Packers for a few years, so he felt I could still be productive and still be a running back and get the job done."

As for negotiations with Lombardi, Jim says, "Well, we had 'em. Probably like any other players that would sit down and they were very, very productive. You felt you should be given credit or be paid for your services, so you felt very strongly that you wanted to try and have the top dollars the running backs in the National Football League were being compensated for their play, whatever that was. Sometimes you don't really know what Jim Brown, or this player or that player, what their actual salaries were. It was kind of a mystery. All I could do is take a consensus and try to figure what my compensation should be for the Green Bay Packers in 1965.

"I didn't throw up any records or throw up any this or that, I just said, 'I just tried to be the best football player I could be within myself and be productive for the Green Bay Packers, and this is it.' There's no ifs, ands or buts about it. I'm just workin' hard. I'd had an injury, or whatever, and I wanted to work hard to get through it, to be on that field, to be able to carry that ball the next ball game."

Taylor insists the negotiations were conducted in a business-like manner, leaving no ill feelings, "No, there was not. There was never any bitter feeling; we were always on a man-to-man, on a business level. Always talking, there was no hard feelings, or anger, or no type of resentment, or no type of any of that, certainly was not."

Packer fans were given a cruel glimpse of the future of American sports as one of their all-time favorites took a business approach to what had been viewed as a game. Jimmy contends that Lombardi knew it was not personal.

# JIM TAYLOR

"I think he knew it was a business decision. We did sit down and we came to the situation knowing that the Green Bay Packers are a 501 3C, a non-profit corporation. He may not be able to do as much as say, the New Orleans Saints in compensation. We were just at a stalemate, he was very, very tough and I just took a position. It was a stalemate. We visited and talked and negotiated things, I think as we left and parted company, he respected me as a person, as a man, as a football player. That was my choice and he accepted it and moved on from there."

The expansion New Orleans Saints wanted Louisiana native son Jim Taylor long-term for much more than playing football. Team owner John Mecom Jr. surrendered a first round draft choice to Green Bay and a huge contract to Taylor that allowed the running back to lock up his financial future:

"It was a long-tern contract, A National Football League contract for four years, and then I extended my stay another 16 years, and tied it into a front office job, with scouting, radio color, and other front office duties and assignments with the New Orleans Saints." A twenty year contact in 1967 was unheard of, "Yes, they wanted to include a long-term contract and deferred long-term monies for the next 20 years."

Like many of his former teammates, Taylor made a trip to Washington, D.C. to visit his dying coach in the hospital:

"Well, I went up and knew he probably was on his death bed, and had very little time left. We had some good talks and good visits, and reminisced about some of our days there with the Packers. He had become the Washington Redskins general manager and then I think he coached maybe one year. I think he knew that he was gonna be moving on, you know, and he was gonna pass on. So, we had an outstanding, great, great visit, things real man-to-man, lots of good memories and things. I went back to the funeral in New York at the termination of his life."

Jimmy was the first player from the great Lombardi teams to be enshrined in the Pro Football Hall of Fame. As testament to his respect for the Lombardi's, he selected Marie to present him for induction:

"Yeah, I chose Marie 'cause I think it was very appropriate. My feelings toward Coach Lombardi? He really instilled in me the player I became and I felt very good about having Marie as my presenter at the Pro Football Hall of Fame induction. Being the first of the Packer players of our years to be inducted, I just felt very good about her being my presenter."

The great coach and general manager Vince Lombardi left a large impression on Taylor unequalled by anyone:

"By far, head and shoulders above anyone else he impacted my life with the direction, and the motivation, and the fatherly image I received from our relationship."

# CHAPTER 12
# MAX McGEE:

*"Well. he scared the hell out of me right off the bat."*

# THE LOMBARDI LEGACY

Max McGee, from Tulane University, played wide receiver for the Packers in 1954 and '57-67. In 1955 and '56, he served as a pilot in the United States Air Force. He was one of nine men who played on all nine of Vince Lombardi's Green Bay teams. An outstanding talent, Max became famous for his quick wit and late night adventures with Paul Hornung. On the field, number 85 was a fine receiver and occasional punter. He scored 51 career touchdowns and led the league in punting in 1954.

His legend as a Packer was secured in Super Bowl I. Called off the bench following a Boyd Dowler injury during the Packers second possession, Max caught seven passes for 138 yards and two touchdowns while nursing a hangover. Not expecting to play, Max trotted the streets 'til the wee hours on the eve of the inaugural Super Bowl.

The first reception for a touchdown in Super Bowl history belongs to William Max McGee. He also caught a scoring pass in Super Bowl II, the last Green Bay game for Max and Lombardi.

From 1979-1998, Packer fans enjoyed Max as color commentator on the Packer Radio Network. He was so popular he was voted Wisconsin's Sportscaster of the Year, an unprecedented 10 times. In 1999, he founded the Max McGee National Research Center for Juvenile Diabetes at the Children's Hospital of Wisconsin, located in Milwaukee. On October 20, 2007, Max fell to his death while cleaning leaves off his roof.

His easy going style served him well in contract negotiations, unlike some of his teammates Max McGee had little difficulty in that area:

"Well, I found it pretty good because he sent somebody up, maybe it was after Jack Vainisi, I don't know who it would have been. They had a certain offer; we're not talking about a lot of money in those days. I wasn't totally satisfied, so Vince said he would talk to me, and I think he forgot the number the other guy gave me because he offered me more than what the guy he had sent out to offer me money did. I decided it was a pretty good deal. But Vince was pretty easy; he actually said something like, "Well, what do you think you're worth? What do you want?" I said a number and he said "You got it." And that was it; there wasn't much negotiation. I didn't ask for a heck of a lot. I had other businesses and I wasn't playing football for money then anyway, I was playing to have fun and get these rings that we have."

McGee was part of the Packer organization for three years in the '50's when the franchise was in the pits, so when Lombardi gathered the team for the first meeting, Max knew this head coach and general manager meant business:

"Well, he scared the hell out of me, right off the bat, you know, because I was late for the first meeting or something; somewhere I got hung up. Well, he read the riot act. I'll never forget. I punched, I don't know if it was Hornung, or Taylor, somebody and said, 'This thing's gonna turn around. I think we really got something here.' Because I could feel the intensity, and you could look at people, look them in their eyes and tell that this is a changed football team. You know, we were coming off a 1-10-1. We won one game and you could just see after Vince's first speech he meant business. I said we're going somewhere and sure enough, we had a winning record that year, 7-5 and then we went right to the 1960 NFL championship."

Max and Paul Hornung were the self-designated party guys, but their high jinks and carefree demeanor served a purpose in the high intensity world of Vince Lombardi:

"I think so. He was so tight. He got the people wound up so tight, he needed a loosener-upper, and that was my job and he accepted that and knew that. So, I could get away with saying some things I don't think I would have said had I been somebody else. I could make that statement 'cause he'd get everybody in these little talks the day before the game, where everybody's tight as a drum. Well, you can't play sports being tight, so I think he kind of liked the fact that I could say something and everybody would laugh and loosen up and have a little fun.

"I think he was pretty consistent. He was a hard bargain. He was

# THE LOMBARDI LEGACY

Vince Lombardi; that's what he was--he couldn't change much, because he demanded the best out of you and he did that right up until he quit. And he quit on a winning note, and on purpose he did that."

Some believe Lombardi found vicarious satisfaction watching McGee and Hornung run the streets and live lives so opposite of his. Max wished he could have had more time with the coach away from the game:

"Oh, I'd love it under certain circumstances. You know, Vince was a fun guy. I don't know if anybody saw that side of him; I think Paul and I did. We were the two bachelors and I think he kind of enjoyed that type of life and we were out there to have fun, we weren't gettin' rich, we were just out playing football, having fun. And if it can't be fun, like I can't think it's so much fun today. I watch these guys play and I can't tell if they're having fun or not. But we were having fun and Vince liked that. He would have liked to have been with us on one of them nights we snuck out and chased the late night show, you know. I had a relationship where I knew when he wasn't really mad at me; he called me Maxie. I just think, without saying a lot of things, he made you understand what life is all about. If you want to be a winner, this is what you do, and if you don't want to be a winner, get the hell out of here. That was kind of his deal, and he taught me how to be a winner; taught me all my life.

"He believed in his religion and he believed in winning, and that was his life. I think he transplanted that into enough of us guys that that's what we did. We won football games and we won championships."

Max developed an extremely successful business career, including co-founding Chi-Chi's Mexican Restaurants in 1975. It was his contention that he would not have been nearly as successful without Lombardi's influence:

"You know, probably not. Knock on wood; I've been pretty lucky in life, but I give a lot of my success directly to Vince Lombardi, just from the fact that he taught you about winning. His famous statement probably didn't really say what he wanted, the one where he says, "Winning isn't everything,

130

it's the only thing," 'because I think he was probably a little different from a coaching standpoint. And I think we carried a lot of it, the effort, one hundred percent. He wanted it all. Leave it all on the field, and that's the way we did it.'

# CHAPTER 13
# VERNON BIEVER:

*"You could feel his way of doing things."*

# THE LOMBARDI LEGACY

The gold standard for NFL sideline photographers is Vernon Biever. He began shooting Packer action in 1941 while attending St. Norbert College in De Pere, Wisconsin. Vernon worked on a freelance basis for the Milwaukee Sentinel for a year and half before serving three years in the Army. By the time he returned in 1946, the newspaper had filled the position. Biever approached the Packers with a unique offer: he would shoot sideline action for free in exchange for a sideline pass. The Packers said the price was right. The rich history of the storied Green Bay Packer franchise has been documented brilliantly and consistently by Mr. Biever. Sports fans, especially professional football fans, owe Vernon a "thank you" for capturing, pictorially the Lombardi Dynasty and freezing it in time.

Much of Vernon Biever's great work is available for purchase from the Gallery of Sports Art in Milwaukee, Wisconsin. Check out the website: www. galleryofsportsart.com.

Biever has roamed the sidelines with every Packer head coach from Curly Lambeau to Mike McCarthy. By his own description, he has shot "thousands upon thousands" of Packer game photos. The quality and quantity of his work earned him induction into the Packer Hall of Fame in 2002, the same Hall that is adorned with so much of his work. Semi-retired and living in Port Washington, Wisconsin, Vernon now shoots Packer games from the press box while son John carries on the family tradition at field level.

Vernon Biever watched Vince Lombardi place the entire Packer organization into a demanding incubator and transform devastation into greatness:

"Well, before Lombardi, you pretty well had the place by yourself to do anything you wanted to do, and I could do that and I did. But once he stepped into the picture, you had to follow his rules, which were a *lot*. He had a lot of rules and regulations, but he got the job done, and if that's what it takes to get the job done, I vote for him."

As much as the new coach could rant and rave, he was somewhat nonverbal with changes that affected Vernon:

"You could feel it--you could feel his way of doing things, and that's the way it worked out. Nothing strange."

The same instincts that permitted him to read Lombardi are probably the same ones that allowed him to capture many classic photos. The head coach would ask Vern for special photos from time to time, but one in particular made an impact:

"Well, that picture of Colonel Krueger and himself, they were good friends from Army. That's where Krueger came from, and aside from that, no, but I did a lot of stuff for him. In fact, I took a picture on 'Lombardi Day' in Green Bay, of he and his wife in the stands. They were there for a while--and Mrs. Lombardi said that was one of the finest pictures she had of him, so I felt pretty proud of that. When he first got to Green Bay, he didn't like to have his picture taken, over time he got used to it though."

He liked the Krueger photo, but did not complement Vernon on a regular basis:

"No, he never did; where as other guys did, like a Bart Starr. In fact, if it wasn't for Bart Starr, I would not be in the Hall of Fame. He pushed pretty hard for that. I always considered Bart and his family very close friends, and we are very close friends."

Because this great sports photographer has been on the sidelines with all the Packer coaches, invariably the comparisons are made between Curly Lambeau and Lombardi:

"Both were excitable on the sideline, Lombardi was pretty noisy. They were a lot alike. It was pretty much what you see on the film clips."

Many people from the Packer Glory Years hold a special tie to each other, trainers, secretaries, and one sideline photographer who remains close to the players of those times. Vernon is part of the inner circle and said:

"I would say so, because, first of all, they kept on winning. And if you had some losers along the way, or a losing steak for many years, they wouldn't be that close. But, because of their good attitude and good competition and good winning they stuck around, where nowadays you've got a revolving door up there. In fact, it's like that in all places and these players do not have a chance to stay together, know each other, like it used to be, which was a lot better."

As controlling as Lombardi was, one would suspect he would have thrown a hissy fit if an injured player would have been photographed:

"No, they weren't strict on that kind of stuff. As a matter of fact, I could work in front of the bench, which nobody else could, and even Lombardi didn't complain about that, which I'm surprised about. He would find a reason to put me on the side, but he never complained about that."

Paradoxically, Vernon's most vivid memory of Lombardi did not involve a direct encounter with him:

"Well, strange thing about that is in the 1960 NFL Championship game we played the Philadelphia Eagles and we lost; Lombardi said, "We'll never lose a championship game again," or "we ran out of time." But after that game, he was talking to Commissioner Pete Rozelle, and very jovial, which is not typical of Lombardi. It was surprising. I didn't expect him to be in that kind of mood, but he was. I can't explain it."

Vernon blazed the way for sideline photographers in the NFL; he is a one of kind original and sees Lombardi the same way: "He was in a class by himself. He was altogether different than most guys. Whatever attitude he had, he won football games, and that's all it takes."

Vernon was becoming great before Lombardi got to Green Bay, but the dynasty gave the great photographer an opportunity to shoot big game, after big game, allowing his work to take on added importance. He knows what he would say to the former top man if he could talk to him:

"Thanks for doing what you did. You did one hell of a job with that football team with a very poor record, which they had. He brought them back to life and all the players will agree that it took Lombardi to do that."

December 11, 1968

Mr. Vernon J. Biever
Post Office Box 209
Port Washington, Wisconsin   53074

Dear ~~Mr. Biever~~: *Vera*

Thank you for the portrait of Colonel Krueger and myself.

It is excellent and will be suitably framed.

Sincerely,

Vince Lombardi

VL:dvdy

LAMBEAU FIELD

1967
1966
1965
1962
1961
1944
1939
1936
1931
1930
1929

MEMBER CLUB NATIONAL FOOTBALL LEAGUE  ●  ELEVEN TIMES WORLD CHAMPIONS
WESTERN DIVISION CHAMPIONS 1938-1960  ●  SUPER BOWL CHAMPIONS 1966-1967

# Chapter 14
# Willie Davis:

*"He never disappointed me."*

# THE LOMBARDI LEGACY

One of the all time great Green Bay Packers, Willie Davis is the quintessential example of General Manager Vince Lombardi's genius. Not only did he acquire the future NFL Hall of Famer for A.D. Williams, Lombardi switched Willie from offensive tackle, to left defensive end. A tremendous bundle of speed, agility, quickness, work ethic and intelligence; Davis became one of the NFL's greatest defensive linemen.

Drafted in the 15th round, he served two years in the United States Army before beginning his career with the Cleveland Browns. Prior to Willie's acquisition, the Packer general manager had already secured defensive tackle Henry Jordan and defensive end Bill Quinlan from the same man, same team, Paul Brown and the Cleveland Browns. Lombardi cleaned his clock.

Willie did not miss a game during his Packer career, he played in 5 Pro Bowls, 6 NFL Championship games, earned induction into the Pro Football Hall of Fame in 1981, and the Packer Hall in 1975.

As a mature, rational, respected leader, Willie's value to young black players in his role as liaison to Lombardi served to galvanize the team during the racially combustible 1960's. He had three of the greatest coaches this country has ever produced; Eddie Robinson at Grambling, Paul Brown in Cleveland and Vince Lombardi at Green Bay.

After joining the Packers, Davis attended the University of Chicago where he earned a masters degree in business. Equal to his success as a player, Willie chronicled a highly distinguished business career. He served on several prestigious boards of directors including, Alliance Bank, Dow Chemical, Green Bay Packers, Fidelity Title & Trust, Johnson Controls, L.A. Gear, Manpower, Mattel, MGM, MGM Mirage, and WICOR. He has also served on the boards of K-Mart, Sara Lee and Strong Funds.

Willie is the owner of several businesses including: All-Pro Broadcasting, which owns WLDB, WLUM and WMCS in Milwaukee and KATY and KCXX in California. He has also owned beverage distributorships and been involved in real estate ventures.

# WILLIE DAVIS

Davis is tribute to using Lombardi's principles in life following football. One can imagine Lombardi in Heaven, looking approvingly on the life and being of Willie Davis. Green Bay's immortal number 87 recalls how he heard he had been traded from the Browns to the Packers following Lombardi's first year of 1959.

"Well, I can tell you right now, I had just signed a contract with the Cleveland Browns and was told by Paul Brown I was going to be the starting left offensive tackle in the upcoming season. I was working as a substitute teacher on the west side of Cleveland. Every day when I finished the day, about three thirty or four o'clock, I'd be zooming home to go and work out, believing I was going to have a chance to be the starting left tackle. Well, I'm driving home one day; I had just signed my contract two weeks before that—and it's like a 'sports flash' on the radio. They said, "Second-year tackle, end, or whatever, Willie Davis traded to Green Bay." Well, I was devastated. Paul Brown, when he was a little bit upset with you, said, "If you don't perform, we can always send you to Green Bay." It was almost considered the worst place. It was the Siberia of football.

"Well, I was so devastated by that. I had a great offer out of college to go to Canada. My first reaction was, 'I'm going to Canada, they showed the most interest in the first place. I chose to go to Cleveland, but now that they've traded me, I'm going to Canada.' If I was around today, I could have accepted it as part of business, but back then, you sign up with teams and you kind of ended up there forever. It was like it became almost a love affair. I'm going, 'Gol darn,' I'm thinking about facing guys that I played with, and just seeing them around, and I think 'Gol darn, how do I explain this?' I got home and I had a couple phone calls waiting for me from Jack Vainisi, who was the head of the personnel thing with Green Bay. The messages said, "Please call Coach Lombardi." Of course I did and I remember to this day what I said to him, "Coach, This is Willie. I had a message to call you."

"Aw, yeah, I gotta talk to you."

# THE LOMBARDI LEGACY

I wanted to tell him right then, "Coach, I have made my mind up to go to Canada."

He responded, "Yeah, we gotta get you up here."

I told Jack when he talked to me I thought I was going to Canada so I'm sure he told Coach Lombardi. I said, "Coach, I'm just devastated by this whole thing."

"What?"

"I had just signed and was told I was going to be the starting offense tackle."

"Let me tell you one thing. This trade was made because of need." And then he asked me, "Did you follow us a little bit last year? Willie, I'll just tell you this, we're going to be a winning football team." He said, "I'm gonna tell you one other thing, there's no one that can come here and do a better job. Just know this, we have no concern about your playing offense, whatever, we just want you to play defense."

"Then he told me about a play I made against the Giants. He said it showed more agility and more aggressiveness than any play he'd ever seen. He said, "Willie, trust me, you come here and give us that kind of effort, and you'll be our left end and that's where you'll play." He was so convincing I could see myself breaking down a little bit with each conversation, so finally, I said, "Coach, I just don't know.'"

"Well, do you want me to call you back in a few minutes?"

"Coach, right now I'm pretty devastated, so I don't know, maybe I'm not even thinking straight."

"Well, I just want you to come to Green Bay."

"I ended up going to Green Bay and it was really interesting because I remember when I walked into his office there at St. Norbert College, where we had the training camp, the first thing he said was, "How much were you making in Cleveland?" I couldn't tell you. It was peanuts in the first place. When I told him, he goes, "Hey—you got another thousand dollars on that

142

right now." I think I was making eighty-five hundred and another thousand bucks. Hey, that's a pretty big raise, but it was just the feeling.

"I would say the greatest thing about Coach Lombardi. He knew how to take a person from this level (motions with his hand at chest level) to another level (raises to head level), and everything he said in that conversation, from walking in his office, getting that raise, and I'm like, 'I'm getting a raise and I haven't even played.' I mean, everything was lifting me. When I walked out of his office, I said, 'Well, I'm gonna start kicking some booty right now.' You know, it went from there. Ten years later, I had started every game for the Green Bay Packers and played defensive left end and felt absolutely it was *the* greatest thing that ever happened to me in pro football."

When Davis met Lombardi for the first time, it was apparent, Green Bay's second year coach was special:

"He had that aura, and you know, he could say something and it was so meaningful to me, it was almost like—it was uplifting, you know, just like he looked at me and he said, (waving and pointing with his finger for exclamation), "You're gonna be--you're gonna be our defensive end." He *used* his finger in pointing. I mean, he made you feel like he was absolutely certain of what you could do, and the fact that now you're gonna do it. Before I walked on the field, I felt that I was playing up to a standard."

Willie had been in the military, spent four years with the great Eddie Robinson at Grambling and two with Paul Brown in Cleveland, before going to Green Bay. Suffice to say not just any old coach was going to have credibility with Davis, but Lombardi did:

"Absolutely, and you're absolutely right by that, too. Coach Robinson was like a father, and a coach. Coach Brown was probably fundamentally, one of the best coaches I'd ever been with, and it was helpful to me that I played those two years in that system, because you did everything, in almost exact science, the way it was. He'd tell you, "Hold up! Move over two inches!" I mean, he was that technical. You got in trouble with Coach Lombardi from a lack of concentration. Mental mistakes. That was his undoing, as far as I'm concerned. If you wanted to get in trouble with Coach Lombardi, you turn up making a lot of mental mistakes. He could go berserk about that. I think he enjoyed, more than anything, seeing a player rise to the next level.

"I remember later in Green Bay, I had made the All-Pro team and I was Defensive Player of the Year. I remember trying to discuss my contract the next year. I'm telling him about all these things, and I said, "Well, Coach, you know, I was at the Pro Bowl game, and I'm talking to David "Deacon" Jones and the other guys there." I said, 'Coach, they're making more money.' He said, "Aw, no, that's not true." You could never really talk to him straight up, he'd find some way to break you down. So, I had written this letter I took to him and I got everything on the letter. He's looking at it and he's just reading and laughing and kind of stopped, and it goes on, then he finishes the letter and he says, "You know what, Willie? Everything you got in there is right. I can't disagree with one thing. You know, Willie, you're forgetting one thing… we helped make you." Oh, my goodness, he got me again. He got me again.

"OK, we go on from there, and we're discussing things, and I'll never forget this. You know, you could hit that moment with him when you went silent and he went silent. It's like, "Who's going to speak next?" I'm checking the walls and finally, he said, "Well, you probably want to get on the road back to Chicago." Funny thing, and to this day I was proud that I formed those few words. I said, "Right Coach, but you know, I was just thinking, the difference in my driving back to Chicago and wanting to stay on the right side of traffic, versus turning into oncoming traffic is the difference in that amount." It was fifteen hundred bucks; and he looked at me, because I felt, as much as he had gotten me; he looked at me and you could always see him reflect. He was one of the most interesting guys that I'd ever been around. You could see him literally, digesting things in his mind, and he sat there for a minute and he looked at me straight in the eye. He said, "Willie, if the difference between you driving back to Chicago, getting ready to come back here to training camp versus wanting to turn into oncoming traffic is fifteen hundred dollars, you got it. Now get out of here." True story—I walked out of there and I was feeling good."

Feeling good is different than feeling like you won a negotiation session with General Manager Lombardi. Davis explains, "You never exactly felt like you won with Coach Lombardi. You felt like you had a temporary victory of some type. Maybe you didn't even try real hard; you wanted to feel all the things that make you feel good about being on a winner. He could do that better than anybody I've ever seen. He started telling you why you were going to be successful and how you could do it and why it was important. He could just make you absolutely feel like you were at the next level."

Serving in the duel capacity of head coach and general manager, Lombardi could have allowed lingering feelings from contract negotiations to spill over to coaching. Davis says, "No, no, not with me, I witnessed it with Jim Taylor, Willie Wood and a few others, Herb Adderley and a few of the other folks where it literally, it carried all the way to the practice field with his hollering and you'd see the attitude, but I never had that problem with Coach. He made you feel that everything he was doing was with a sense of fairness, and this was the way."

Vince Lombardi's accomplishments on the football field, as great as they were, may be dwarfed in importance by his contributions to racial progress. The infusion of black players into the Green Bay Packers was accomplished without incident, a tremendous testament to his diligent attention to the entire issue.

Davis relates, "I've said kind of quietly to myself that in many ways, what Coach Lombardi did in Green Bay, all the way from helping us find a place to live, he understood what our problem was and he wanted to make a difference. I remember he called me up, and said, "We're gonna find you guys a place. You remember that Paul Mazzoleni? "I'm gonna call Paul." He actually was the one that helped us. Lombardi was very bothered, he said, "It's just a shame that the people want and expect you to come and play and the next minute, they almost don't care enough to find a place for you."

Lombardi's attention to detail is beyond question and in the important area of fairness and equality he made the historic decision to have Willie Davis serve as liaison between the black players and himself. It was a mutual agreement, Lombardi wanted him and Davis said, "I somewhat volunteered, I said, 'Coach, I know it's time', because they had the problem with Marv Fleming, dating the white girl. Her dad had called and said he was going to shoot him. I remember going to Marv and saying, "Hey man, you better cool it." Imitating Fleming in a high-pitched voice Willie said, "Hey, man I'm from California."

"I don't give a shit where you're from you'd better listen."
"Coach called me in and said, "Willie, I feel almost conflicted. If Fleming wanted to see my daughter I wouldn't like it; I wouldn't want it. But there's just something in me that says I couldn't totally prevent him from doing it." And he asked, "Do you understand?"

"Yeah, Coach, I do understand and I'm gonna make sure Fleming understands."

"You know more and more with some of our black players coming in, some of you older black players are going to need to pull 'em aside and talk to them."

Some forty years after retiring, the team's black elder statesman offered a retrospective on racial progress within the team. "We had Lionel Aldridge, who was interracially married. This was just at a time when some of this stuff was starting to break down. When I first went to Green Bay, the few black players went here; the white players went someplace else. By the time we were shutting down 10 years later, it had almost just dissipated—this whole racial thing—I mean, there were white players, black players, still totally intermingled from food to whatever, going to the restaurants."

# WILLIE DAVIS

The ideal fit of Lombardi and Green Bay allowed events to occur that may not have been possible with another person in another place, especially involving race relations in the 1960's.

"Well, you just raised the issue that I say to this day was so critical, and it's always important in racial and other pretty intense situations, one of the things is to have success in the process. The other one is how you approach it. Coach Lombardi made it pretty clear that he would not tolerate any prejudice considerations at all. And you know, it was really interesting to players like myself, when things were just starting. In Cleveland, there had been a black and white situation, the players from the Southeast Conference, and things, and it was just not a natural coming together.

"I think when I went to Green Bay there was not that *natural* coming together. As we drafted black players—first Adderley and Robinson, just their draft position helped break down the situation. He was aware of guys showing up at other places creating a problem, with image and everything else. I think he would have been totally, totally disappointed if there had been a racially explosive situation in Green Bay that ever got out. I mean what racial problem that existed then, probably felt so compressed in the system that they didn't dare break out. You had guys that probably accepted a lot of what they never would have accepted if they didn't have a concern. They knew to create a problem would be to blow up Coach Lombardi in a way that he would have them out of there in a New York minute.

"I tell you right now, Green Bay would be totally, totally misled if they felt for a minute that Lombardi didn't blaze the way, open the way for black players. Not only in Green Bay, but for the rest of the league, because he took black players and built us into champions. I think the league started to look around and see these black players make a difference in Green Bay. You saw 'em pop up more frequently in other places, and I think, to that extent, it was definitely driven by him."

Lombardi had a unique talent for putting the right people in the right places. So it was that he selected Willie Davis as defensive captain, not because he was black, but because he was suited for the role.

"I would say there's probably some truth in this. I was explaining to a guy a couple days ago something about what I consider leadership. I was either co-captain or captain of every team I ever played with—high school, in the military, college and in the pros. This is not from an ego, but it's from my belief that I've always exuded leadership. You know we'd run the sprints and do other crap and I was always there, finishing first and doing things with my group. I saw Dave Robinson and other people come in, and it was kind of interesting to me, I was happy to see them kind of press the (racial) issue. I was not going to go to them and say, 'You need to do this.' I wasn't going to go to them and say, 'You shouldn't do this.' To me, Dave, Herb and Lionel and some of these guys—as you saw them take a whole different approach to where they were going to live and what they were going to do, it made the whole situation more aware and more prepared to deal with it. I mean, in many ways, it made my role very easy, because frankly, many times when I talked to them, I was talking about them playing and not so much the social life.

"People like Robinson, again, he was married anyway, so it wasn't that much of a situation. It was just situations of knocking down little craziness that had existed before. They said a black couldn't play linebacker and all this crap. Dave came right in and blew that out of the water."

That was 1963 when only three rookies cracked Lombardi's roster. They were bright, articulate, assertive and black; Dave Robinson, Lionel Aldridge and Marv Fleming. Willie could not resist taking a poke at one of those guys.

"Well, I don't know if you've been around Dave Robinson much. Any group that Dave's in, he's going to enlighten them with some factual things about life, be it engineering or what. He's going to make them believe that he's a pretty special guy, and I will tell you right now, the greatest years I had and the greatest time I had was playing next to this guy (Robinson). I played there with Dan Currie, and about half the time, the play would be snapped and Dan would still be hollering, "Yeah, Willie."

"No Dan, play the play." With Dave, we had a minimum of communication *by need*."

There was a complicated powder keg of potential trouble in the Packer locker room in the person of Lionel Aldridge. He was a black defensive end who had not yet been clinically diagnosed, but those near him sensed there was something wrong. He had a mental illness that would become full blown later in life. As a team captain, Willie needed to monitor and manage the situation. If there would have been an incident, it could have been attributed to race rather than psychological disorder.

"Yeah, yeah, and you know it was so interesting because you do feel a responsibility. I mean, I felt as if I owed it to these guys to be honest with them because some of the more interesting conversations I had was really with the white players. Lionel Aldridge, who played for us, I don't think anybody quite ever understood Lionel, and obviously he was later diagnosed with the schizophrenia and everything else. There were players--a number of the white players that said, "Hey, what's the deal with Lionel?" And of course, he played the other defensive end, he kind of felt that I took away some of what otherwise would have been glory moments for him, and so I had to walk a very careful line so I didn't say or do the wrong things.

"Many times when players come to me, I'd go back and say, "Hey, look, you just need to be careful. You need to be careful because we don't need it. You need to be careful what you say to Lionel, and if you don't feel comfortable you probably just don't say anything. But it was a situation where the wrong thing—it could upset him, yeah."

Davis was a central figure in a ground breaking development that went virtually unnoticed because it worked so well.

"You know Jerry Kramer and I, we were the first two integrated roommates. We didn't necessarily do it because of accomplishing it. He lost his roommate, and it was kind of a fun thing, because we used to talk and kid around a lot, and we just ended up being roommates. I know we were the first in Green Bay for darn sure. Coach Lombardi worked so hard to maintain and control and he didn't want to find out the wrong way-- what a racial issue would do in Green Bay. And you know I will say to you right now, the greatest example in this country is really what sports have been able to do in breaking down race situations."

Willie Davis loves a laugh and loves to laugh, and recalls a couple lighter incidents. Lombardi had carved out his place in history being one of the famous linemen at Fordham University. Summarily unimpressed by Lombardi's football technique, the hearty, fun side of Willie Davis could not resist giving his old coach the needle.

"The Seven Blocks of Granite", if you saw a picture of 'em they look like seven individualists and someone said you should tease Lombardi about the position he had, because you could never even block anybody sittin' back in that little squatty position. He enjoyed exposing a certain amount of that to us, it's almost like he was saying, "Hey, you guys should know this is not totally strange to me," and I said, 'Gee, coach you need to keep that as a fun thing, you don't need to make it like it's a serious event."

With all the success in his own businesses, sitting on prestigious boards of directors, untouched by scandal and so much more, Willie Davis tells what it would be like if he could spend a day with Vince Lombardi:

"You know, I think knowing what I know now, it would be extra special and important to me if I had a chance to spend a day. I think one of the things I would say is, 'Coach, how am I doing?' I would almost want his evaluation of how I'm doing and am I doing it right or what else can I do to change the situation? So it would be a special day in my life, as it was in the past. There's no question in my mind that things that he exposed you to were not only good for football, but they had almost an equally important meaning to you as you went forth in business. One of the things he used to

# WILLIE DAVIS

say was, "The way you play this game is a reflection of how you'll live the rest of your life." And he said, "If you don't get it done here, you're not going to just walk away from here and just all at once start to do it someplace else." So he was a great trainer, if you will, about life. And these things just don't happen; that you make them happen, you help make them happen. And he was impressive in that dimension of it. He could make you feel like you were playing out kind of a life story of what you would do now, but also what you would do later. There's almost not a day that goes by in some way, especially with something to do with winning or success that I don't think about Coach Lombardi. I'll bet on average it happens twice a week at least, and that's all year. I can be home lying in bed, and I think, what would coach Lombardi think you should do? I literally love Coach Lombardi, and his toughness on us in practice. He never disappointed me. He just never made me feel like he missed an opportunity to make a difference. Maybe some did dislike him for the wrong reason but any individual that was serious about playing football, about being successful, to dislike Lombardi would have been to me, a sense of major disloyalty."

Difficult as it was, the good Captain Willie Davis made a final trip to see his coach and general manager in September 1970. Three distinguished people spent a powerful few minutes together as Vincent Thomas Lombardi's life neared its end. Willie explains, "It was really interesting—when I went back to Washington to see him in the hospital, I guess I was the last former Green Bay Packer to see him alive, and I remember walking into his room with Mrs. Lombardi—and he looked at me and he was so deteriorated that I couldn't have recognized him from before. And I never will forget this; he said to me, "Willie, you were a hell of a football player, and you were the best deal I ever made." And he said, "Hey Willie, you played great football for me." He started to cry, and said, "Willie, I want you to pray for me."

"I'm thinking, 'Oh, my God.' I was just knocked, and I said, 'Coach, I came back to make a deal with you--you get up and come back and coach

151

and I'm gonna come out and unretire.' He kind of cracked a smile, he looked a little bit more and he started to cry again. He told me and Mrs. Lombardi, "Leave, you guys, leave." And we went out and this is all in less than 10 minutes. Mrs. Lombardi said, "Willie, I'm convinced of one thing--all you guys that he saw that were a part of the Green Bay success when he was totally in charge, the greatest thing for him now is to see you and for you to see him and he's not in charge." You know, I think that resonated with me more than anything. Now he's a man lying helplessly on his back and he is almost, in a sense, saying to you to do things for him other than play football, and it was tough. It was tough for him, and it was every bit as tough--at least as far as I'm concerned—to every player or former player."

Being told by Lombardi that he was the best deal he ever made ranks near the top of all things Willie heard from his coach and general manager. "That surely was one. I used to go up in his office; many times he would invite you up just to talk about what his concerns were for the week and the status of certain things. I remember once when I went in his office and he was telling me he had applied for the Notre Dame opening and he never even got a response. He was saying, "Willie, you came here and I know in your mind after we talked you had something you wanted to prove. I'm gonna tell you, I know why you play the way you do every week. Because it's important to you that you meet all the standards that you set for yourself. You know why I know that? Because I lived through the exact same thing. I tell you-- there's nothing more important to me than making the Packers winners. It was my one opportunity, and finally I got it, and now I got this chance—I'm not going to blow it. I was so lucky that I had good players. But I'm going to tell you, absolutely, that I understand why you have to play this game the way you do. A lot of you guys, he probably went through a good third of the team all I need to do is just give you guys the game plan and I know you're going to come ready to play because of what's in you."

"Boy was he ever true about that. He said to me once, "You know, you're a better football player than we realized we were getting," whatever that meant. But I remember him saying that."

# CHAPTER 15
# PEGGY KOSTELNIK SPALDING:

*"My gosh, the power of that man,
that's incredible."*

# THE LOMBARDI LEGACY

Ask a Packer fan to name the defensive players on the great 1960's Green Bay teams and they will probably miss one of the linemen. If they need a clue, tell them it's a guy who was on all five championship teams. Two more hints; his number was 77 and his wife's name was Peggy. Yep, Peggy Kostelnik's husband Ron is one of the toughest ones to name. The big defensive tackle out of the University of Cincinnati, was a second round draft choice for the 1961 season. An unheralded selection by Lombardi, Kostelnik was a solid run stopper during an eight year Packer career in which he missed just two games. Of his former teammate, linebacker Dave Robinson says, "Without Ron our defensive line would have been a sieve; he was quick, impossible to trap and took care of the screens and traps. If Henry Jordan was double teamed, Ron had the quarterback on his back." Kostelnik's cheerful, boyish face always belied the competent competitor within.

Peggy Fey grew up in Cincinnati and graduated from the University of Cincinnati having earned a BS in Education. Graduation ceremonies were on a Friday night and she and Ron were married the next day. She earned a Master's Degree from Northwestern University in Evanston, Illinois. The former Ms. Fey taught for 24 years until taking over Ron's company following his death in 1993. Her teaching career began at Hughes High School in Cincinnati and finished at the University of Wisconsin-Green Bay where she taught College Composition and Expository Writing. Since 1995, she has lived in Menasha, Wisconsin with her husband John Spalding.

The story of Ron and Peggy is true Americana, hard working, honest and humble; not from wealth or glitz, and not phony. Ron Kostelnik came from coal mining country about 80 miles east of Pittsburgh; he was an obscure late bloomer in college who was overshadowed at Green Bay by the array of perennial Pro Bowl players. Lombardi is not given much credit for his draft selections, but the 1961 rookies of Herb Adderley, Elijah Pitts and Kostelnik were vital ingredients in the Packer Dynasty. All three are members of the Green Bay Packer Hall of Fame, with Ron's induction occurring in 1989.

# PEGGY KOSTELNIK SPALDING

The Kostelniks were what Lombardi people were supposed to be: very hungry and solidly dedicated to the Green Bay Packers with an industrious eye cast to the future in order to lead a productive life in a post football world. Their story captures the essence of Lombardi's lessons of preparation with an ability to overcome life's cruelest blows. Peggy's perseverance is high tribute to the Great Coach.

Despite being taken in the second round, Ron Kostelnik was probably a "reach" at number two, not having been a highly touted or decorated college player. Peggy Kostelnik Spalding recalls the rapid changes in Ron's football life:

"All this happened so quickly, he never thought of playing pro ball until he had that one game. He was unsung and then all of a sudden, he had this game against North Texas State where he had something like nine tackles and was named Associated Press Defensive Player of the Week. He made All-American Honorable Mention and it changed rapidly in maybe a two week period and then he was drafted."

Green Bay selected Kostelnik in the second round, whereas the Buffalo Bills of the rival AFL waited until its 14th pick. Buffalo never stood a chance and Lombardi struck fast by sending Defensive Coordinator Phil Bengtson to get Kostelnik's signature on a contract. Shortly after the draft, Ron took Peggy to his hometown of Colver, Pennsylvania to meet his parents. Peggy explains:

"When we got off the train, Coach Phil Bengtson was there to meet the train. So, he went out to meet Ron's parents, they were meeting me for the first time and Coach Bengtson. He literally signed Ron then, except Ron was only twenty years old, so his mother had to sign for him and she wouldn't do it. She said, "Oh no, he'll get hurt playing football, I do not want him to play professional football." So they had to go up in another room, they had to keep talking to her, and talking to her, and talking to her to try to convince her to sign that contract. She kept that contract until the day she died and she willed it to my daughter. I know for a fact he took his bonus and went out and bought me an engagement ring. I would say the bonus was maybe a thousand dollars."

The entire experience of professional sports was brand new to both the Kostelnik and Fey families and they did not know that being drafted and signed did not guarantee Ron a spot on the Packer roster. Peggy needed to explain that to her own father, "When Ron signed his contract, my dad believed, 'OK, he signed a contract he's on the team.' At that time, I was student teaching and he was driving me to my class, we were just having a conversation and he found out that Ron had to make the team. My dad stopped the car and said, "Oh, oh Peggy I think you should put off that wedding." He didn't know that he had to make the team."

Peggy's side of the family held a send-off for the young couple before they left for training camp in 1961.

"Prior to going to Green Bay my grandma had a breakfast for me. We were all packed and all ready to go. All of the relatives came, but nobody had ever heard of Green Bay. They were crying and giving me all these electric blankets, I don't know where they thought I was going."

Having just graduated from college, no money to speak of, the young Kostelniks had to find a way to get to training camp as Peggy recalls, "We used Ron's parents' car and drove to Green Bay and then the car broke down when we got there, so we had *no car* until Ron got his first check.

"The first time I met Mr. Lombardi and Mrs. Lombardi would have been after the exhibition games when we would go to St. Norbert's and they would have a wonderful buffet, at the Pfister Hotel if we were in Milwaukee. They would have ice carvings and all that.

"I was intimidated by the other wives when I saw them. They were all so cute and they were all these Southern Belles. I can remember my mom was taking a train up to visit me and I actually called her and said, "Mom you've got to bring me some new clothes, I don't have the right clothes up here."

# PEGGY KOSTELNIK SPALDING

High draft choice or not, Kostelnik still had to make the team, which was not an easy chore as the Packers became a powerhouse. Peggy recalls the anguish of the first training camp: "Every single Monday morning when that cut list was posted it was painful, there's no other way to describe it. Ron would come home and I'd ask, 'Did you make the cut?' We really worried through that *every single week*. When we finally made it to the point we were on the team, the relief was unbelievable."

Then as now, contracts were not guaranteed, so each year it was high drama until the final cuts were announced.

"You know what, that never really ends. You worry about it in the beginning, I'd say for the first three years and then you worry about it at the end." Peggy could not have agreed more when reminded of another milestone year, that magic fifth season that qualifies a player for a pension. For pro football families in the 1960's, a paycheck from the team was one of at least two that were needed to live and raise a family. The player invariably worked during the off season and the wife many times had a job as well.

For Peggy and other Packer wives, game day was a little unusual: "The very first thing we had to do was make this *special breakfast* that included, for some unknown reason, pancakes and cling peaches. Mr. Lombardi believed this would give you a boost in energy. Ron always left very early, he got very nervous. When they were in Milwaukee or Chicago, we would take the train down to the games as a group. For road games, we'd get together at each other's homes and watch the games."

Ron was somewhat lost in the cavalcade of stars at Green Bay as the team stacked up a pile of championships, but it was different back in coal mining country as Peggy describes, "I don't think we ever felt famous until we went back to Colver, Pennsylvania. Ron's relatives all lived on the same street, it was called Twenty Row and they were all coal miners, so he was famous there in his environment and in his high school. We didn't feel famous, we just felt grateful."

# THE LOMBARDI LEGACY

The power and influence of Vince Lombardi can only be known to those who felt it, not even a wife like Peggy could totally grasp his dominance: "I'll tell you an image of Mr. Lombardi that will always remain in my mind. Mr. Lombardi had an edict that players had to wear a hat. We had an apartment in De Pere and we were walking down the street pushing a baby buggy. All of a sudden Mr. Lombardi drove by and he spotted Ron, myself and our baby. He stopped, backed up, opened the window and pointed to the top of his head; Ron didn't have a hat on. Ron, without saying one word, turned around, walked all the way back to the apartment, got a hat on and came back. I thought, "My gosh, the power of that man, that's incredible." Mr. Lombardi drove off, he knew he'd go back and get a hat, and there was no doubt in his mind."

Ron Kostelnik knew football was a tenuous occupation that would be short at best and could end immediately with an injury. Peggy relates how her husband prepared for the future: "The first three off seasons Ron went back to the University of Cincinnati and they were kind enough to structure a Master Degree program for him so he could get the masters in three off seasons. After that, he did promotional work for Main Line Industrial Distributors, which he eventually bought and became sole owner. Once he bought that company, he did run it under Lombardi Principles." The company had been owned by John Spalding, who Peggy would later marry.

Lifelong friendships developed with other Packer wives: "Well, definitely Olive Jordan and I right from the beginning, because Henry and Ron were best friends. We're very, very good friends today. Ruth Pitts and I had so much in common because we were teachers and I really like her, she's really funny. I'll tell you one story about Ruth. Elijah Pitts, Ron, Ruth and I were thinking how lucky we were this was happening to us and we knew it at the time. We knew when they were playing ball that we were *really* lucky. Ruth said, "One time I went in my backyard and put my hands on my head, looked up to the heavens and said, "Oh thank you God" and I hope he's not going to take all this away from me." I always remember her saying that, because it's the truth.'"

Kostelnik was traded to the Baltimore Colts in 1969 leaving the Packers with a hole to fill in the defensive line and Ron and Peggy with a house in Green Bay that needed to be occupied. Peggy recalls what happened to their home: "When we got traded to Baltimore, we rented our house to Marv Fleming, who's a very, very good friend. Marv was and still is a real 'neatnik.' When Baltimore played the Packers and Ron was back in Green Bay, he went over to see Marv at the house and Marv said, "Ah, you're gonna have to take off your shoes to come in the house." When Ron told me that, I was thrilled because I knew the house looked great."

Vince Lombardi's death occurred during Ron's first year of retirement and he, like many of the Great Coach's players, was deeply affected and attended the funeral in New York. For Peggy, the loss of Lombardi was powerful, but when Marie passed it was more so:

"I remember being in a car when I turned on the radio and heard that Marie Lombardi had died, I was *so sad.* I don't know why, it just really affected me. Ron and I had just visited her in Florida, I was sad about Vince, but it affected me more profoundly when Marie died." Her high respect and regard for Mrs. Lombardi is equivalent to that of Olive Jordan's.

Peggy Kostelnik and Olive became close friends while in Green Bay; many times they sat side by side during games while their husbands played side by side at the defensive tackle positions. When Olive lost her husband unexpectedly in 1977, it was Ron Kostelnik who rushed from Wisconsin's Fox River Valley to the Jordan home outside of Milwaukee to made sure the pragmatic details were taken care of in a time of turmoil; things like insurance and other unspectacular, but necessary details. His attention to the Jordan family's needs is perhaps a perfect reflection of Ron Kostelnik the man, unspectacular, but rock solid to the core.

The two families were close both on and off the field; both planned well for long happy lives after football, both were adjusting exceptionally well to life after the NFL, but both men died way too young of heart attacks. With no prior history of coronary problems, Henry Jordon passed at age 42; Ron Kostelnik was just 53 years old.

On January 29, 1993, as Ron and Peggy were driving on I-75 near Georgetown, Kentucky, traveling from Florida to Cincinnati, she unfortunately experienced what Olive endured 16 years earlier. Peggy said, "He was in perfect health, obviously he wasn't but he looked it. He was talking about how beautiful the sunset was and all of a sudden just turned the car and said, "Oh, oh." And that was it, we hit a construction site and the car flipped three times and we landed way back in, I don't even know where. I was really fortunate that the sunroof blew out and it was the only way I could get out. I didn't realize Ron had died; he must have died instantly right before the accident. I wasn't able to get anybody to find us so I had to crawl back in the car and get a beach towel. I went up on a hill to wave it. When two ambulances came, I thought that was strange, but the one man said, "No, no, no, I'm here for you, your husband will be fine, I'm here for you." They had to get the Jaws of Life for him, but they didn't say he was dead. I didn't find out until that night and it was very difficult, along with being quite injured in the accident and the sudden shock of it."

In the most horrible time in her life with Ron's funeral and her own medical issues, it was predictable who would be with her in a time of need. Peggy said, "Olive came and organized everything. I had a quite a few broken bones, she organized everything."

God it seems unfair. This unheralded football player from the coal mines of Western Pennsylvania who took his bonus money to buy an engagement ring for the love of his life rather than a car he needed, lived a championship NFL career, planned for his future, followed the plan, and then died so early. He lived his life the way athletes and non-athletes should and it ended prematurely on a Kentucky interstate highway. It also left Peggy's life upside down, literally and figuratively:

"I didn't know this, but Ron had named me as the CEO and Chairman of the Board of his company. I had to take a leave of absence from my teaching job and try to run that company and position it for sale which is what I really wanted to do."

It was a two year procedure that saw Peggy complete the task and thus, in true Lombardi fashion, overcome adversity in dire times. In the process, she met her present husband, John Spalding. Peggy explains, "That's where John comes into the story because he was a widower and had originally owed the company. I ran into him in a restaurant and he was doing mergers and acquisitions and I kept pumping him with all these questions. So he put together the team that actually sold it." The quality of Peggy Kostelnik Spalding can be measured in any number of ways, including the management of her life following a personal and professional catastrophe.

The relationship with John Spalding blossomed into marriage as they united in 1995. In a quirk of fate, John's brother, Father Bill Spalding was Vince Lombardi's parish priest at the Church of the Resurrection in Green Bay's suburb of Allouez. General Manager Lombardi served on the board of Resurrection and initiated the annual Bishop's Charity preseason game apparently due to the input of Father Bill.

In a later chapter of this book, Donny Anderson says of Lombardi, "he oughta be really proud of a lot of guys." Very true Donny, and the Lombardi gals also, including Peggy Kostelnik Spalding.

# CHAPTER 16
# LORI KECK:

*"He would never admit it, but he liked
that I talked back to him."*

# THE LOMBARDI LEGACY

Lori Keck's remarkable 48 year Wisconsin sports career ranks with the most unique and distinguished ever compiled. She joined Vince Lombardi's office staff in 1961 and continued with the organization through 1971. Physically located in close proximity to his office, Lori held a ringside seat to the many dimensions of his personality. A spirited individual in her own right, Ms. Keck offered Lombardi a rare departure from the "yes people" who would not butt heads with him. The legendary Packer Coach and General Manager sometimes amused himself with Lori's feisty reactions to his good natured taunts. Initially she was undaunted by the NFL's emerging great figure because she didn't know he was one.

A non-sports fan in her youth, after leaving the Packers, Lori worked 37 years as Executive Assistant to Allan H. (Bud) Selig when he owned the Milwaukee Brewers, and during his tenure as the ninth Commissioner of Major League Baseball. She sat witness as the large foot prints of Messrs. Lombardi and Selig marked the Wisconsin and national sports landscape.

By her own description she had virtually no interest in sports growing up in Sturgeon Bay, Wisconsin, "I went to one high school football game in my life; I was not sports oriented at all. I just didn't pay attention; I can't explain it." When she interviewed with the Packers in January, 1961, Lori didn't know if Lombardi was a football man or an entrée at an Italian restaurant.

She was employed by the Packers for over 11 years, seven of those working directly for Lombardi. Her specific duties as correspondence secretary to the head coach and general manager included taking dictation, typing play books and speeches, but the bulk of her work was with the coaches and Public Relations Department. Chuck Lane headed the PR Department for several of those years and much in keeping with the closeness among Lombardi's former employees, Chuck and Lori hold each other in high regard and have remained in contact throughout the years. Both left the Packers when former Coach and General Manager Dan Devine bumbled and stumbled with his ineptitude in the early 1970's.

# LORI KECK

While in her first job out of business school, Lori was working as a secretary in the Buyers Department at H.C. Prange's Department store in Green Bay. After being at Prange's for five months, the employment agency she had registered with called to tell her the Packers were looking for a girl. She asked, "What are the Packers?" Being twenty years old, when she was told it was a professional football team she says, "All I could think of was men in tight pants, so I thought I would check it out."

She interviewed for the job with Business Manager and former Packer great Vern Lewellen while Lombardi was out of town and was told she needed to come back to be interviewed by Lombardi. Several weeks went by with no word from the Packers so she called back and scheduled an interview with him. Lori details what happened following the session:

"In those days I didn't have a car so I walked home; it took me about 15 minutes and another 15 minutes after I arrived home, they called and told me I had the job." Apparently she was a breath of fresh air, "I didn't know anything about Lombardi at all. As a young woman, I had a pretty smart mouth, I didn't know who Lombardi was or what I was really getting into. So, I answered everything quite honestly and perhaps with an attitude and I think that was something he was looking for. I only had five months actual working experience, so he was taking a chance on me."

When she first started, the Packer offices were in the Downtowner Motel, so the quarters were tight with a lack of privacy. In just her second week, she was at the mimeograph (copy) machine that was located very close to his office when; "All of a sudden I heard some *horrible* language coming out of Lombardi's office. It was the first time I had heard him angry. I finally figured out he had Ray Nitschke in there and he was screaming at his player. I began to wonder what I had gotten myself into because he scared me. I remember him saying, "Goddamnit Ray if you can't handle your drinks, you don't drink." The night before, Nitschke had thrown a glass of whiskey in a woman's face and it got back to Lombardi. Lombardi was not pleased and it never happened again."

It sounds as if Lombardi had his own alcohol treatment program; short-term, out patient, low cost with very high recovery rates. Despite the shocking introduction to Lombardi's managerial style and communication skills, leaving the organization was not considered by Ms. Keck, "Never. Never, never crossed my mind. If he would have ever talked to me that way I may have considered it. As long as it wasn't directed at me...."

There was however an incident that did draw the Old Man's attention to her, "Everybody's heard of "Lombardi Time," which is 15 minutes earlier than the appointed or scheduled time. My one main fault is being on time for work, anyway this one particular morning I rolled in, I was no more than five minutes late and it was probably only a couple minutes. There was a bus in the parking lot to take the team to the airport for an out of town game, it was parked at the front door and I thought, "Well, I'm not walking through that." I parked by the back door and thought I was home free. Lombardi had seen my car (from the bus) and sent Tom Miller (business manager) in to the office to tell me if I couldn't get to work on time they would find somebody who could. Of course, that was a warning and I improved after that."

When Lori started, she was secretary for the Director of Player Personnel for nine months, at which time Lombardi's secretary left to have a baby and did not return to the organization. Ms. Keck was offered the job and took it without hesitation. She was not in awe of the man; he was not a full blown legend in '61 and as a matter of fact she says, "It took me almost two years before I knew what was happening. The first year '61, when we won the championship, it was exciting, but it took the second one ('62) when I said, "My God, I am working for somebody who is making history and someone who will go down in history as something really special."

Lombardi tried to treat females better and differently than men, but according to Lori, it didn't always work, "He was a little different around women, they still took the brunt of his anger if he was upset with them, but he was a little more diplomatic. The business offices at the stadium were upstairs and there was a glass front so we could see the expression on his face when he came up the stairs. If he was looking down and just kept walking, we kept our heads down and didn't say a word to him. If he smiled and said good morning we knew we were going to have a fairly descent day, at least until somebody screwed up."

Ms. Keck recalls the Packer office was not conducive to all who tried to work for him, "There was one girl who was only with us for a couple of months because she could not emotionally cope with Lombardi. As soon as she saw him, she would get so nervous she would start screwing up and, of course, that only incurred his wrath. As soon as she saw him, her body would visibly start shaking. After two months she said, "I can't take this anymore" and she quit."

Lori did not, however, find the situation completely tranquil as she developed a bleeding ulcer while working for Lombardi. When she advised him of her ailment he said, "Hah, I've never had one." From her perspective it was proof positive he was a carrier. Most office staffs will moan and grumble about the boss behind his back, but according to Lori, "I don't think we ever really discussed him other than to make sure that we were doing everything right in order not to incur his wrath. We never talked about his personality or his home life; we never discussed 'Lombardi proper,' we wanted nothing more than to please him and do things the way he wanted them done." That's the same response he got from his good players and he only kept the good ones.

The conference room, meeting room and film room were right across the hall from the general office that housed the secretarial staff, so Lori was very close to some of Lombardi's football meetings and could hear the commotion. "The Monday after a game, we very often didn't know if we'd won that game the day before or not. It seems his language would be worse after a sloppy win than after a loss. He hated sloppy play as much as losing."

# THE LOMBARDI LEGACY

Lori recalls an episode when she got splashed with the boss's language:

"We had a little kitchenette and you had to pass the film room in order to get to it. I was going to get a cup of coffee and as I went by the room he was unleashing a line of expletives and saw me and said, "Sorry Lori," and kept right on going.

"What I liked is you always knew where you stood, even if you didn't like where you were standing, you knew where you were and you knew what he wanted. It was tough; it was very tough because you were not allowed to make mistakes. Actually you could make a mistake *once* but if you did it a second time you were gone. He was such a perfectionist he drove me to perfection. Everything had to be done a certain way and if you tried to change anything, he fought you on it and you would end up doing it his way. He was very organized, everything had to be in its right place, everything had to be his way and if it wasn't, he'd tell you about it and you would do it his way. Even if you thought you had a better way, you kept it to yourself." She could not resist taking a jab at her old boss from 40 years away, "He was a creature of habit, but he was able to chew people out in a variety of ways."

His emotions were always an incident away from surfacing, and for his former secretary, "That was the beauty of working for him because you never knew what to expect. It was not a hum drum existence. You were on your toes and walking on eggs most of the time because he did have a volatile temper and you didn't know when it was going to explode. You just wanted to be sure it wasn't going to be directed at you. Fortunately, it was never directed at me." Lori was among the very, very few to avoid his anger and she credits him for that, "I never had any serious mistakes with him. I put in a lot of overtime on my own just to make sure things were done the way he wanted. I never wanted to disappoint him. He made me that good." One of the most consistent qualities of the Lombardi people is their genuine, core confidence. Lori's comments are not arrogant or self promoting. They come from a woman who worked extremely hard to be better than she thought she could be and caught excellence while chasing perfection. She has lived what he taught.

In true times of need, he was a realist, "I saw the human side of him when my mother became ill. He was *extremely* considerate. He told me to take care of her and do what I had to do. He was very understanding, which I found surprising after watching him around the office and not really seeing the personal side of him. While he was conscious you had a family and a life, he didn't necessarily want to hear about your trials and tribulations. If it became necessary for you to tell him about a family illness or something legitimate, he was very understanding, but he didn't want to listen to you dumping your problems in his lap; he would stop that immediately."

His raw intelligence surprised those around him and not just every now and then, according to Lori, "Constantly, because he didn't just know football, he could discuss any subject extremely intelligently and know what he was talking about. For instance, it was very easy to take dictation from him; he spelled everything and even put in the punctuation."

His capacity for finding errors is illustrated in an example recalled by Ms. Keck, "There was a word in one of his letters, and to this day I cannot remember what the word was, but it was very unusual. He used a lot of Latin phrases too and I had to do a lot of research to make sure I had the spelling right on those. But there was this one particular word, because it was so odd, I looked it up in two dictionaries just to make sure I had it right. When I gave him the letter he said, "That word is spelled wrong."

"No it's not."

"*Yes it is.*"

"I looked it up in two different dictionaries; that word is *right.*"

Pointing that famous finger of his, he said, "Look at that."

"I had inadvertently transposed two letters within the word while typing it and of course he was right as he always was. His penmanship was horrific, especially when he used Latin phrases, which he used a lot. It took a long time to decipher some of that stuff."

He could compartmentalize, organize and separate issues, tasks and events. According to Lori, he did somewhat the same thing with his personal appearance, "He dressed immaculately. He always wore a suit into the office; of course he would change into coaching attire when he was involved with coaching duties. He *very rarely* came upstairs with those cloths on. He would change back into his business suit after practice and team meetings were over and then come upstairs."

Lori Keck is an accomplished Executive Assistant with decades of experience in the world of professional sports. It is difficult to envision her as anything but confident, but she says it was not always so, "No, it's all due to Lombardi. He brought it out of me. After he won a few championships, and I realized who I was working for and that I was able to cope and do what he wanted and what he expected, it built a lot of confidence in me. Figuring if I could work for him and hold my own then I must be pretty good."

Lombardi's office staff did not completely share in the gifts that were given to player's wives for each championship, but they were not totally forgotten by the team's leader. "We received a charm in the shape of a football with a gem stone in it, the last year it was a diamond. It had the Packer "G" with the championship year inscribed. It's something quite special because it's one of a kind; I've got five of them and great memories of each of those years."

The league office fought Lombardi initially regarding gifts to the wives, but he eventually won out. However, when he tried to distribute championship money among the office staff, Commissioner Pete Rozelle would not relent, "There was one year and I actually typed the list of names of people in the office who were to receive it; my name included, and I was excited. Lombardi decided he was going to take one championship share and split it between the girls in the office and I think Al Treml (Film Director, Photography). It was submitted to the Commissioner's office in New York and the Commissioner turned it down, he said, "Absolutely not, it's for the players." It was one of the very few times he did not get his way, but he fought for his people."

Green Bay's head man has been called a master psychologist thousands of times and apparently used that talent to amuse himself by baiting one of the few people who would snap at him: Lori Keck. "I had a pretty good temper. I think that is the one thing Lombardi really liked about me, I didn't 'yes' him like everybody else did. Everybody said, "Yes sir, yes sir, yes sir," and that's all the conversation he would get out of people. He would never admit it, but he liked that I talked back to him. Everybody would laugh at his jokes just to get on the good side of the Coach. I sometimes would fire back and he would purposely bait me and I didn't realize it in the beginning, but he would bait me just to see how far he could get before I lost my temper. Of course, I had to watch it because I knew I was speaking to Vince Lombardi, but I still gave him more fight than a lot of other people did."

When Lori would take her lunch break and read a book to relax, her leisure time provided the ideal situation for his good natured taunts. It creates a visual picture of mischief, Lombardi at his desk with Lori in the little kitchenette close by, but out of each others sight. It is easy to imagine him sitting behind his desk with a smile on his face as he asked a question of her intentionally interrupting her reading for one purpose; to trigger an explosion. Then another question, tick, tick, tick; then another. She says, "Yea, I'd answer back exactly the way I felt, "this is my lunch hour, this is my time, I'm trying to read a book, could you just hold off." If only it could have been captured on video tape.

Lori said, "He liked people who gave him a little fight, but they better be clear on what you were fighting about, otherwise he would just dismiss them. He might say, "Come back and talk to me when you know what you're talking about." Mostly he would just wave them off."

Without doubt, Lombardi respected her as is evident by this story, "He went to Bermuda or Jamaica, and before he left he called the girls into his office and said, "I don't want any sloughing off on the job while I'm gone." Lori said, "*I just bristled.* I didn't say a word about it, but he knew I was upset, he knew it."

"Lorraine" (Lori).

"What?"

"Well?"

"Well who has?"

"Well, I'm just telling you that's what I expect."

"He then called a day or two later while on vacation and asked to talk to me and he asked, "Are you still mad at me?""

"Well I didn't understand why we had to be told that because we don't do that, we don't slough off when you're gone." He said, "Maybe *you* don't, but there are others in the office and I wanted to make an example, and I thought you would understand."

"Well I didn't at the time."

His ability to read people boggles the mind and he did exactly the same thing with players; rode the ones who could take it to teach the others. There was one difference however, the players didn't talk back while Lorraine (Lori) did and he respected her for it.

Rumors were swirling in 1968 that the Great Coach wanted to return to coaching and become an owner; it was a very poorly kept secret. Whispers had Edward Bennett Williams of the Redskins offering Lombardi even more power, combined with ownership. Lori recalls what it was like to think about the possibility of his leaving, "Terrible, terrible, nobody wanted him to leave, nobody wanted to face the possibility of going on without him. It was a tension filled awful time and when it became true it was even worse." When it happened on February 4, 1969, Lori Keck was among the very first to know, "He called me into his office to take some dictation and he started dictating his letter of resignation." As the interview for our book *The Lombardi Legacy* was conducted on August 8, 2009, Ms. Keck was overcome with emotion and began to tear up. She said, "Well, I didn't expect it to affect me so strongly after all these years. Back to the dictation, when I realized what he was doing, tears started running down my face and I was having a little trouble seeing what I was writing. Thankfully he got a phone call he had to take, so I went into the bathroom and dried my tears. I came back out, he finished the letter and when he was done I asked him if I could go to Washington with him. He said no because part of the agreement that was made with the Packers to gain his release stipulated he couldn't touch anybody for a year. And that was that, it was an *extremely* sad time in that office. Nobody wanted to be there without him, it was like losing a member of the family."

The office staff threw a going away party that was not fun according to Ms. Keck, "It was like attending a wake and it was awful. The bookkeeper told him we were having a farewell party he said, "No please, not another one." She told him he had to do it because we had the cake and everybody was expecting it. Nobody knew what to say, you know, nobody wanted him to go and we knew there was nothing we could do about it; it was like being at a funeral. He didn't say much, because he felt bad. He tried to keep the spirits up, tried to be jovial, but it was probably one of the saddest events I've ever attended. Obviously losing my parents and sister were worse, but it was awful." As for his physical office, one that Lori had gone into thousands of times, "Desolation, we had lost a member of the family and it was sad, I didn't want to go in there."

In 1970, despite efforts by the Lombardi family and Washington Redskins to keep news of the great man's dire illness under wraps, word got to Green Bay and Lori remembers, "Didn't believe it, *did not* believe it because he was invincible. He was invincible, it couldn't be happening to Vince Lombardi; no way." Then on the morning of September 3, 1970, "I always wake up to my radio and the first thing I heard was Paul Harvey saying, "The Heavens in Green Bay are weeping for the loss of Vince Lombardi." It was raining that day. I turned over and started crying. I was devastated."

Lori worked for Green Bay during the Phil Bengtson era and spent another year when Dan Devine was allegedly at the helm. She then left the Packers as Devine sat in his paranoia while allowing the once proud franchise to meander into disarray. Ms. Keck moved to Milwaukee and applied for about 30 jobs, being offered some of them, but according to her, "There was always something missing, I didn't know what it was, I couldn't put my finger on it. The employment agency called one day and said the Brewers were looking for someone. They didn't say what it was. I thought I would check it out, but I didn't think I wanted to get back into sports." She interviewed with the Director of Finance who was not sure what position he was evaluating her for, either secretary for the President or public relations. Milwaukee Brewers owner Bud Selig made the decision without meeting her; his reasoning was based in logic, if she was good enough for Vince Lombardi, she was good enough for him and his Milwaukee Brewers. For every second of every day for 37 years, he knew he made the right decision.

Inevitably Lori is asked to compare the two huge sports figures, "They are both equally dynamic and dedicated, but very different. Where Lombardi wanted absolute control of everything, as does Commissioner Selig, the Commissioner allows his people the freedom to do things on their own and come up with their own ideas to solve problems. Ideally, in my situation it was best to take care of something before it became a problem, before it reached his desk. Lombardi was more controlling, he didn't allow the freedom, he had his thumb on everything."

Lori Keck will leave her own legacy on Wisconsin sports; it will be low profile, it will be excellent and like her, it will be real. She cannot be anything else.

*Green Bay Packers*

1265 LOMBARDI AVENUE / GREEN BAY, WISCONSIN 54305 / AREA CODE 414 494-2351

February 4, 1969

To Dominic Olejniczak, President, and the
Board of Directors of the Green Bay Packers:

It is with sincere regret and after many hours of deliberation
that I am requesting a release from my contract with the Green
Bay Packers.

This was not only a difficult decision, but a highly emotional
one. I have made many close friends in Green Bay and in Wisconsin. Many of these are among the Board of Directors and the
Executive Committee. I sincerely hope we will continue in that
friendship.

My decision was based upon a number of factors. One was the
equity position with the Washington Redskins and I do not believe
I need go into the advantages of a capital gain position under
today's tax laws.

The other factor was really altruistic in that I need a challenge
and I have found the satisfaction of a challenge is not in main-
taining a position, but rather in attaining it. I can no more
walk away from this challenge than I could have walked away from
the one ten years ago. I am the same man today I was ten years
ago.

The future of the Packers is in good hands; the front office,
ticket office and the football field. The Packers have a good
football coach who will be a better one without the pressure
of having Vince Lombardi looking over his shoulder and without
the players wondering how the man upstairs might have done it.

LAMBEAU FIELD

MEMBER CLUB NATIONAL FOOTBALL LEAGUE ● ELEVEN TIMES WORLD CHAMPIONS
WESTERN DIVISION CHAMPIONS 1938-1960 ● SUPER BOWL CHAMPIONS 1966-1967

Each of us, if we would grow, must be committed to excellence and the victory, even though we know complete victory cannot be attained, it must be pursued with all of ones might. The Championships, the money, the color; all of these things linger only in the memory. It is the spirit, the will to excell, the will to win; these are the things that endure. These are the important things and they will always remain in Green Bay.

There has never been a question of remuneration. After making a decision a year ago not to coach, I think you all can well understand the impossibility of my returning to the field in Green Bay. It would be totally unfair to coaches and players alike.

I have spent ten happy years in Green Bay. I know I will miss the city, the team, but most of all, my friends.

                                        Sincerely,

                                        Vince Lombardi

VL:lsk

# CHAPTER 17
## PAT PEPPLER:

*"He broke down and cried like a baby."*

# THE LOMBARDI LEGACY

Pat Peppler was Vince Lombardi's Player Personnel Director beginning in 1963. His contributions to the Packer dynasty were monumental as he had a hand in acquiring the following players: Donny Anderson, Ken Bowman, Zeke Bratkowski, Bob Brown, Tom Brown, Lee Roy Caffey, Don Chandler, Carroll Dale, Gale Gillingham, Jim Grabowski, Doug Hart, Bob Jeter, Chuck Mercein, Ben Wilson, and Travis Williams. Pat worked closely with Lombardi and saw the way he operated as general manager.

Following a nine year stint with Green Bay, Peppler was Director of Pro Personnel for Don Shula and the Dolphins for three years. He moved to Atlanta and served as General Manager for two seasons, as well as, interim head coach for nine games. Then, it was on to the Oilers for four years as assistant general manager to Bum Phillips before concluding his NFL career with Phillips and the New Orleans Saints, again as assistant general manager for five years.

Pat was directly and intricately involved with player acquisitions for much of Lombardi's reign. In this chapter, Pat clarifies several issues including what really happened with the Jim Ringo negotiations, how Donny Anderson was signed as well as a recollection of an emotional time for Lombardi in 1968, when the former coach "cried like a baby."

A sports lifer, Pat was a three sport star at Shorewood, Wisconsin High School, went on to a distinguished Michigan State University career in baseball and basketball. He also played minor league baseball before becoming a successful high football coach in East Lansing, Michigan.

Peppler was a college assistant coach at North Carolina State for eight years before moving to Wake Forest.

Prior to scouting combines, professional teams worked closely with collegiate coaching staffs to find and evaluate potential NFL talent. Pat Peppler explains his connection to and subsequent hiring by the Green Bay Packers, "I was at North Carolina State and later Wake Forest where I would report to the pro clubs. They would send you what they wanted and they'd pay you like a hundred dollars for a one or two-page report. I always worked with the pro teams when they came through. They didn't care how many clubs you reported to, as long as you gave them what they wanted. The Packers were one of the teams I reported to, and I always worked with the coaches when they came by for spring practice. When Vern Lewellan died, Vince replaced him with Dick Voris. Dick Voris had been the coach at Virginia, and we had gotten to know each other and he had offered me a job as defensive coordinator one time. He knew Vince from the Army days, so when I was reporting to him he spent a lot of time with me. I had a disagreement with the head coach at North Carolina State and after eight years, I moved to Wake Forest, we were 0 and 10.

"I went on a recruiting trip for Wake Forest, and when I came home, my then-wife said, "You're supposed to call Vince Lombardi anytime of the day or night," but she said, "First call Dick Voris." I called Dick and he said, "I wanted to go back in coaching and the Forty-Niners' gave me job. I'm leaving and I recommended you to Vince Lombardi. He always liked your reports because they were clear and concise and he thought they were good appraisals of the talent."

"I called Vince and he said, "Meet me in New York at the Regency on Wednesday" --this was Monday night. He continued, "Or I'll be in Miami Beach on Thursday."

"Well, I'll be in New York if at all possible." I said. Somehow he kind of liked that; that I wanted to do it as quickly as I could.

"Dick told me, "Now one thing, please don't accept this as a stepping stone to get back into coaching. Vince wants to make sure you know that he'd be disappointed if someone wasn't ready to quit the coaching part of it."

"I went there and I met him and he asked me to stay over 'til the next day 'cause he had to interview a couple other people, but he said, "I'm pretty sure the job is going to be yours." So that made it a little more anxious to wait. Thursday morning he said, "The job is yours." I was in a state of shock. That was before the '63 season.

"I was making about eight thousands dollars at Wake Forest--he said, "I'll pay you ten thousand dollars," which I was a little surprised it wasn't more, but I wasn't gonna turn him down for a two thousand dollar raise coming from a 0-10 team. He also said, "I'll give you a thousand dollars for the All-Star game." That's what they allot to the assistant coaches and personnel and so I got eleven thousand dollars that first year.

"I went home and by the following Monday, I was in Green Bay. I walked from the YMCA where Vince put me up in splendor, to the Packer office five blocks away. I was frozen stiff by the time I got up there."

When Pat joined Green Bay, the club had won back-to-back world championships and Lombardi was looking for more. Peppler walked into a pressure cooker situation. "Well, I didn't look at it this way; I thought it was great to be with the worlds' champions, and I was sure I had a lot to learn, but it's a lot better to be with a great head coach; anyplace else in football is second-best. There wasn't any question about power. Power was all with Lombardi, you wouldn't expect anything differently. He told me what the duties were and he didn't say a whole lot about negotiating contacts but that was the first thing he had me do when I got to Green Bay. The first thing he said, "Well, you're gonna have to do the contracts and do the contract talk." A lot of the groundwork had to be done, and he couldn't do all that. Now he might settle things, when they needed to be settled."

When Lombardi negotiated his initial contract with Green Bay, it was done with the understanding he would run the organization and he made sure he flexed his power early and often to train people he was in charge. According to Peppler, "The first thing Vince did, as I understood it, was get rid of the 150-some-man board of directors. He said, "I can't work with that many people." He made a suggestion to them—and a pretty strong suggestion that they cut down the size of the board—six or seven. Ole' (Dominic Olejniczak) was the President of the Board of the Directors, so

# PAT PEPPLER

Vince would talk directly to him. You're never stronger than you are the first day on the job and a lot of people know that intellectually, but don't put it into practice. He put it into practice. He took all his chances right away. It was before I was there, but I heard the story that Olejniczak came down to the field with a list of things he said the Board of Directors said were wrong in the 1959 intra-squad game. Reportedly, Vince took the paper, crumpled it up and threw it away and said, "I'll coach the goddamned team." You're never stronger than you are the first day on the job."

According to Peppler, Lombardi had a clear idea of what he wanted in regard to players and how he was going to get them, "He was looking to fill holes--what you need now. He never really separated that thinking, it was not his style to say, "Well, this was the best athlete," he was looking for the best football player, and he was focused on that. We prepared as a staff pretty thoroughly. The coaches were a big part of the personnel, and they scouted college games on the weekends and they covered spring practices and they were our in-house scouting staff. And then, we had the college assistants who reported to us, like I was reporting when I was over at North Carolina State, and that was valuable to the thing. Over time, Vince built up a feeling for the different guys whose reports we read, very thoroughly and very lengthy as a staff."

As dictatorial as he was, Lombardi wanted people to express their opinions and challenge his mind, "Yeah you could stand up, but basically he knew what he was looking for. I was really both college and pro personnel with Vince, but he set the tone for what he was looking for. For example, when we lost Jim Taylor, Vince had already had his eye on a replacement for Jim Taylor and we wound up with the fullback from the Los Angeles Rams, Ben Wilson. When he needed something, he paid the price, he didn't quibble around, he bargained a little bit, but he paid a second-round draft choice for Ben Wilson and probably most people would have said that it wasn't worth it, but we needed a fullback and he was a pretty darn good one.

# The Lombardi Legacy

"Confrontation was never a problem, and it's not my style anyway. I would just give the pros and cons of a person and whatever he took from that--in some cases he agreed with it. Every now and then when the coaches and I would disagree with him, he'd say, "you people must think I'm senile or something," but he would always pay attention, in other words, it wasn't a contentious thing. During the draft, that was a time where there wasn't time for niceties, when the draft was going on, you'd have to speak your mind pretty fast if you wanted to do it, and he respected that. He never hesitated to say whether he thought it was right or wrong."

Seldom would rookies play on a regular basis for Lombardi, they made too many mistakes, but they were part of the future, Pat said, "Vince dealt with rookies very good. He made the famous speeches that, "If I don't win, I'll be gone and if you can't help me win, you'll be gone." But then, he also had a way of recognizing the fact they were gonna learn and gonna make mistakes and the way you handle your mistakes is important. Of course they were in awe, but he was good with them."

Pat also saw the influx of black players onto the Packer roster and gives his old boss high marks for his ability to make it work, "Vince was really a fair-minded person and always recognized the other guy's side of the thing. There was a thing in the league, I'm sure some of it was prejudice, but some of it was just really not knowing; people not knowing. Like you wouldn't want a certain type of player, people didn't know how to handle the race thing, and Vince handled it by being the way he was, straight-forward." Peppler gives strong approval of Lombardi's management of race relations, "As good as it could have been handled, and should have been a model."

Part of the Lombardi folklore has to do with center Jim Ringo. As the story goes, Ringo showed up for a contract negotiation with an attorney, supposedly the first time Lombardi had been confronted with an agent. According to legend, the Packer general manager left the room and traded Ringo to the Philadelphia Eagles within five minutes. It did not happen that way. Pat Peppler was involved in lengthy negotiations with the cantankerous Ringo. Pat says, "Well, in the first place, Ringo didn't have an agent. By then, I knew what Vince wanted done, and I started calling, contacting players to talk about their contracts, and Ringo was one of the first ones to call back. Jim had been very dissatisfied at the end of that '63 season; he complained about a bunch of things and he wasn't particularly happy with a lot of things. When I talked to him, he started to complain which he had a perfect right to do. I offered him his ('63) contract and told him, 'This is what Vince offered,' because I didn't have any credibility with the guy—he didn't know me from a cord of wood. I said, 'I made you the offer that Vince gave me' and you said, "No, I want this, this, this, this and more," and I went to Vince and he said, "Give it to him." So he gave you everything you asked for. Then Jerry Kramer had an offer from the other league that was four or five thousand dollars more than we were offering him.

"So, when Ringo came to camp, under the contract that he virtually negotiated himself, Vince called him in and gave him an extra thousand dollars. He said, "Kramer held me up on the contract, and that's not fair to you because you had been around longer." So I told him, "Jim, you got nothing to complain about last year. Let's talk about this year."

"He said, "All right," and he's mad, half-mad, which made him a good player, I guess. He was competitive. And he said, "Gimme twenty-five thousand dollars or trade me." So he was probably making twenty from that previous year. So I went to Vince and I just reported it just as it was. A lot of times, I'd soften up players comments, like when Dan Currie said, "you tell that Dago SOB…," I said, 'I ain't gonna do that to you, Dan.' I just reported it like it was.

"Vince liked to create the impression, when it was beneficial, that he made snap judgments. But he had been talking to Philadelphia about a possible trade, which was a logical place, very close to Jim's home in Eastern Pennsylvania, and in the Eastern Conference, where it didn't have quite the talent of the Western Conference. Within an hour Vince called me into the office and said, "I just traded Jim to Philadelphia. I'm calling him and I want you to be in here and listen in on the conversation, so everybody is on the same page." He called him and Vince was genuine, he told Jim, "You did a great job here and I think this is going to be good for your career, being in the Eastern Conference and being near your home." And he brought it off very well. But there was no agent involved.

"But, see, Vince had a league meeting and some stories that would come out of that were funny. I remember him saying that one of the owners said to him, "Vince, what are you gonna do if a player walks in with an agent?" Vince said, "He'll walk out with an agent." So that story, put together with the Ringo thing, made it look like that's what happened. And I don't think Vince wanted anybody to think any differently. He thought that had a greater effect for him on the situation and all. So, that's how the story kept going, and I would hear it from people, and I knew--knowing the whole story, but Vince never wanted to publicize the real story."

During Pat's first year in Green Bay, he got caught in the middle of a conflict between team President Dominic Olejniczak and Lombardi regarding a vote at an NFL meeting, "Well, Detroit had lost a couple quarterbacks, and they had gone to the league on the basis of, "We won't be putting a very good product on the field, because we weren't going to have as good a chance of winning." They had this technique whereby they could have a player that they technically wouldn't have had the right to acquire, I forget the details. But anyway, that was an issue at the league meeting, and Vince told me to go with Olejniczak. Vince was concerned about the decision, and he wanted us to oppose that thing. Olejniczak's telling me to say this, and say that. Well, the league put all kinds of pressure on us and the vote didn't go that way, and I didn't even know the rules, whether it had to be unanimous or what. Ole told me to say something rather than him say it. If I had been smarter I would have abstained, which would have been the same as a 'no' vote without

Packer offices in the Downtowner Hotel.
*(Jim Hurley photo)*

Lombardi and Art Daley of the Green Bay Press-Gazette review the first Packer
Year Book in 1960. Of Daley's creation, Lombardi said, "Oh good,
that will help us sell tickets." *(Art Daley photo)*

1960 Western Conference Champions. The second year coach gets a ride in the L.A. Coliseum. Gary Knaflec (84), Dan Currie (58), Hank Gremminger (46) Max McGee (background) Emlen Tunnell (background), and Jerry Kramer (64). Notice the helmets without a logo. *(Gary Knaflec photo)*

Wives of the Packer assistant coach's pose in front of the Lombardi fireplace. (L to R) Goodie (Bill) Austin, sitting Barbara (Norb) Hecker, Kay (Phil) Bengston, Pat (Red) Cochran and Marie Lombardi. *(Courtesy of Pat Cochran)*

Defensive backs, Jesse Whittenton (47), Hank Gremminger (46), Herb Adderley (26) and Willie Wood (24). Jesse and Hank were with the team when Lombardi arrived. *(Vernon Biever photo, copyright)*

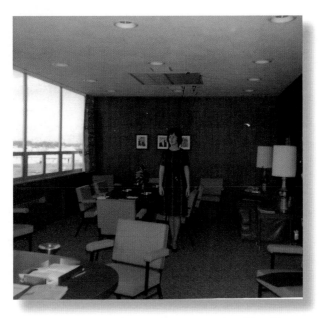

Secretary Lori Keck standing in Lombardi's office, site of many short contract negotiating sessions. *(Courtesy Lori Keck)*

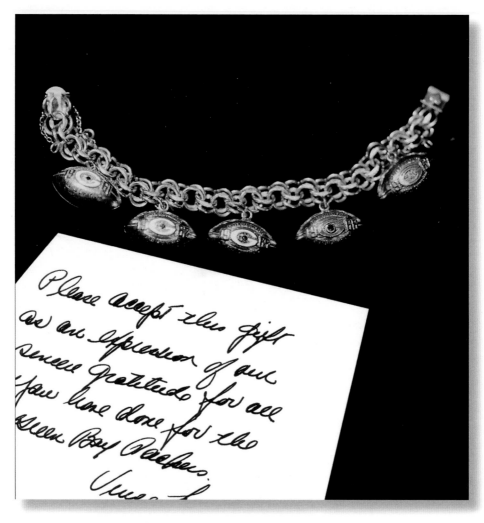

Five charms, five World Titles. Lombardi recognized wives and
office staff for their contributions to greatness. *(Courtesy Lori Keck)*

Elijah Pitts and Ruth Bellinger at Philander Smith College.
*(Courtesy Ruth Pitts)*

Elijah Pitts serving in Army Reserve as many athletes did in the '60's.
*(Courtesy Ruth Pitts)*

Ruth Pitts Litman, 2009.

Quaterback Bart Starr (L) and the dean of sideline photographers,
Vernon Biever. *(Vernon J. Biever, copyright)*

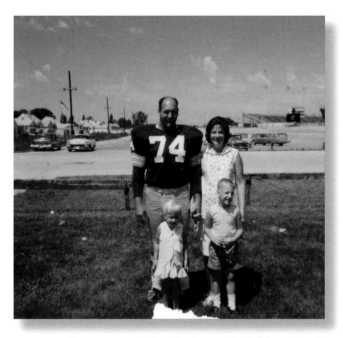

Henry and a pregnant Olive Jordan with children Butch
and Suzanne. Lombardi had patted Olive's enlarged
stomach and said, "Good." *(Courtesy Olive Jordan Frey)*

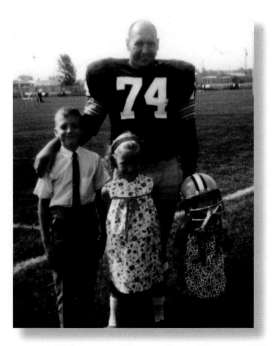

Henry, Butch, Suzanne and Theresa at Picture Day, *(Courtesy Olive Jordan Fry)*

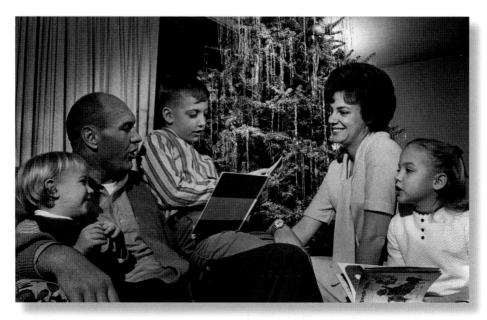

The Jordan's in Christmas spirit. *(Courtesy Olive Jordan Frey)*

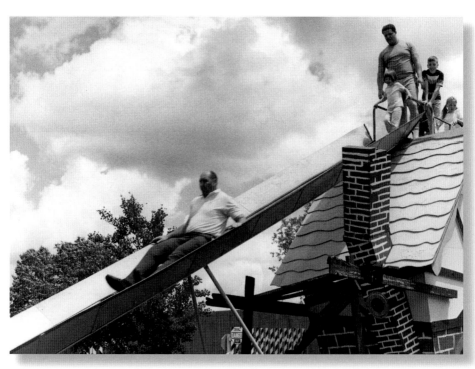

Henry Jordan on slide at Wisconsin Dells, Wisconsin. Ron Kostelnik and youngsters wait at the top. *(Courtesy, Olive Jordan Frey)*

Olive Jordan (L) and Marie Lombardi (R) at Marie's Florida condo.
*(Courtesy Olive Joran Frey)*

Olive Jordan Frey 2009.

Wives gathered to watch televised Packer road games. (L to R) Cherry (Barr) Starr, Pat (Carroll) Dale, Pat (Boyd) Dowler, Mary Ellen (Ken) Bowman, Olive (Henry) Jordan, Pat (Don) Chandler, Jackie (Ray) Nitschke, Barbara (Jerry) Kramer, Marilyn (Doug) Hart, M. E. (Zeke) Bratkowski and Peggy Kostelnik, standing. (*Courtesy Peggy Kostelnik*)

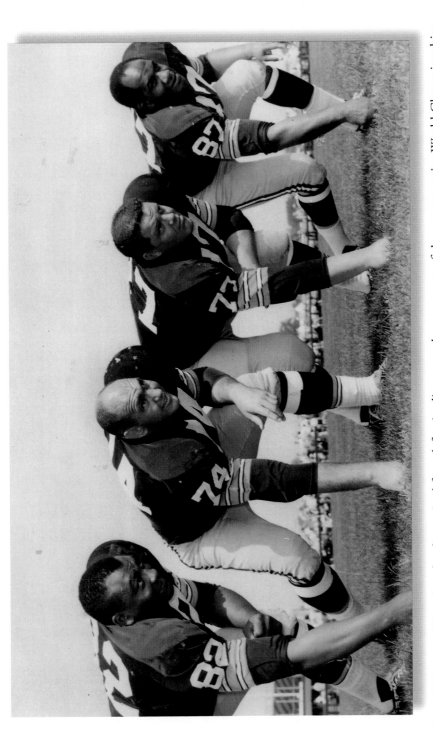

General Manager Vince Lombardi acquired four defensive linemen who were part of three consecutive World Championships. Lionel Aldridge (82) Henry Jordan (74) Ron Kostelnik (77) and Willie Davis (87). *(Courtesy Peggy Kostelnik)*

Jim and Helen Taylor at home in Baton Rouge, Louisiana, 2009.

Pat Cochran, 2008

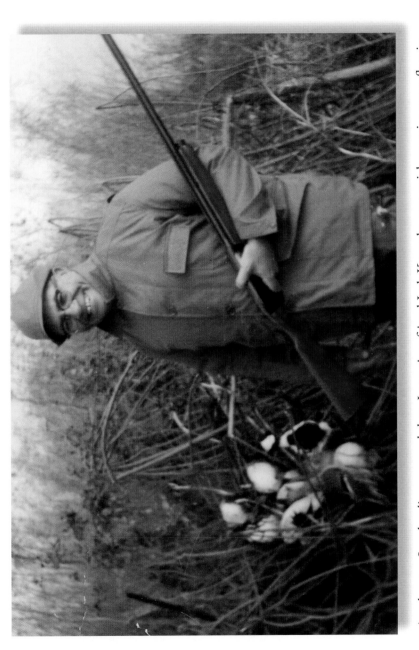

As a hunter, Lombardi was a good shot. Long time friend Jack Koeppler was quick to point out a flaw in Lombardi's hunting attire. The coat is supposed to be inside of the waders. (*Courtesy Dianne Koeppler*)

Jack Koeppler (L) and Lombardi (R) spent hundreds of hours together away from football. Mostly on the golf course, but shown here on a duck hunting trip. (*Courtesy Dianne Koeppler*)

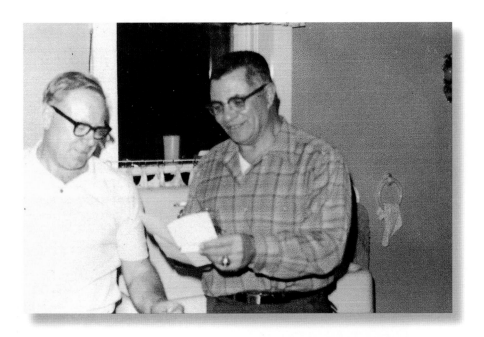

Judge Robert Parins and Lombardi in 1966. Pictured at Ed Beland's hunting camp near Banat, Wisconsin in Menominee County. *The Lombardi Legacy is grateful to Dianne Koeppler for sharing this precious photo.*

Player Personnel Director Pat Peppler joined the Packers in 1963. He was called, "the best football man here," by Vince Lombardi.

Lombardi gave this money clip to Jack Koeppler shortly after the 1961 Championship Game. Jack carried it for 47 years. (*Courtesy Dianne Koeppler*)

Gerald "Dad" Braisher designed Packer "G" logo. A wonderful man.
*(Courtesy De Pere Historical Society)*

"Dad" Braisher made room number 17 in the Union Hotel home for forty years.

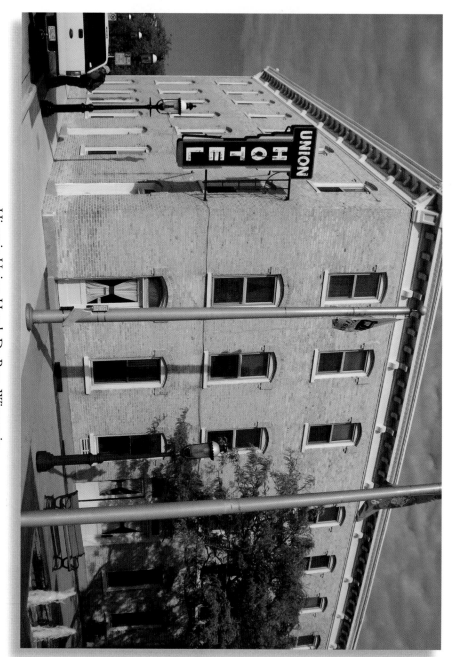

Historic Union Hotel, De Pere, Wisconsin.

Jim Boyd of the Union Hotel made sure the Packer logo was placed on "Dad" Braisher's head stone. Oak Hill Cemetery, Janesville, Wisconsin serves as final resting place.

Wide receiver Bob Long (L) and tight end Marv Fleming (R) celebrate following Super Bowl I. They have named this photo, "On Top of the World."
*(Vernon J. Biever, copyright)*

One of Lombardi's valuable acquisitions, Don Chandler hits an extra point in Super Bowl I. Notice empty seats in the Los Angeles Coliseum.
*(Vernon J. Biever, copyright)*

Tom Brown was the first person to play major league baseball and participate in two Super Bowls. *(Courtesy Tom Brown)*

Topps baseball card number 311 of 1964, switch hitter Tom Brown. *(Topps)*

February 28, 1968, Vince Lombardi resigns as Green Bay Packer head coach becoming general manager only. (*Courtesy Art Daley*)

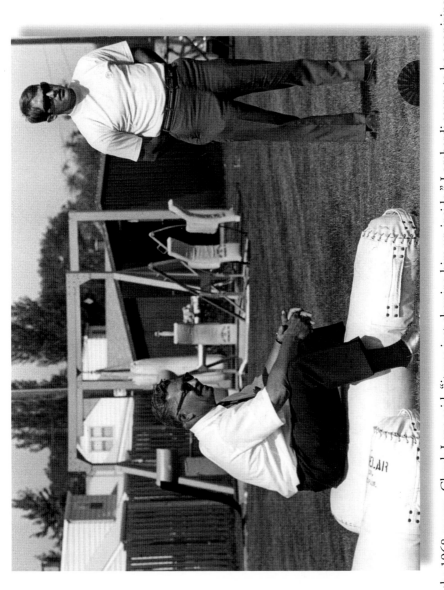

Of the 1968 season, Chuck Lane said, "it was just chewing him up inside." Lombardi seems to be agonizing watching practice as general manager, while twenty-five year old Lane shares the misery. *(Vernon J. Biever, copyright)*

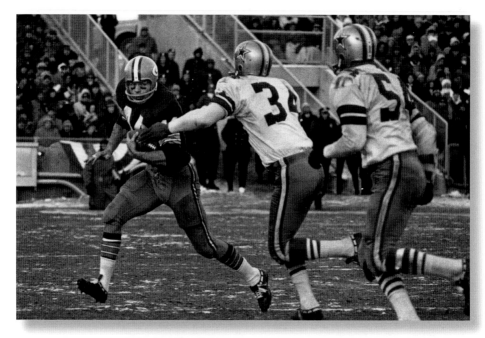

Donny Anderson in the Ice Bowl. Following the game Lombardi told him, "Today you became a man." *(Vernon J. Biever, copyright)*

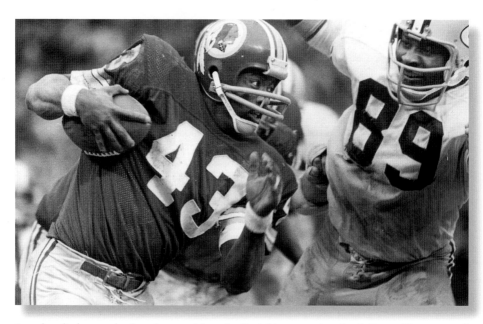

Lombardi detected a hearing problem in Redskins running back Larry Brown, and number 43 became the leagues MVP. Dave Robinson and his friend Larry Brown are shown about to share a moment. *(Vernon J. Beaver, copyright)*

Baseball's ninth Commissioner Allan H. "Bud" Selig  and Executive Assistant Lori Keck.

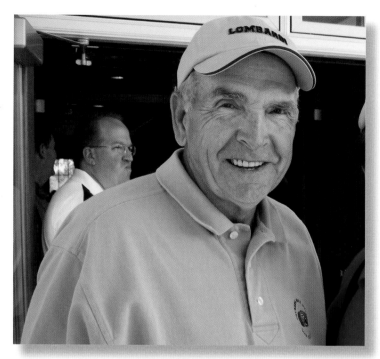

When Lombardi traded for Carroll Dale, he added a long ball
receiving threat and outstanding man of character.

Peggy Kostelnik Spalding spending time with grandson Vinnie Biskupic.

Dave Robinson - Green Bay Packers 1963-'72.
Washington Redskins 1973-'74. *(Dave Robinson photo)*

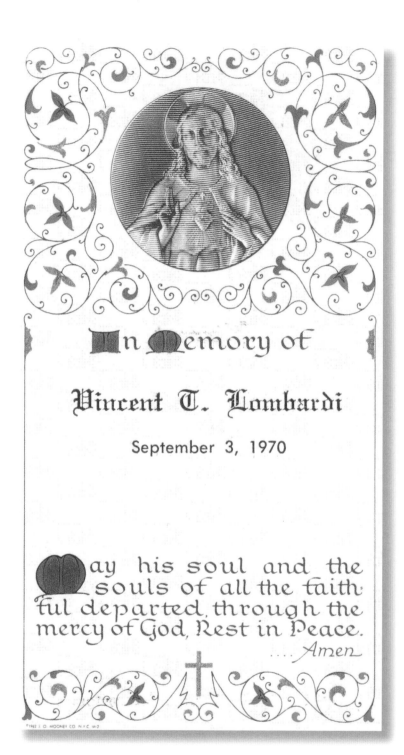

In Memory of

Vincent T. Lombardi

September 3, 1970

May his soul and the souls of all the faithful departed, through the mercy of God, Rest in Peace.
....Amen

Dave Robinson's ticket for attendance
at Vince Lombardi's funeral

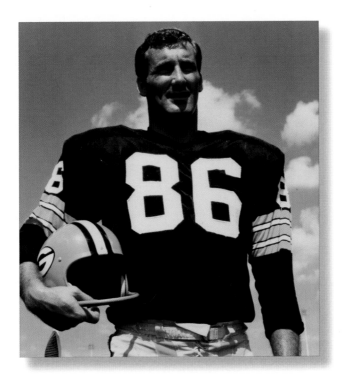

Boyd Dowler in Packer and Redskin uniforms show how similar Lombardi
made them. Washington helmet has an "R" like you-know-whose.

Sportswriter Bud Lea, 2009

Paul Hornung, 2009

That's just Kramer.

Vicki Aldridge Nelson, courage personified.

(L to R) Marv Fleming, Dave Robinson and Bob Jeter. 2008

actually saying no.

"NFL Commissioner Rozelle put a lot of pressure on, and Ole kept saying, "Say yes, say yes." So I finally said, 'Yes.' I went back to Green Bay and I thought, 'Oh, no.' Lombardi was really mad. I went to Ole and said, 'Hey, I'm a young guy and just new to the job and I made the head coach mad.' Of course, I didn't realize the whole situation with Ole. And I survived it. I just told Vince, I said, 'Hey, I screwed up, and it won't happen again.' He was probably thinking, "I ain't gonna give you a chance to let it happen again."

Probably the most publicized personnel move Lombardi ever made was the signing of the "Gold Dust Twins," Donny Anderson and Jim Grabowski and no one saw it coming, "Donny Anderson was what we called a junior eligible or a red shirt, and so we drafted him when he still had another year of college eligibility. And we had two first round draft choices, and it was quite a shock, even to people on the staff, when Vince took Donny with our number one choice. In those days, we were drafting toward the end of the preceding season, that particular year, '64, we drafted in a Chicago hotel. We drafted for 22 hours, straight through. That was the draft when Vince went to bed and told me to make the last pick, "and do something funny." Players said I did something funny because I drafted Bill Curry. Bill was a junior-eligible, and the next year he had gotten a little bigger and became a good player from Georgia Tech; probably would have been a second or third-round draft choice. Vince was always complimentary, his standard saying was, "Pat, you did a helluva job on this and I was a horse's ass as usual." So what do you say? 'No, Coach you weren't really a horse's ass. I'm glad it worked out good, Coach.'

When the AFL and NFL were engaged in their bidding war, the Packer general manager had two issues to deal with; an aging backfield of Taylor and Hornung in addition to the ongoing battle with the upstart league. There has been speculation for all these years that part of Donny Anderson's contract was paid for by each of the other NFL teams. Both Peppler and Anderson don't think that happened, partly because other teams were in the same bidding war trying to sign their own draft choices, "I've heard the story that the league did. I doubt that very seriously. The Packers had enough money.

"When he became eligible to sign, after a year of sweatin' him out, he came back with a big increase over what we had been offering. We had offered some kind of a $400,000 package and there was probably some deferred—most of the contracts, even Joe Namath's had some deferred money in it to take some of the sting out of it. He came up with something like a $600,000 package. I'd gotten to know him pretty well—and I was recruiting him, and I was double-recruiting him because his dad worked for Phillips 66, which was owned by Bud Adams. Houston had the rights to Donny in the AFL, and the owner of the Oilers was the employer of Donny's dad and three uncles. So I had my job cut out for me, and I stayed close to Donny and developed a relationship. After they made the offer, I was upset it was that high. I said to Donny, "Donny, how in the hell much money do you have to have?"

He said, "Pat, I can get anything I want from Bud Adams, and you know that. I wanna be with the Packers." So, that was good news and bad news. I called Vince to tell him what the offer was, and he cussed a little bit and he said, "*Alright, give it to him and get the hell out of there before the price goes up.*" Well, I couldn't get the hell out of there, we had some loose ends, but that's how it went with that. And Donny, he really wanted to be a Packer, he was delighted."

Entering the 1965 season, Lombardi knew he had an excellent team with a two significant needs. He needed to make a couple moves to put his club back on track to win championships. Paul Hornung had been suspended for the '63 season for betting on games, when he returned in '64 he hit an unacceptable 31.5 % of his field goal attempts. Place kicking may have cost the '63 title and '64 was a down year defined by key injuries. Two of the most important deals made by General Manager Vince Lombardi were the acquisitions of kicker Don Chandler and wide receiver Carroll Dale. Chandler made nearly 65% of his attempts in 1965 as the Pack returned to championship standards. Dale added a deep receiving threat. There would not have been three consecutive championships without those two players. Peppler explains, "Part of the Donny Anderson story was we acquired Don Chandler, who was a combination punter and place kicker. We were deficient there. Although Jerry Kramer filled in, he was not a full-scale guy. Don Chandler was an excellent punter and place kicker—conventional place kicker, very important part of that and I think we gave a third-round draft choice for him."

The Packers and Giants talked about a couple different ways to do the deal according to Peppler, "The Giants wanted to get a number one for one of their tight ends and Chandler. The coaches and I were not high on that. That was one of the times Lombardi got kind of mad at us, 'cause he said, "Well, we won't get Chandler if we don't do this." I said, 'Coach, let's take a chance and see. Let's ask the Giants if they will trade us Chandler for a third without having to involve the first-round draft choice.' He listened to that, and of course, I was just echoing what the coach thought."

Because the trade for Chandler involved giving up just a third round selection, Green Bay kept its number one choice which was later used to select Donny Anderson.

Pat said, "Carroll Dale we got for Dan Currie. Dan was getting down at the end of his career. Vince used a technique of trading players when they still had some value and get younger people to keep things going with the club, and that's what he did with Dan. Dan only lasted another couple years with the Rams and Carroll Dale was still playing in the league in the early '70s."

Not many people truly defied Lombardi, but fullback Jimmy Taylor did by playing out his option during the '65 season, freeing him after '66. Taylor was nearing the end of a great career, was not the dominant force he had been in the early '60's, but still critical to winning the unprecedented third consecutive title in 1967. Peppler gives some insight into the departure of Taylor, "We needed him and Jim would have been, not financially, but he'd been a lot better off with the Packers when he had maybe another two or three years left to play. He was more valuable to a good team than he was to expansion team like New Orleans. But he was from down there; he was from LSU, and Saints owner John Mecom wanted him badly, and I think a lot of promises were made prior, because he was playing out his option. Vince tried very hard, and I don't know the particulars, I'm sure he kept upping the ante for Jim. As Jim turned him down, Vince would re-think it, because he really didn't want to lose him. But finally it became apparent that Jim had probably made an agreement, if not actually signed a contract. When Vince kept upping the ante, Jim was in kind of a dilemma, 'cause he really would have rather played for Green Bay."

Green Bay missed a golden opportunity to win three consecutive championships when the strong '63 club fell just short, therefore 1967 offered Lombardi his last realist chance to run off three straight. The team was old, injured and probably a little burned out having endured eight years of his heavy hand. Pat and the general manager did a tremendous job patching holes to get that final title, "That was very important. Ben Wilson was a good football player and unfortunately, he got hurt, and so we wound up in the Ice Bowl game with (fullback) Chuck Mercein, who we got off the Washington Redskins' cab squad. He had been with the Giants and Well' (Giants Owner Wellington Mara) was a good friend of ours and a fine man--a great loss to the league when he died (2005).

"We talked to him about Chuck, and he said he was a good player, he strongly recommended him to us as a smart player as well as being a smart student--sometimes they aren't the same. And, geez, he came in and did a great job. To show how smart Chuck Mercein was, Bart called "thirty-one wedge" but didn't give the ball to Mercein, he just ran behind the same blocking that the fullback would have run behind, and it was a better play when no one knew it was the sneak. We had great blocks between Ken Bowman and Kramer, who got under Jethro Pugh, who was the one who played the highest. Plus, we had a great cut-off block on the back side which was not that well-known, Dallas end Bob Lilly was over there and we had a good block by Forrest Gregg. But Mercein went up there intending to get the ball, but he pulled off because he realized that the worst thing that could happen would be if the officials called "assisting the runner," 'cause Bart was going to make it without Chuck anyway. And he didn't want to take any chance at all, and I thought that was pretty damn smart." The famous end zone photo of the final Ice Bowl touchdown, taken by John Biever, shows Mercein with his arms in the air, not to signal touchdown, but to let the refs know he *did not* assist Bart.

"Yeah, he just knew it right away. He'd done a fine job. He caught a pass during the final drive. The field was slippery as the devil and came down in the left flat and went down the sideline; he would have been better off with ice skates on."

The team that won it all in 1967 was nowhere near one of the best Lombardi era squads; however, it showcased the combined skills of Head Coach and General Manager Vince Lombardi. Peppler comments, "Well, it wasn't me that put it together, but I was thrilled to be a part of it—Vince did. We got a guy one time, red-headed guy —good player. Red Mack was probably a 175-pound guy who came in and did a great job for us on special teams, just tickled to death to be a Packer. He'd been in Pittsburgh and they weren't good in those days and we got a hold of him, and that's the kind of thing that happened. Guys played better here."

After controlling nearly every aspect of the Packers for nine years, Lombardi loosened his grip in 1968 by turning the head coaching duties over to his hand picked successor Phil Bengtson. Acting solely as general manager, Lombardi did not want to obstruct Bengtson as Pat explains, "He bent over backwards not to interfere. Too far, I thought, which I told him one time. He would talk to me, 'cause he knew I could keep my mouth shut. Phil wanted Richie Moore, a defensive lineman in the draft. He thought he was another Merlin Olsen. Well, I didn't share that opinion, nor did people in the league. Phil expressed his interest and he liked him and he was trying to justify it. No one else on the staff would go along with it and so he seemingly acquiesced. We planned that chart very thoroughly in preparation for the draft. Positions were all in order from best to worst. We went through a very lengthy process, just like we did with Vince and then Phil violated that whole principle and jumped up and used his position as head coach when Vince wasn't in there. Vince stayed away, in my opinion, he stayed away too much. And when Phil did that, I was really upset about the way it was done, because we had a process, and we worked it through and argued it and everything else, and then he violated the principle."

The most poignant description of Lombardi's misery in 1968, as he watched the team decompose under Phil Bengtson, is given by Peppler, "I'll tell you a story you probably haven't heard. The Packer locker room, it was like a conference room and then the coaches' locker room was behind that. Well, late in that year with Vince as general manager, we were just about out of it, and we were gonna play the Vikings. We had about two or three games left. Vince told Phil he wanted to talk to the team and he went in and he talked to the team. I was in that office and I was on the phone doing some things in there when Vince came out of that meeting. I found out later what he said in there, but he was trying to stir 'em up. He came in the room and he looked at me and he said, "Goddamnit, I don't know why I have to whip 'em all the time to get 'em to do it." He sort of looked at me a little bit and I said, 'Coach, you trained 'em with a whip. You can't put it down.' He said, "Yeah." He went over and he took his chair, faced it into the corner, like a kid sittin' in the corner, and he broke down and cried like a baby. Then, he finally got straightened out, and he said, "There is so damn much I wanted to tell 'em." He felt like he had let 'em down. He was just so upset. I mean, Vince was emotional anyway, but he was really upset."

Despite Lombardi's extensive control in Green Bay, he could not wield total power at the NFL meetings. Only owners were allowed to vote at league gatherings and he needed to become one. According to Peppler, there was an ownership offer made to Lombardi before he took the Washington job, "Vince had some offers, and Rankin Smith, who I worked for in Atlanta, told me he had a handshake from Lombardi on 13 percent of the Atlanta Falcons as part of the deal. He was critical of Lombardi to me, which didn't go over that big with me, but he was my new owner. I tried to soften it up, and which I think was true—I said, 'I think Pete Rozelle interfered with the thing,' because it wasn't easy to move from a club those days--those rules favored the owners very much, and Pete was a little bit autocratic about it as well. I think Rozelle told Vince that in order to move, he should sit out a year. I couldn't swear to that, but I have that sense, knowing Rozelle and the way things were then, it was probably somewhat justified."

In the pre free agent world, Rozelle didn't want players moving from team to team, thus driving up salaries. Also, he could hardly let the league's greatest coach do it and then stand up to the union to oppose player free agency. Pat says, "In all, it could have cost Vince a lot of money. Turned out, he made a good deal with the Redskins. Marie told me, she moved to Miami when I was with the Dolphins, and she was a guest in our press box, and she said, "You know, Vince left me seven million dollars," and most of that was achieved in probably the last three or four years of his life."

As he was leaving Green Bay, Lombardi told the Packer Executive Board not to allow one person to hold both the head coach and general manager positions. They did not follow his advice. Peppler had wanted the GM job when Lombardi left for the Redskins, however Bengtson got both titles much to the detriment of the franchise. The former colleagues, Lombardi and Peppler, had an opportunity to meet, chat, reminisce and discuss the entire issue of Lombardi's departure from Green Bay. Pat explains, "He called me in 1969 and asked, "Are you coming east this year?" It so happened I was going there, but, of course, if I hadn't I'd have gone anyway to see him. It was the last time I saw Vince alive. He just wanted to talk about what happened when he left Green Bay. He still felt guilty about that. He told me, "I had to promise the Packer Board of Directors I wouldn't take anybody with me to Washington. But you've done a good job, and if there was any way I could take you, I would do it. I told them that you were the best football man here."

At that point in our interview, Pat Peppler, veteran of many NFL experiences, had his eyes fill with tears. "I was shocked. Some of 'em tried to pass it off. They said, "Well, he said that to more than one person." I said, 'Well, all I know is he said it to me.' I told Lombardi, 'Coach, that's worth more to me than being able to go with you.'

"He knew he had to give the job to Phil on one hand, on the other hand he told them 'don't make anybody head coach and general manager again; it's too big a job now.' And I know he had reservations, complete reservations about Phil becoming the general manager. He knew I was much better qualified for all the nuts and bolts of trades and waivers and league rules and all of that kind of stuff. Just like Phil was a lot better qualified to be a defensive coordinator than I was.

"I got to say some things when I went to Washington that I couldn't say under any circumstances. I did thank him in the incident when he told me he recommended me and all of that. He said, "You were smart not to come out for the general manager job." Part of which, if I failed to get that, I'd probably be looking for a job. Because Phil had come out strongly to become the general manager and Vince didn't think he was qualified, and frankly, I think he had severe reservations about him as head coach. Phil was second-in-command and we'd been successful, and the defensive players really had confidence in him, so Vince was locked into that."

194

# PAT PEPPLER

Pat Peppler deserves a special place in Green Bay Packer history. Somewhat like Jack Vainisi before Lombardi arrived, Peppler was instrumental in acquiring quality players while the Great Coach posted the three-peat from 1965-'67. It has been fashionable to dismiss Lombardi as an ineffective general manager, but when you consider the injection of talent that was needed to sustain the greatness, performance is its own proof. He was constantly drafting late because of the winning, therefore top talent was not readily available. He and his Director of Player Personnel, Pat Peppler, put rosters together that allowed the Packers to win three straight World Championships. It hasn't been done since and Lombardi did it with, "the best football man here."

Great job Pat Peppler, great job.

# CHAPTER 18
## RUTH PITTS LITMAN:

*"Lombardi would not be able to discourage
him very easily."*

# THE LOMBARDI LEGACY

Elijah Pitts was a 13th round draft choice in 1960 and played on the first Vince Lombardi World Championship team. Described by Boyd Dowler as, "mistake free," Elijah was a long shot to make the club in 1961. The halfback position was well stocked with Paul Hornung and Tom Moore, so an obscure back from equally obscure Philander Smith College in Little Rock, Arkansas, had little chance to crack the roster. He not only made the team, but played on all five of Lombardi's championship squads. Elijah was not a headliner or superstar, but he was a rock solid Lombardi type player. According to quarterback Bart Starr, Elijah made an immediate impression, "His commitment, it was very obvious after a very few days that this man was very, very, very committed to be the best player he could be. Boyd was absolutely correct, he studied uniquely lengthy and as a result he was practically error free."

Pitts was the first black player to have a significant offensive role on the Lombardi Packer Dynasty. Playing in Green Bay from 1961-'69, and again in 1971, he scored 210 points, including a touchdown in the 1966 Championship game against Dallas, and two rushing TD's in Super Bowl I.

Elijah and his number 22 were inducted into the Packer Hall of Fame in 1979 as tribute to the versatile running back who was a valued receiver, outstanding special team player, and tremendous blocker in the Lombardi Sweep. He knew the system well enough to be plugged in at either halfback or fullback and not miss a beat. Most of his play was at halfback because durable Jim Taylor was the fullback.

Academically Elijah earned a music scholarship to Philander Smith, a Methodist College where he found two great loves: Ruth Bellinger and football. He was devoted to both for the rest of his life. Elijah and Ruth met in a music class when he was a junior playing tuba and she was a freshman on the trombone. Their relationship withstood the separation while Elijah was in Green Bay, and Ruth worked to earn her teaching degree in 1962.

The words "Elijah Pitts from Philander Smith" have a comical sound, however, his former teammates tell of a great natured running back who was utterly dedicated to perfection. Without exception he is complemented for his lack of mental errors; a required trait for anyone attempting to play for Vince Lombardi. As Dowler said about Green Bay's players, "guys were football smart and basically intelligent people."

In Buffalo, Pitts is viewed as a treasure. He served as an assistant coach with the Bills for an astonishing 16 years. He was named assistant head coach in 1992 and served as interim head coach for three games in 1995 when Marv Levy took a medical leave.

Ruth and Elijah married in March of 1962, and remained as one until stomach cancer claimed his life 36 years later, on July 10, 1998. They had three children, daughter Kimberly, and sons Anthony and Ron who had a five year NFL career and is a Fox television football play-by-play announcer. Today Ruth lives in Palm Desert, California where she is an avid golfer with a bright, bubbly personality and a youthful look belying her years.

News traveled relatively fast on the campus of Philander Smith in 1960 when Elijah was drafted by Green Bay. Ruth Pitts Litman explains, "I knew pretty much right away. I believe he called, which would be one of the few times. During those days you weren't on the phone all the time; long distance was expensive. It was in December because that's when the draft was held. He was happy and I was happy for him. There had been talk that he might be drafted, but coming from a small black school, everybody was saying, "most likely you won't get drafted and even if you do get drafted you're not gonna make it." So there was a little talk, a little hype and it was an exciting time for both of us."

Just as there was no certainty Pitts would make the team, there was no guarantee the young couple's relationship would survive, "Well, who knew? We were twenty some years old, who knew. As it turned out there was a lot of separation and a lot of things to do. I had to finish school; he was going to see if he could make the team, so our life was in transition and we were young, we didn't know what anything would be. We were happy it happened, but we had so much more to do."

Ruth said contact between the two was conducted the old fashion way, "There weren't cell phones, there were letters. We wrote each other all the time. I was at school, he was in training camp and when he got a chance, he wrote, and I wrote. You couldn't just pick up the phone and call in those days. I have letters that say, "They cut two guys today—five guys are gone, I'm still here," you know, all that kind of stuff. He did say he would lay in bed at the dorm in training camp and there was a guy with these big shoes and you would hear him coming down the hall and you would just hope he wouldn't stop at you room." The guy was training camp's Grim Reaper who delivered news to players they had been cut from the roster. Mr. Reaper always passed by the room of Elijah Pitts from Philander Smith.

Back home Ruth Bellinger had an obstacle in the way of her relationship with the young football player; Reverend Martin Luther Jones Bellinger. Some preachers do not want an aspiring football player as a son-in-law and Ruth's father was not overjoyed with the prospect: "Oh not at all, not at all. I told him I had met someone and felt pretty serious about it and so forth and so on. My dad said, "Well what does he do?"

"Right now he may play football."

"What does he do, what's he gonna do?"

"Dad, he's gonna play football."

"He's not gonna make a living at that."

"But eventually as he met him and life went on, they became the best of friends and they really loved each other."

There was so much going on at the time for Elijah and Ruth, not only had a pro football career begun, but he was leaving the South for the first time as the country was in the throes of racial turmoil. Ruth said, "I think when you're young you don't think about all those things. We thought about the opportunity; he had really accomplished something pretty good to come from where he had to make that team. So it was something to look forward to. I think we looked at it in more positives than negatives. As far as racial things, we both lived in the South we knew all of that, I don't think we went there looking for that kind of thing."

Packer flanker Boyd Dowler spent lots of practice and game time with Elijah and came to the conclusion Pitts played well partially because he did not want to bring disgrace to his race. Ruth concurs, "If he played well it would be a reflection naturally, but that's how he was anyway. He just didn't like to do anything half way once he got into something like that. Also, you have to think he thought, "I don't have room for a lot of mistakes. I have to do it well the first time." He was already in a situation that seemed somewhat impossible. He was black, coming from a small black college that nobody was interested in, he goes to a team that had just come off one of the most profound seasons they had in years. They just barely missed beating Philadelphia and were loaded with talent. So, he went into an almost "no win" situation.

"He was very, very strong in his mind." Lombardi's training camps were designed for many things, including eliminating players who would quit. Ruth says the physical appearance of her husband disguised the tenacity of the man, "Lombardi would not be able to discourage him very easily. Although you wouldn't think that, because he always had a smile on his face and he was so good natured and humble, but he was very strong of character."

Lombardi made a concerted effort to address racial issues on the team and in the community; Ruth believes there were issues that did not surface. She said, "He may not have even known about some issues that came up. Also, remember the team was winning so there wasn't a lot to be dissatisfied about. But, why would he know when all of the black players were living on the out skirts of town, in one place, because no one would rent to them? Did he know that, or did he feel, "maybe that's how they want it." I don't know."

Tony Canadeo was a great Packer running back and member of the team's

Board of Directors. His brother had an apartment complex and according to Ruth, the black players rented from him: "They rented that most of the time, but that was when the guys were by themselves. As the black girls began to move to Green Bay, others would come because we would be company for each other. At one time Elijah told me, "The black guys are not bringing their wives here, so I'd rather you not come either. I would not want you to be here by yourself." But as some began to come, then others came, and we found housing. Housing became better as time went by, it actually changed. I noticed housing changed with Marv Fleming, Lionel Aldridge and Dave Robinson because they decided, "We've got to have some housing and we're gonna make some noise up here if we don't have some descent places to live." So the housing conditions changed."

In addition to housing, there were other black specific issues like hair cuts. Ruth said, "If you don't have a population then you don't cultivate services for that. We had to go to Milwaukee most of the time; players had Monday's off so they'd go down there early on Monday. The black females had no services either. We went to several beauty shops in Green Bay and they would be accommodating, but if you don't know how to do something, you don't know how to do it. We would go to Milwaukee or just try to do it ourselves. We learned to live with it, but it was inconvenient."

Players had an advantage because they would travel to large metropolitan areas during the season as is detailed in the next chapter by Dave Robinson.

Lombardi's roster was very stable throughout most of his nine years; therefore, families had years to build relationships. Ruth had several close women friends, but there was one special person with whom she built a bond, "Oh, Peggy Kostelnik, she's my buddy, we were rookie wives together." The 1961 rookie class was Herb Adderley, Ron Kostelnik and Elijah Pitts. Ruth and Peggy have been friends for years, not only because they entered the league together, they were both school teachers.

As for the relationships with other wives she says, "It doesn't matter black or white, there's some women gonna get along and there's some that's not. It's all up to the individuals basically. So there's some you got along with, and some you didn't, and that's just life."

During Packer home games the wives sat together and at times needed each other for emotional support as Ruth explains, "To sit there and have your husband being talked about, called "no good" and all that. Sometimes you can't take it. So, any number of times somebody may have done something, thrown a program at somebody. I may have done that and I'm not the only one. After awhile you cannot sit there and have someone you love be criticized and ridiculed, it just really hurts, but you do have to learn to be quite. Thank goodness they were winning."

In an effort to promote team unity beginning early in the season, Packer families were invited to attend a buffet following home preseason games. Also, a large Thanksgiving gathering was held back in Green Bay after the traditional game in Detroit to celebrate the holiday, and get the families together. Core members of the team were around for so many years, so they literally saw each others families grow up. Ruth said the gatherings served as a purpose for Mrs. Lombardi, "Marie would come by and see you, see how you were doing and always encourage you to keep your family together. That was always a good message for all of us, it wasn't just because I was a black wife, she said this to all of us. I always felt welcome, the Lombardi's were warm and welcoming. There was a little distance there, I think given the time in our history they did the best they could with it." Of Mr. Lombardi Ruth says, "He was scary at the time because he did have your life in his hands, but as time went on he wasn't as scary as he'd like you to think he was. I think he had a pretty warm heart.

"One time I was waiting for Elijah outside of Sensenbrenner Hall during training camp at St. Norbert College, we were going to go to dinner on a night off, and Vince came by. I reached my hand out to shake hands with him and I had one of the championship rings on that he had given Elijah and he said, "Aah what's that on your finger?"

"That is very special and I will always cherish it."

He just laughed and said, "Have a good night." He always was concerned that the wives were happy; he made an effort to help make that happen. For instance, we were engaged and going to be married and I got the mink stole for the 1961 championship."

For Ruth and Elijah Pitts, a significant chapter of their lives ended on September 3, 1970 when Vince Lombardi died. The overwhelming feeling was, according to Ruth, "Sadness, it was a sadness, something that you cannot really express. You feel sadness and you feel a loss of this person who had touched your life in a positive way. It was something you couldn't really accept; I remember Elijah saying he was a *great* man."

In some important ways, the life of Elijah Pitts and his career were a reflection of each other, or maybe they were the same thing. He and Ruth had a dedicated long-term relationship and marriage; he and the Packers had a smooth, harmonious, stable association. For an unheard of 16 years, he was an assistant coach for the same team. When stomach cancer claimed the life of Elijah Pitts on July 10, 1998, an outpouring of love and appreciation from the Buffalo Bills and their fans served as tribute to his remarkable association with the team and community. Likewise, Ruth and her children received support from many members of the family Lombardi built, "Oh phenomenal, phenomenal, all of them who could, came to Buffalo. Of course, Peggy Kostelnik was there. You could feel the love. Bob Skoronski, Fuzzy Thurston, Bart and Cherry Starr, Olive Jordan, Dana Caffey, Dave Robinson, all of them that could be were there. The friendship and the love, quite a family and it always has been."

An important part of the family was the reliable, steady, joyful, mistake free Elijah Pitts from Philander Smith.

# CHAPTER 19
# DAVE ROBINSON:

*"We couldn't get a hair cut in Green Bay."*

# THE LOMBARDI LEGACY

**EDITOR'S NOTE:** This thumbnail biography was compiled completely by co-author Royce Boyles with no editing by co-author Dave Robinson.

Dave Robinson is one of the greatest linebackers in Packer history and many feel he should be in the Pro Football Hall of Fame. Former defensive tackle, and long time Packer assistant coach, Dave "Hawg" Hanner said, "He was the best linebacker we had." In addition to tremendous athletic talent, Robby possessed a high IQ, high football IQ and instincts that allowed him to make big plays. Of the great linebackers during most of the Lombardi period, only Ray Nitschke was on the roster when the new coach arrived. General Manager Vince Lombardi drafted Robby in the first round of the 1962 draft and acquired Lee Roy Caffey, in a trade with Philadelphia in '64. NFL Films selected the trio as the sixth best in the history of the league.

The biggest, least publicized play in Packer history was turned in by Robby in the 1966 Championship game against the Dallas Cowboys. Dallas was on Green Bay's two yard line, trailing by seven points with less than a minute remaining. Blitzing from his linebacker position Dave forced quarterback Don Meredith to launch a wobbly pass that safety Tom Brown intercepted to cement the win, as the clock showed 28 seconds. The victory earned Lombardi's team a trip to Super Bowl I, but unfortunately the great play is mostly lost in Packer annals.

Attending Moorestown High School, in Moorestown, New Jersey, Dave was a four sport star in football, basketball, baseball and track. In all, he earned 12 letters, in three years, in addition to being selected All-State first team, in basketball, baseball and second team football, as a senior. His prep basketball team lost one game in three years and the football squad was undefeated his junior season. He was flooded by scholarship offers to attend Ivy League schools, in addition to those with powerhouse football programs. Dave filled out 26 collegiate scholarship applications and was accepted for every one. He says the best offer was from Colgate University, but he wanted

# Dave Robinson

to play big time football at a school with a good engineering program, and still be close to home in case of family emergences. Robby chose Penn State University where he attained a 3.2 grade point average in civil engineering, and was a consensus All-American tight end.

Dave began his college career as an offensive guard and nose tackle before settling in at tight end and defensive end. The Nittnay Lions featured Head Coach Rip Engle with a coaching staff which included eventual legend, Joe Paterno during Robby's collegiate years. A perennial national power, Penn State played in a post season game each year of Dave's career, compiling a 24-8 record. Robby was inducted into the College Hall of Fame in 1997.

He wore number 89 with distension in Green Bay for 10 years (1963-'72), and concluded his stellar career by playing two years for the Redskins before retiring after the '74 season. The Packer Hall of Fame opened its doors to him in 1982.

Late in his playing career, and during retirement, Dave held several positions with the Joseph Schlitz Brewing Co., including Director of Minority Relations and eventually became owner of a beverage distributorship in the greater Akron, Ohio area.

In recent years, and while compiling this book, Dave has felt the tragic loss of his wife Elaine to a stroke in 2007 followed three months and four days later by the passing of his 42 year old son Richard to a heart attack.

Dave and namesake son, David Junior, reside in Akron just a few miles from the Pro Football Hall of Fame where Robby serves on the Hall's Board of Directors.

An east coast native, the Packers grabbed *his* attention when he was a junior in college. Dave Robinson explains, "In 1961, the Green Bay Packers came out of nowhere and had beaten the New York Giants 37-0 in Green Bay. I was born and reared in New Jersey about ten miles from Philadelphia. All my friends were Philadelphia Eagle fans, so quite naturally I had to be different and rooted for the New York Giants. I thought the Giants were a

207

great team. This Green Bay Packer team, coached by Vince Lombardi who had been a Giant's coach, came up and just destroyed my Giants 37-0, so I thought right away the guy was a genius. The team was awesome; I thought it was the number one team in football. I wanted to play- that day- I wanted to be a Green Bay Packer."

When Robby was drafted for the 1963 season, the AFL-NFL signing war was escalating, but would not reach its peak until 1965. He negotiated his own contract having to deal with both leagues, "I was drafted by the San Diego Chargers of the AFL, they came out and offered me a contract, bonus, first and second year contact of 10-10-10, thirty thousand dollars. Green Bay came out with 12-12-12, thirty six thousand. Up until that time, I had decided I was not going to play pro ball; I was gonna pursue a career outside of football. I told my fiancée, later my wife, 'what we can do is play five years and get some money to establish ourselves, and then I'll retire. Once I play five years, and get vested for the pension, we'll have a secondary pension, I'll come out and go to work full-time with Campbell's Soup.' Well, after five years you know what happened.

"Al Davis was doing the negotiating for the San Diego Chargers, and I was talking with Dick Voris of the Green Bay Packers, they both were going up and up in increments, very small. My wife had already told me, no matter what, she wanted to go to San Diego because of the weather. She said, "I'm not going to that cold Green Bay, I'm going to San Diego." I said, 'OK.'

She said, "String 'em along, get all the money you can, we're gonna sign with San Diego."

So, we got up to $38,000 and Al Davis came to me and said, "Listen, we signed two of the top three draft choices, we're out of money, we can't go any higher than $38,000, but Ralph Wilson's got money up in Buffalo. What we're gonna do is continue to negotiate and whatever agreement we come to, Wilson's gonna pick up your contract, and you'll be a Buffalo Bill. And I said, 'OK'. So I called my wife, she was my girl friend, I said, 'Baby, guess what, we're not going to San Diego, it's gonna be Buffalo or Green Bay.' She said, (high squeaky voice) "Buffalo? To hell with that." She damn near hung up on me. The rest is all history, we kept negotiating, I finally held 'em up and I got 15-15-15, $15,000 for a bonus and $15,000 a year for the first two years.

"But then, Lombardi put a little quirk in it, if I wanted a no cut contract, he couldn't give me 15. Vince said if I wanted a no cut contract, which they offered me in the AFL, he said he'd only go $15,000 bonus, but only $12,000 a year. I was a little worried about that and I think Dick Voris sensed I was being a little apprehensive. He arranged for me to have dinner with former Giant and Packer great Emlen Tunnell. Emlen lived in Philadelphia and was one of my heroes from the time he was with the Giants. I had dinner with Emlen Tunnell, and he said, "Dave I'm gonna tell you something, Vince Lombardi is probably the biggest egotist you ever saw in your life. If you are the worst football player in America, he won't cut you and tell the rest of the world he made a mistake. So don't worry about the no cut, go for the money." I said, 'OK Emlen, don't worry about it.' So I said I'd sign for the 15-15-15 and not take the no cut.

"Right after that I signed and I got married. Before I got to camp, my wife's pregnant with twins. And I said, 'Holy cow, no cut contract, I gotta make this team.' The thing is, coming out of college; you never know how good you are. That was the thing; I didn't know how good I was. I knew the Green Bay Packers were the greatest team in football, these guys are better than anybody I ever played against. I didn't know how good I was and it's a hell of a thing, you don't know. Rookies didn't start. Vince Lombardi did not play rookies. Lionel Aldridge was the first rookie to start for Vince Lombardi. He said every rookie costs you three games. In fact, I did start at the end of my rookie year because on Thanksgiving Day, the fullback's coming through the line and Ray Nitschke slammed him with his hand and broke his arm. As I told Ray later, 'Bad break for you Ray, good break for me.' So I started the rest of the year."

# THE LOMBARDI LEGACY

Robby was versatile, having played tight end and defensive end at Penn State and as he relates, Green Bay was not totally clear where to play him, "I had been told by defensive coach Phil Bengtson he wanted me to play linebacker because they had a real need for linebackers. They didn't have a back up linebacker. Bill Forrester was planning to retire; in fact, Vince made him come back for the '63 season because Nelson Toburen was hurt. Bill Forrester was playing the right side, Dan Currie was playing the left side and Ray Nitschke was well entrenched in the middle.

"I went to the Coach's All-American game in Buffalo, Phil Bengtson was there and he gave me the linebacker play book. So, I go home and study everything I can about being a linebacker. I went to the All-Star game in Chicago. Your home team directs the All-Stars where to play you. They told me they wanted me to play defensive end. Evidently in Packer camp, Lionel Aldridge started looking pretty good at defensive end, so they call down to All-Star camp and said, "Move Dave to tight end." I said, 'What's this defensive play book I got--burn it.' Then Marvin Fleming started looking good in Packer camp, so Green Bay called the All-Stars and said, "Move Dave to linebacker." I moved to linebacker and that's where I stayed. All of that explains why Dave wore uniform number 89 while other Packer linebackers were numbered in the 50's and 60's.

Contract negotiations with Lombardi provided Dave with several lessons and he got to know the man as general manager when they hammered out a deal: "One-on-one. Vince was *way* better prepared. The second time, he blew me out of the water. The first time I went from fifteen thousand to twenty, he gave me $20,000, but I'd been hurt. He said, "I'll tell you what, I'll give you $20,000 provided you are in the top 22 men in minutes played." In other words, if you're hurt again, you won't get the $5,000 bonus, you only get the 15. I said, 'OK Coach,' I went along with it.

"I went back the next year and Vince said, "You made 15 last year so we're gonna offer you $16,500." I said, 'Oh coach, wait a minute, hold it, I made 20 last year.'

"Oh no, you made 15 with a $5,000.00 bonus," he told me.

"Coach, we sat across the desk, you and I. I thought we agreed that I was gonna make 20, unless I got hurt, then it was gonna revert back. I was under the assumption I was making 20 for the year."

"Finally he said, "I'll give in, use 20 as your base and I'll offer you 22 this year."

"So, my fourth year in the league I made $22,000.00. That's when I knew you had to cross all of your T's and dot all I's, that's when I went in the next year fully prepared to get all I wanted from Vince Lombardi. He had the statistics right in front of him, right in front of him. It's amazing.

"So that year, '66, I had one of my greatest years. I went in the next year, I said I was gonna get a $15,000.00 raise, that would take me to 37. I walked in and Vince offered me 30, and he said, "How's that?"

"Well Coach, I really wanted a little more."

"Wait a minute," he said and pulled out his book and flipped through it.

"Now, the average grade for a linebacker in any one game is a minus two. Linebackers have more opportunities to make more mistakes than anybody else. Well, for the year, a 14 game season, I was a plus 26. And Vince brought it up and he saw that, we went back and forth, he offered me 35 and I signed.

"Vince liked the person to speak their mind. If you said something ridiculous, Vince would discount it and kick you out of the office probably. But if you had sound reasoning for it, he respected it, he wanted to go toe-to-toe, he wanted fighters on his team. He didn't want namby-pamby type people; so consequently, it was a way for him to judge your character in negotiation.

"Then he told me something, he said, "Every year you know we're gonna make extra money." He was right; every single year I played for Vince Lombardi, I got an extra playoff check in April. Then told me, "I'll tell you what I'll do, if the *team* wins 10 games, I'll give you $2,000.00, if the *team* wins 12 games, I'll give you another $2,000.00, and if the *team* wins 14 games I'll give you another $2,000. So, you could make possibly $6,000.00 more." He asked, "Do you think we can win 12 games?"

"Oh, yea."

"That's $4,000.00 right there, now the four thousand, plus the $13,000.00 raise, you'll be making $17,000.00 that's more than the $15,000.00 you came in asking for." I had to shake my head and say, 'This guy's a hell of a negotiator.'

"See, you didn't sign your contract. When you reached an agreement with Vince, you stood up, you shook hands with him and then you left. Then later, in about a week or two he'd put the contract in your locker, you were expected to sign it, get it back to him. But, he always told you when you got done, "Your contract is the most private thing you're ever gonna get, no one needs to know what's in your contract. Don't talk about it." I thought he was joking, I said, 'Don't worry about it coach, I'm as embarrassed about it as you are.' He laughed. But no one talked about their contract."

To illustrate the point, Dave tells how his fellow linebacker, Lee Roy Caffey spilled the beans about his contract during a game, "I can't remember what year it was, but I know we were playing St. Louis, and it was a 'nothing game.' St. Louis was out of it, we were already wrapped up and we were playing them in Green Bay. It was either the 10th or 12th game and I've got the $2,000.00 bonus riding on the game. We're in the huddle, and Lee Roy Caffey comes in the huddle and says in his very high squeaky voice, "We gotta win this game fellas. I wanna buy a watermelon farm, and I need the $2,000.00 for my 12 game clause." Somebody says, "You got a 12 game clause?"

Willie Wood says, "I got a 12 game clause."

Somebody says, "I got a 12 game clause."

"I got one." The whole defense had a 12 game clause; we didn't know that, he promised everybody $2,000.00 if the team won 12 games." Imagine all the time those guys spent together in training camp, on road trips, at team parties and still did not know about each other's deals.

Team incentives were used to promote team unity and achievement. In all matters, the team mattered more than an individual. For years, Dave was the team's union representative and offers a fascinating look at Lombardi's involvement with labor issues. "Vince was against the union, he thought unions were the worst thing that ever happened to professional sports. In 1968, the very first strike, Browns owner, Art Model suggested the league have replacement games. Vince said he wasn't gonna have it, he was gonna lock the Green Bay Packers out. He said, "You guys (NFL owners) do what you want to do, but I worked too long and too hard trying to make a unit out of a bunch of ball players I inherited in 1959, now I'm not gonna break them up. They are either gonna stay out as a unit, or come in as a unit. If there's a provision allowing some people to come in, I'm gonna lock my team out." At the time, we were defending World Champions and were locked out, so we were like the tail that waged the dog. The whole league voted to lock the players out. I think we missed one or two games and the strike was settled; and the season went on. But, he said he did not want the team to be segmented, didn't want the team to be broken down into those who crossed the picket line and those who did not." Additionally, there were absolutely no ill feelings between General Manager Lombardi and union rep Dave Robinson.

Early in the civil rights movement the racial ball was moving forward slowly. Dave clarifies the state of racial affairs in his rookie year of 1963, "To put it in context, the Civil Rights Act was signed by President Lyndon Johnson in '64. It didn't take effect until 1968. When I got there in '63, there was nothing. You call somebody in Green Bay and say, 'I see you've got an apartment for rent,' they'd say, "we don't rent to blacks." Click. It was not against the law, that was it, that's all there was to it.

"In fact, when I came to the National Football League in 1963, there were no starting linebackers in the National Football League who were black, none. The rumor was at the time that blacks couldn't play linebacker. Now, the AFL had linebackers in it—the AFL was way ahead of the NFL with the racial relationships.

"I told you, I was moved around in training camp and they finally put me at linebacker. When I came to training camp, Vince Lombardi came to me and said, "Phil wanted you to play linebacker all along. I'm the one who had you moved around and I'm very happy. I think you can be a great linebacker." He said, "This year, ('63), we're trying to win our third consecutive World Championship, the first team ever to do that, and we don't need any distractions, we don't want anything that's going to disrupt the flow of the team. Winning three consecutive championships is the most important thing around here. The reason why I didn't want you to play linebacker at first was you'll be the first black linebacker in the National Football League and I don't want a bunch of reporters going around writing stories about that and not about us winning the championship. So, if anybody comes to you and asks you about being the first black linebacker, you just refer 'em to me." I said, 'Fine Coach, I don't mind,' and I did every time somebody asked, I just refered'em to Vince. There never was an article that I knew of anyway. He did something about it, but we didn't win anyway, and that's it."

By that time, Lombardi had been involved in more racial issues than we will ever know, but Robby shares this, "In the early years, he yielded to things like, when the team would go to New Orleans. He had black players stay in the black hotels instead of everybody staying together. Because the team was in two hotels, they were separated. It bothered him. In later years, when we went to New Orleans, he looked around to find a place where the whole team could stay together. We stayed in a hotel out by the airport in New Orleans, the only one that would accept integrated living."

Anonymity for a white ball player in Green Bay was difficult; impossible for a black according to Robinson, "When you walked down the street and you met a guy, any guy, a lot of people didn't look at you as being black, or white; they looked at you as being a Green Bay Packer. If you were black in Green Bay, you either came in on a train, because the porters came in on a train, you came in on a boat, because Green Bay is the furthermost western port coming down the St. Lawrence Seaway, or you played for the Green Bay Packers. Most of the guys over six foot and over 200 pounds, played for the Green Bay Packers.

"Let's say you go to the store to buy something, some guys knew you were a Packer when you walked in the door, and they gave you a break, they gave you ten percent, or twenty percent discount. Other people knew you were a Green Bay Packer; they'd jack the price up twenty percent. Other people just didn't care. You were always on guard, you had to be very guarded about everything you did and said. And when our wives came to town—our wives told us, it was like a joke with them. They'd walk down the street and some farmer coming in from the outskirts of Green Bay, into the "big city" for the first time, they'd see one of the players wives on the streets and they'd say, "Where you dancing dear?" The only black women in town were dancers. And they'd ask where they were dancing. All the wives got accused of that, and they were very insulted by it. I had twin boys; my wife would take out the twins and roll the twins down the street in the stroller. People would come up and rub their heads and stuff for good luck and my wife would be pissed. She'd be furious. I'd come home and she'd be slamming stuff around the kitchen, "You like this place don't you?" She'd tell me one of those stories, and I said, 'What are you gonna do, you can't stop it.' Most of the stuff they did innocently. I found out over a period of time the people in Green Bay were biased because they didn't understand, they'd never really been exposed to blacks and they took all the stereotypes not knowing what they were. You know, there's good blacks and there's bad blacks, there's good whites and there's bad whites, and they didn't understand. Unfortunately, all they saw on TV and read in the papers was the negative side."

# THE LOMBARDI LEGACY

The stereotypes also affected housing as Dave relates, "I had a landlord tell me one time, "This house isn't much, but it's probably better than what you've got back in Jersey." I told him, 'Not really, my friends and I wouldn't even live in your house, let alone the one your renting. I said, 'All my friends have houses nicer than yours.' And he was taken aback, like I was lying or something, but it was the truth, because of economic reasons I hung around with people who had decent homes in Jersey. And that was it, they assumed that when we lived in Jersey, we all came from the ghettos somewhere; I didn't. There wasn't a ghetto in my town to tell the truth."

The transition to a small northern city in the early '60's offered the obvious racial challenges to blacks, in addition to some basic obstacles according to Dave, "Well, the biggest thing was, we couldn't get a hair cut in Green Bay—couldn't get a hair cut in Green Bay at all. We used to look at the schedule, and we'd see, "We're gonna play in Pittsburgh, we can get a hair cut there, then we play at home, then we go to Cleveland, we'll get a hair cut there." We tried to figure every two weeks where we're gonna be—certain places we knew where the barber shops were. There were only nine of us on the team, so we'd all get in a couple of cabs, and we go to the barber shops, we'd get a hair cut and —you're gonna be in the "black neighborhood"— we'd go to a restaurant, or something and eat until the last guy got his hair cut, call the cabs, all get in the cabs and go back to the hotel.

"One time we were down in New Orleans and it was our turn to get a hair cut. That's when the racial situation in New Orleans was a little strong. Vince said he did not want us to leave the hotel, nobody leaves because we're way out by the airport, and in New Orleans you could not get a cab, they would not pick up blacks no matter what. So Willie Davis was our representative, black liaison, went to Vince and said, "Coach, the guys need hair cuts." Well Vince said, "I don't want the guys to go down there, I don't want an incident." Willie finally told Vince he had some friends from Grambling University, so Vince told Willie if he got his friends from Grambling to come

# DAVE ROBINSON

to the hotel, pick us up in private cars, take us to the barber shop and bring us back, then it was OK, and that's how we got our hair cuts that week."

Either at home, or on the road, from the beginning of time some guys have trotted the streets, the same was true for black players in Green Bay: "The streets were pounded, just like anything else, some guys ran the streets and some guys didn't. There could have been a lot of trouble. I remember once I talked to Vince and he said, "We never had any problems in Green Bay." And I told Vince, 'Coach, we don't have any problems in Green Bay because we're winning. If we ever start to loose in Green Bay, there will be all kinds of problems pop up.' From 1959 to 1967, racial problems and losing were not allowed in Packer land.

Awareness is the first step in the change process and Robby noticed an inconsistency when he joined the club in 1963, "When I came to Green Bay, I was the ninth black guy to come in, I came in from the All-Star camp, everybody had been paired off; the other eight guys all had black roommates. I came in, I was the odd man. There were only 38 men on the squad, an even number of guys on a squad, but I had a room to myself. Rather than have me room with a white guy, they gave me a room to myself. I knew at that time, somewhere in the hotel, there was a white guy that was rooming by himself, rather than room with me. And all the way through college, my roommate had always been white, Dick Anderson, the other end, was white and he and I were roommates all the way through college. When I told that to Vince, he said, "OK." The next year, as general manager, he set up the rule and that was it, the policy was dead and people could choose roommates they wanted. The first two integrated roommates were Willie Davis and Jerry Kramer, they voted and became roommates. After that, guys had roommates in training camp and roomed right through; white and black were integrated roommates."

What few racial problems issues arose, Lombardi handled quickly as Robby explains, "I can think of one guy who had a problem, a real serious

217

problem, and Vince did trade him. He got something for him. I was there, I don't want to say anything about it. I don't want to get too far. But the biggest problem we had wasn't usually with the player, because most ball players aren't biased. You know, you get hit in the mouth by a black guy, or a white guy, you still got hit in the mouth and spit out the blood. It was the wives; the problem came with the wives. A guy who comes from the deep South, usually marries a girl from the deep South, who has some very strong racial beliefs. This is why most of the problem had to do with the wives"

At one time, the Packer Executive Board seemed to have a problem with Lombardi selecting black players with high draft choices. Dave explains how the issues were resolved, "He had drafted Herb Adderley for the first round in '61, then Earl Gros (white running back), then he had drafted me in '63. They called him in and said, "Vince, you're wasting draft choices. You don't have to draft black guys in the first round; you did that two out of three years. Black guys are gonna be available on the third round."

"Vince said, "I'm drafting football players, I'm not drafting white or black, I'm just drafting the best players out there. You guys run the business end of the thing, and I'll run the Green Bay Packer football operation."

"Also, there were some places in town that did not particularly want to see the black Packers come into their place, be it a restaurant, or anything else, and the word I got was Vince Lombardi put the word out to all the businesses in town, if you don't want to serve the black Packers, I'll put your place 'off limits', and no Packers will come in. In Green Bay, as small as that town was, it was a great, great asset to any restaurant, or any place else to have Packers come into your restaurant. That's like the Mecca of Northeastern Wisconsin, and salesmen would come in and they could stay out all night long, as long as they went back home to some little town in central Wisconsin, with a handful of Green Bay Packer autographs. They went to places they knew the Packers would frequent. If your place was off limits, you lost a lot of business."

# DAVE ROBINSON

From 1940-1963, the Packers played the Washington Redskins in preseason every year, except 1941 and 1950. The long time agreement between those two clubs came to an end over a racial incident directly involving Green Bay's Head Coach and General Manager. It's important to remember Lombardi, being Italian, was of Mediterranean skin and had course hair. Additionally, during training camp, he was out in the sun with his ball club conducting two a day practices, therefore, developing a deep tan. The '62 game was scheduled in Columbus, Georgia and the Packers went to North Carolina to spend time during the week before the contest. At the time, George Preston Marshall owned the Redskins. Marshall was a raciest and integrated his team only after being threatened by the United States government. In 1962, Interior Secretary Stewart Udall gave the team an ultimatum to either sign a black player, or be evicted from the new District of Columbia Stadium.

During the Packers stay in North Carolina, Vince and Marie Lombardi went to a restaurant for dinner and encountered a situation that set in motion a string of events that ended the Green Bay-Washington preseason agreement. Dave Robinson tells how a maître d' refused to seat the Lombardi's, "I wasn't there, but paraphrasing he said, "Well we don't allow blacks in this restaurant." Vince said, "I'm not black, I'm Vince Lombardi." The maître d' said, "I don't care who the hell you are, you're not bringing that blond woman in this restaurant and have dinner."

Having been refused service, Lombardi called Marshall and told him of the incident at which time George Preston Marshall laughed at Lombardi. Marshall's bad idea of laughter was followed by an innovative one by Lombardi.

In those days, players were only paid $50.00 for each preseason game; the Packers were world champions and sold out huge stadiums even for exhibition games, so the teams split a lot of money. Dave tells how Lombardi made his point to the bigoted George Preston Marshall: "We end up playing the Washington Redskins in 1963, in Cedar Rapids, Iowa at a high school football stadium. Frank Budd, a black track star and world's fastest human being was trying to make the team with the Washington Redskins. There were like a hundred press credential requests, and the press box could accommodate about twenty. The lights were so low, all the punts and half the kickoffs went above and out of the lights. It was terrible, the locker rooms couldn't handle it, both teams lost their shirt, after that the contract was ended."

The Redskins and Packers took turns in alternating years selecting the location of the game. Following the Cedar Rapids contest, Lombardi reportedly found George Preston Marshall and told him the game would be played at the same high school stadium every other year, at which time Marshall asked Lombardi if he would like to break the contract. Apparently, Lombardi didn't have to tell him it was as clear as black and white he wanted out of the deal. The lack of black players on Washington's roster was probably a large contributing factor for their abysmal record during that time period.

As Boyd Dowler mentioned in his chapter, Lombardi had a sharp mind and progressive approach to running the organization. Robby discusses Lombardi in those terms, "Very, very, very smart man, but he loved gadgets. Somebody sold him on the idea of personality tests, so Vince gets these personality tests, the first thing he did was administer the tests to all his football players. The word I got, when he got the results, he looked at the linebackers, Caffey, Nitschke and myself and he said, "Holy shit, look at these guys, their manic depressive or something." Based on that, that was the standard he set when linebackers took the test. He looked at it and asked, "Will this guy be a linebacker—his attitude." He loved it. Also, he looked at how say, a Forrest Gregg graded out, and Bob Skoronski, and looked for similarities when he drafted a tackle. So, he had an advantage of having guys he really trusted and he used his team as the criteria. He used the tests."

General Manager Lombardi also used his players as a scouting system

# DAVE ROBINSON

designed to evaluate players around the league: "After every game you were given a sheet, and you had to evaluate the guy you played against—how good he was, how quick he was, anything. You had to list three or four good things about him, and two or three bad things about him. Vince kept that on record. And let's say we're talking about you, and I played against you. I list you, and then all of a sudden your name comes up on the waiver list, or he wants to trade for you. First thing he did, get in and see, "What do my people who played against him think about this guy. He was dumb, I could fool him, or he was really tough, he comes off hard even though we were winning he kept fighting right to the end." Lombardi had a line on you before he picked you up."

In 2007, New York Giants Coach Tom Caughlin increased rapport with his club by establishing a liaison with the locker room and received high praise from the media for the 'innovation.' Lombardi had three ways into his, two formal and one not so much. Robby explains, "He had certain guys. He didn't have a wire or anything, but certain guys ran back to Vince, anything went on in that locker room, Vince found out about it. I mean you could just make a joke and he found out about it. I don't know who they were, there were some rumors, people said it was, "such and such and so and so," but he had somebody, he had the locker room snitched so to speak.

"We had an executive committee, five man committee, four players and Vince Lombardi. That's so there would never be a tie on the votes. Most of the votes went 5-0. Everybody waited to see how Vince voted, then, the other four guys fell in line. The offensive and defensive captains were on that team, then he took one offensive and one defensive leader." Additionally, Willie Davis served as liaison for the black players to Vince Lombardi, truly an innovation for the times.

As general manager, Lombardi both overtly and covertly maneuvered his team players into a position to win. Dave sights a couple of examples, "In '63, Bart Starr broke his hand, and Vince pulled a real big thing when he got

221

Zeke Bratkowski. We needed a quarterback bad, and the trade deadline was over. So, he arranged with the Rams to put Zeke Bratkowski on waivers, and everybody in the league knew if they claimed Zeke, the Rams were going to withdraw the waivers. We got Zeke Bratkowski off of waivers, and then when the season was over, in the first week or two, we traded center Kenny Iman to the Rams for, like a 17th round draft choice. That was a Zeke Bratkowski for Kenny Iman trade being fulfilled because he couldn't do it during the season; it was after the trade deadline.

"When you're the World Champions, needs aren't always that great. He figured his team was set, but he was drafting somebody for backup. There's an old story about how he and Dave 'Hawg' Hanner went to a draft session, and there were 20 rounds in the draft then. They get to round 17 and he turned to 'Hawg' and he says, "Hawg, I think we addressed all of our needs, didn't we?" And 'Hawg' said, "Well coach, we didn't draft any linebackers." And Vince says, "Linebackers? We don't need any linebackers, we got Robinson, Nitschke, Caffey, and (Tommy Joe) Crutcher for the back up, we're gonna go with those four, that's it." Hanner said, "Coach, Coach, we need some linebackers for the intrasquad game. So, Vince drafts like four guys, and picked up a couple free agents.

"He did some other things. After Super Bowl I, Max McGee was quoted as saying, "What a great game for me to retire on. That's it, I'm done." The reporters went to Vince and said, "Max says he gonna retire after this game, he had a great game, it's gonna be his last game." Vince said, "I think you may have misheard him." He wanted Max back 'cause he wanted to make that run for three in a row. But he did things like that."

After winning the third consecutive World Championship in 1967, Lombardi stepped out of coaching, and into the singular role of general manager, something that was painful for Robby to watch: "Yes, in fact, I like to say in '68, when he was just general manager, it was like somebody had torn half of his heart out. You could see he really wanted to coach, you could see he was fighting himself not to second guess Phil. Something would happen and Phil would say something, or run a play, or make a decision and everybody would look to Vince to see if he was gonna correct it, or do something different. Vince really had to fight with himself, especially on the practice field, not to say something, 'cause he wanted it to be Phil's team. That was very difficult and I could see why he went back to coaching football."

For Dave Robinson, the permanent stamp of Lombardi is deep, wide and obvious, but one lesson stands above all the others. Dave said, "Coach would tell us, "At the beginning of the season everybody's in first place, zero, zero, zero and in life. At the end of the season there's one winner, there's no such thing as second place. The minute you accept second, it's gonna be easier to accept third, the minute you accept third it's gonna be much easier to slip into fourth. If you take any sense of pride in being number two, that's the day you become a loser. And this county's built on winners. Americans like to win. The joys of winning are only a joy if you've tasted the bitterness of defeat.

"The team, when I got there, a lot of guys had been around for that 1-10-1 season. They remember what it was like when you had to sneak downtown after a game to keep from getting hollered at and everything else. They really understood it. That's why winning every game meant so much to them and they passed it on to us, that's the pride Vince brought into the locker room."

It may not have felt like it at the time, but playing for football's greatest coach was a life changer for the Penn State linebacker, "Looking back on it, I think it was the fact he gave me an opportunity to play in the National Football League and to play for him. It's kind of funny, my wife came to camp and she went down to talk to Marie Lombardi, and Marie said, "How do you like it in Green Bay?" She said, "I like it here OK except when Vince hollers at Dave. He comes home and hollers at the kids and I and I'm having a terrible time." Marie said, "You tell Dave that Vince only hollers at people who have potential, when he stops hollering, go home and pack your bags, you're outta here."

"From then on, when Vince hollered at me I thought, 'Hey, he likes me.' He liked me a lot evidently. That's the thing about Vince Lombardi, you thought you knew the man and every day he would say something new, and different, and kept you on your toes."

For Robby, there is no limit to what he would give to spend some time with his old coach: "As much as I could, as much as I could scrape up. When he slipped away, I realized there were so many things I never asked him, so many things I didn't get his advice. He had great advice. The best thing said when he died was, you should not feel sorry for Vince Lombardi, you should feel sorry for the people who were never coached by him, who never touched him, people who never met the man."

If Dave could talk to him he would say, "I would probably tell him, 'I love you Coach.' My father died when I was fifteen years old and I was at a real crossroads in my life. I hung out with a kid who later ended up going to jail for murder, he was my best friend. I could have gone that way, or could have gone the other way, and followed sports. My father, on his death bed, on Thanksgiving Day, asked, "What are you gonna do now that football season is over?"

"I don't know dad."

"I wish you'd go out for basketball. Your mother worries about you hanging out with certain people after school; she knows where you are when you go to practice. I wish you'd go out for basketball so your mother doesn't worry about you."

"That Monday, when I had to make my decision whether to go to basketball or not, they called me out of school around 11:00, my father had passed away. From that moment on, you can count on one hand, the amount of times I came home directly from school. From football, to basketball to baseball, and track. I ran four sports, I got twelve letters. Four sports a year for three years. Went to practice every night and on top of that I was in college preparatory course, I knew my mother couldn't afford to send me to college. I *had* to win a scholarship to go to college.

"That's what I'd tell Vince, 'Vince Lombardi, you filled a big need in me.' My father was very stern, as Vince was stern. Like my father, Vince Lombardi, when things were going good, nothing was too good for his family. We were the first team to stay at the Waldorf Astoria, everything was great with us. But, if he had to administer punishment he was very, very good at it. He was a big Italian father, like my father. He loved us to death, do anything for us, but step out of line, and he brought it down on you big time. I'd tell Vince over and over again, I'd like to thank him for taking a boy and making me a man."

# CHAPTER 20
# VICKY ALDRIDGE NELSON:

*"Totally a racial pioneer."*

# THE LOMBARDI LEGACY

Defensive end Lionel Aldridge, a black man from Louisiana and Vicki Wankier, a white Mormon from Utah, were about as unlikely a romantic couple as could be found in the early 1960's. Lionel joined the Packers in 1963, having been drafted in the fourth round out of Utah State. Playing all 14 games at right defensive end in 1963, he was the first rookie allowed to start on a Lombardi team from the opening game. Lionel played with Green Bay through 1971 and finished off his pro career in 1973, after two seasons in San Diego. Wearing number 82, Aldridge played right defensive end well enough to enter the Packer Hall of Fame in 1988.

The profound story of Vicki Aldridge Nelson and her marriage to Lionel is a rich mixture of triumph and failure. She was on the receiving end of taunts, cat calls, name calling, and deafening silence. Her heart wrenching story of rejection combined with an uncommon courage to marry the man she loved is a definition of commitment foreign to most.

Looking at their marriage from the outside, all seemed to be going well in the Aldridge household as Lionel was making a smooth transition to radio and television broadcasting with Milwaukee's WTMJ. He appeared destined for a stable post playing career. It was anything but.

Lionel's struggle with depression, paranoia and schizophrenia tore apart the marriage, broadcasting career and his very life. Like other significant issues that seem to afflict just one individual, mental illness is a family dynamic; all of the members are affected. There is much documentation regarding Lionel's battles to put his life together, including a forth coming book by Vicki. Lionel and Vicki divorced in 1982 and she married Joe Nelson in 1987. The big defensive end suffered a premature death, at age 56, on February 12, 1998.

For purposes of *The Lombardi Legacy*, our focus is on Vicki's ordeal to be with the man she loved, Lionel, and the man she would come to love in the process, Vince Lombardi. The courage and fairness of Green Bay's former head coach and general manager can be measured in large degree by his unwavering support of the interracial couple. The combination of Lombardi's principles, decency, strength, defiance, loyalty and commitment to team unity regarding this issue has gone largely unnoticed, but not unappreciated by Vicki Aldridge Nelson. She begins her story on a University campus, "We were dating in college, at Utah State University, and he was probably one of the six black people on the campus. Me, being raised Mormon, did not quite understand the black/white issue. I was a part of a dance group—we used to practice at the field house—one of his jobs was to sweep the field house. That's where he saw me. He found my name in the registry and called me, and of course, I said, 'No' at first, and he kept calling. I kept saying, 'I'm busy, I'm busy, I'm busy.' And he said, "Well, when aren't you?"

"Well, probably a couple weeks from now."

"I'll take it."

"If you can call dating in Utah with a black guy--driving around the outskirts of campus, because that's basically what we could do--and we just talked and yik-yakked. I knew nothing about football. I'd been a cheerleader in high school and they'd say, "First and ten, do it again," and it would be for the other team. When I very first met him, I knew he was a star, so I went to the library, checked out a book on positions that football players play. We started seeing each other and that was my spring quarter of my freshman year. It was his junior year. Then that ended, and we came back to school the following year and didn't think anything more about it. He looked me up again, after we got back into school, and we started seeing each other again. Word got back, not only to the campus, but to my hometown. Things were very prejudiced back then. I was called "nigger-lover" a lot--but we kept it going and we became very good friends. Then, his last year of eligibility, they did not allow him to come back to school anymore. So, he tried to get into another university in that area, and they black-balled him"

Unequivocally, Vicki says the relationship was the reason for Lionel's scholarship being pulled: "Because of the dating, I think he lacked two quarters of graduating, because they would not let him enter any of the schools in Utah."

Vicki said obstacles and setbacks hardened the couples resolve, "I think it probably made us dig our feet in even more. If we'd had people saying, "You know, date and get to know each other and whatever," because sometimes when people say, "No, no, no," you only see the good, and you don't really weigh the things that might not be so good, you're so busy defending your decision, at that point in time. So yeah, I was disowned."

Resistance to Lionel and Vicki's relationship was displayed in Green Bay, during his rookie year of 1963, and it did not come from the players, or organization. "The first time I went back to visit him, we were engaged. He and Bob Jeter shared a place—apartment, if you want to call it—and I was staying at a hotel. After the game, we'd all gone to a party at Henry Jordan's, and all of the wives were sitting in a circle, and all the guys, of course, were over at the bar. I was sitting next to (hesitation) Dixie Taylor." Not Jimmy's present wife Helen. "Yep, Jim Taylor's ex wife. She turned to me and she saw the engagement ring on my hand, and asked me who I was here with, and I told her, "Lionel Aldridge." She got up and moved to the other side of the circle, and then really nobody much talked to me. Olive Jordan was always sweet and darling to me, always very nice. Peggy Kostelnik, Ron Kostelnik's wife, was always very sweet and nice to me, but it was my very first introduction as not even a wife, but just as an engaged person to Lionel. From early on Kathy (Jim) Grabowski and Mary Ellen (Ken) Bowman took me in and really took care of me, made sure I was included in on all the parties and that I was a part of the organization from very early on."

It seems so long ago that some of us were first learning about race relations through experience. In the 1960's, the wave a racial change was so rapid, so intense, that we would sometimes get confronted by it and be amazed how it looked and how we reacted. In 1964, the Packers made a significant trade with the Philadelphia Eagles and acquired outside linebacker Lee Roy Caffey. Lee Roy and wife Dana, natives of little Thorndale, Texas, had very little interaction with blacks throughout their early lives. Grade schools and high schools were segregated; Lee Roy attended Texas A&M where there was no integration. Dana paints a vivid picture of what happened when she attended her first Packer home game and discovered there was an interracial relationship in the family. She said, "At that time there were several of us who were together at the game and I didn't know anybody. The first person I met was Barbara (Forrest) Gregg, she was sitting with me, and Vicki was sitting on the left side of me. We were all just sitting there introducing ourselves to each other and Vicki asked, "Who is your husband?" I said, 'Lee Roy Caffey, he's number 60, and now who are you?' She told me her name and said, "I'm with Lionel Aldridge." I told her I didn't know any of the guys or names, so she pointed him out. She said his number was 82, and I just stopped breathing. I *did not say a word* and she didn't say a word, I don't think we even talked the rest of the game. I absolutely had no response at all and I was just stunned."

Dana's description of her shock, and taking a gasp of air that refused to leave her lungs, is priceless. The two couples became good friends, Lionel played defensive end and Lee Roy was a linebacker right behind him for six years. Over the years, the two women have reminisced about the incident and Dana says, "She told me later she knew I quit breathing. We've had some good laughs about it. It was just my small town up bringing; racially mixed dating just never entered my mind, we hadn't been exposed to it."

As astonishing as interracial dating was in 1963, the Richter scale was needed to measure the shock of such a marriage. Vicki explains how she and Lionel proceeded, "We didn't get married until a couple years' later. At that point in time, we decided we were getting married and Lionel went in to meet with Lombardi because the first interracial couple (player) that had ever gotten married in the NFL had been blackballed from any team in the NFL." The player was rumored to be Cookie Gilchrist who later played in the AFL. Vicki confirmed, "Cookie Gilchrist… mm, hm. And so Lionel just wanted to find out what was going to happen if we got married, so he went in and met with Lombardi.

"From the rumors that I'd always heard about Lombardi, he was always very non-prejudiced—he had one goal in mind, and that was to win. He was very fair. I had not talked to him up until that point, because, again, I was just engaged. Lionel called me and told me that Lombardi said, "You know what, I don't care who you marry, as long as you keep the Green Bay Packer team clean, your nose clean, and you play good football. Don't worry about it—the same thing won't happen to you that's happened to Cookie Gilchrist."

Lionel's conversation with Lombardi and subsequent support made all the difference. Vicki does not believe the marriage would have occurred had Lombardi been neutral or opposed to the union, "No, no. As much as Lionel and I loved each other, I know Lionel loved his football. I know that would have been a very hard decision for Lionel to have to make between me and football, and if I hadn't have had the backing of Mr. Lombardi, I don't think I would have survived in the organization, with the wives, with the husbands, with anything. I don't think it would have been possible."

Make no mistake, interracial marriage in 1965 was a very big issue for the National Football League, so much so, that pressure was applied on Lombardi to stop the marriage. According to Vicki Aldridge Nelson the message was delivered in person, "Yes, the commissioner (Pete Rozelle) came into town and tried to stop it. And Mr. Lombardi said (to Rozelle), "Absolutely not, this is my team. My team is who my team is and nobody can tell me what I can, and cannot do." Lombardi defied the commissioner on a critical social issue at an extremely sensitive time in our country's history.

Vicki says additional pressure was applied, "My parents wrote him a letter and tried to get Mr. Lombardi to stop us from getting married. Mr. Lombardi wrote them a letter and said, "I'm not going to do that, this is a family affair. As long as they are happy, and they love each other..." Number one is religion, and number two is family, and three is the Green Bay Packers --that's what he cared about. And so, he stuck out his neck a lot, for his beliefs, and I'll always, always love him for that."

In Vicki's mind, Vince Lombardi's place in history should include something in addition to coaching, "Totally, totally a racial pioneer. I don't think he believed in any kind of racial discrepancy, I think he believed in, "You're not playing well, you're not using your abilities well, you're not using your intelligence well," but I don't think he had anything—any *care* at all about color. I think he was color-blind, as far as, that was concerned. He came up and talked to me, he would ask me how things were going, make sure everything was going OK, and always seemed to care, always seemed to be concerned and make sure that nobody was treating me really bad."

There is a saying that power corrupts and absolute power corrupts absolutely. By 1965, Lombardi's power was at its zenith, he could have chosen to use it like an axe to destroy Vicki and Lionel's hopes and dreams. Vicki says, "Totally. Totally could have, and everybody would have been on his side, and that's the thing of it, everybody would have been on his side if he'd have done that. But he stood up and said, "No, this is not right. I don't believe this, and I'm going to stand up for what I believe in," is what helped me stand up for what I believe in.

"I think he helped me be a pioneer in my beliefs, because he defended the cause of not being prejudiced, because of a person's color, or a person's religion—things that they cannot help. I think he definitely helped me be a pioneer in my belief that all people are equal. I think he was very fair. I'm very fair-thinking, I like everybody to be treated equal and fair, and I feel like without him, because he was so powerful, I don't know if any of this would."

"I'm writing my own book. I grew up Mormon, Lionel, he grew up Baptist—he grew up in Louisiana, I grew up in Salt Lake City. It will be about how we met, our college days when we were in a Mormon School. Very hard on us, and like I said, he was dropped--his eligibility ended after

# THE LOMBARDI LEGACY

he played his last year of football in the fall semester. It was while playing for the Green Bay Packers, and then later on, when he developed paranoid schizophrenia, so it should be a pretty interesting book."

The wheels of racial change were turning slow; Lionel and Vicki lived it, as those around them adjusted to their interracial marriage. Vicki recalls, "Yeah, it took some time. I think a lot of those things are so ingrained in people they don't even realize they have those kinds of feelings until they are confronted with it. I think a lot of times, they don't even know why they have them. I think after a while, getting to know me and getting to know I'm an OK person, and maybe a nice person, and have something to add, yeah. We finally started to get along much better.

"About the last year of Elijah Pitts' playing with the Packers in 1969, we were all at a party at a hotel, and Ruth Pitts came in, called me in, went into the bathroom and said she had something to say to me. She apologized for how the black women had treated me, how unfair they had been to me, she was so sorry, and if she could do it over again, she would certainly try to make my life more comfortable up there."

Much of Vicki's life has been defined by her relationship with and marriage to Lionel Aldridge. Lombardi was a critical key to making it work because he intuitively knew how to handle it. Vickie agrees, "Yeah, he was such a powerful influence; he was probably the best psychiatrist/psychologist I've ever met. I remember, Lionel used to come home and say, "When we would win, that's when he would cuss us out—when we would lose, he'd never say a thing, 'cause he knew that we felt worse than anybody." And yet, he had an ability to know exactly what buttons to push on Lionel to get him to perform his very, very best, and I think he did that with everyone—not being vindictive or mean, but just knew people—he was a master of knowing people."

Vicki Aldridge Nelson, if given the opportunity to speak with Lombardi today would say, "Well, I don't know if I could say too much. I would hug him

234

and kiss him and thank him so much and maybe kiss his ring like everybody else did. I know he was probably one of the greatest influences in my life, as a Packer wife, and somebody that helped me stand up for my beliefs, backed my beliefs. A person that has that kind of power, that can help you back up your beliefs—gave me a lot of self-confidence, I couldn't thank him enough. He was the most wonderful man. I love him."

It is a select few who have the courage to stand, in the face of heavy social pressure, in order to live their lives according to their convictions, and help change the course of history in the process. While moving in a land of giants, Vicki held firm to her beliefs when she was barely out of her teens. Her resolve and fortitude were gigantic, with the grandest of the giants standing by her side.

# CHAPTER 21
# MARV FLEMING:

*"I remember one time the 'N' word was brought up."*

# THE LOMBARDI LEGACY

Imagine a black student attending the predominantly Mormon University of Utah in the early 1960's. That's Marv Fleming.

The AFL-NFL signing wars were cranking up, when Marv Fleming was drafted, in 1962. He was selected number two by the Denver Broncos, and rumors circulated he had signed before the NFL draft a week later, therefore was not taken until the 11th round by Green Bay. Marv, Dave Robinson and Lionel Aldridge were the only draft choices to make the team in '63. Doug Hart was on the taxi squad for the '63 season, having been claimed on waivers in preseason, before making the team in '64. The three "modern day" blacks impacted the club, both on and off the field. They were informally known as "The Book Ends" due to their signing talents. Lionel was quite good, while the other two tried. They took the words from the 1963 Drifter's hit song, "On Broadway" and adapted it to their situation. Remember the words? "They say the neon lights are bright on Broadway?" The revised version goes, "They say that I will be a star in Green Bay."

Coincidentally, in the mid 1960's Packer team pictures, the three can be found in the front row with Robby and Marv sitting on each end and Lionel somewhere between them, befitting the place of a lead singer. Ladies and gentlemen, those were the Book Ends.

Marv played seven years, 1963-'69, in Green Bay, and five more for the Miami Dolphins. He was a member of the Packers three consecutive championship teams, including the first two Super Bowls. He played out his option in 1969, to join Miami. As a Dolphin tight end, Marv appeared in Super Bowls VI, VII and VIII, winning the last two. He was the first NFL player to perform in five Super Bowls and was a member of the 1972 undefeated Miami club.

For Lombardi's Packers, Marv began his career as Ron Kramer's backup, but became a starter when Ron went to Detroit. The transition from Kramer to Fleming is testament to team unity as taught by Coach Lombardi and the professionalism of Ron and Marv. The tight end position, vital to the running game, was Marv's responsibility from 1965-'69. Green Bay's number 81 is an engaging, bright man with a wry sense of humor.

Despite being drafted second by Denver, Marv Fleming wanted to be a Packer, "Well, let me tell you—just coming to Green Bay—seeing the Green and Gold, was a big thing to me. And playing—beginning to play for the Green Bay Packers was just unheard of, because, they were champions. I wanted to sign with the Packers, even though I didn't know who was playing tight end. Not knowing Lombardi personally, but knowing of him, what I'd heard of him, I honored him—I looked up to him. My first experience with him was when I got drafted. They called me and said, "Marvin, have you signed with Denver?" Denver drafted me number two.

"No I haven't," because they drafted the week before.

"Well, we're going to pick you up now because Denver put out a line that they had signed you."

"No, I haven't talked to anybody from Denver. Who is this?"

Lombardi says, "Is this Marv Fleming.?"

"Yes, who is this?"

"Coach Lombardi."

"Yeah, right." I was wondering, "Why would a guy of his caliber call me?" He gives the phone to Bill Austin, and Bill says, "Uh, Marv, this is Coach Austin with the Green Bay Packers." And I said, "Excuse me, who was that?"

"That was Coach Lombardi."

"That was Coach?"

I didn't even know Coach Lombardi. "Tell him I'm sorry, I didn't know it was him--I'm getting a lot of phone calls," and blah-blah—that was my first impression--my first incident with Coach Lombardi."

Marv wanted to be a Packer and Denver wanted him to be a Bronco, "They offered me a lot more money, a lot better contract than the Green Bay Packers did." Fleming was aware Ron Kramer was Green Bay's number one tight end. Backup Gary Knafelc had moved on to San Francisco, so there was a pretty good chance of making the team, although he did not know that when he signed. After retiring, Marv became an agent and says, "That's the first thing I looked at, 'Can you make the team?' You can sign with these people, but that doesn't necessarily mean you are going to make the team. I just wanted to sign with the Green Bay Packers."

However, he was judicious during the process, when in 1962, team representatives met with him in California to secure his signature. "They were going to give me a two thousand dollar bonus, or five thousand, "If you sign right now." I said, 'I can't sign right now, I have to wait until my mentor looks at the contract.' I didn't sign. When reminded that three thousand dollars was at stake for an immediate deal, Marv told them, 'I'm sorry, I can't sign right now. I've never had three thousand dollars and three thousand dollars doesn't mean anything to me right now.' See, when you've never had it, you don't know the value of it. So when my mentor, Harry L. Skinner came and they sat down and we went over the contract, my mentor Harry said, "Well, I don't see the extra money you promised Marv if he signs right now. I realize it's been three or four hours, but I don't see it here on the table." They said, "If he's going to sign right now, we'll give it to him." I wouldn't have gotten it if he wouldn't have done that for me." Denver offered Fleming ten thousand dollars more to sign, but he took less money to wear green and gold.

Fleming and Aldridge knew each other fairly well and liked each other whereas, Marv had heard and read about Dave Robinson. Marv explains the difference in the two relationships, "I knew Lionel from high school and we played against each other in a Northern California versus Southern California all-star game. I was player of the game, thank you. I knew him very, very well." Marv was not getting a lot of national press coverage in Utah despite his excellent college career. His teammate to be, Robinson, was getting lots of ink according to Marv, "Dave was a tight end, a consensus All-

# MARV FLEMING

American at the big school of Penn State. Dave Robinson, Dave Robinson, Dave Robinson. That's all you read about tight ends was Dave Robinson. When Dave got drafted, I saw he was drafted number one. Here I am drafted eleventh. I knew I could play tight end. So, here we are going to the Hula Bowl, I knew who Dave was, he didn't know who in the hell I was, he never heard of Marv Fleming. On the plane going over to Hawaii, guess who's right in front of me, Dave Robinson. He talked *the whole way*, pissed me off. He's a number one pick and I'll be facing this guy in a couple months. I'm just pissed. Can you imagine six hours of being pissed going over? Here I am in the back seat right behind Dave Robinson and he's talking and talking and talking and talking. At some point on the way to Hawaii, I kind of step out of my seat and I said, 'I'm gonna be the tight end.'

"When we went to training camp, I *really* saw I had a good chance. Ron Kramer was going to be number one, they had another player, Jan Barrett they drafted him number six, but he couldn't block his way out of a paper bag. How I won the job? I saw that Mr. Robinson was a heck of a football player for defense. He was really aggressive on defense; that I liked. He had the intelligence of a defensive player, which I liked. They put Dave on defense at linebacker, he was a good athlete, but he wasn't a tight end." At this point, Marv yelled, "Yea," laughed and then made a special request, "Please use this quote, 'Marv Fleming is still clapping and happy Dave was moved to linebacker. He was a number one draft choice, they always keep those guys. To this day, Marv Fleming is in love with Dave Robinson because he played another position.' I'm still clapping about that." In all seriousness Marv says, "Dave was largely resposinble for making me a better player, because every day I had to face him in practice. He was the best linebacker I ever faced in the NFL." They are best of friends and have been since 1963.

There was still another item to be tended to; Marv had to beat out Barrett for a roster spot. In the exhibition finale, each of the tight end prospects played a half to settle the battle as Marv said, "Ron Kramer gets sick before the last preseason game, then it was up to Jan Barrett or Marv Fleming. I blocked my ass off, I was making one and two blocks on a single play, and I caught the ball, almost made a touchdown. In the second half everybody came over to me and said, "Wow," because I was doing so much in the first half you know. Willie Wood came over and said, "Welcome to the team."

"What do you mean?"

"Welcome to the team, take a look at that out there."

Jan Barrett was missing blocks, missing passes and all that stuff, so that's when I made the team." The official word came the following week, "We had a master meeting, then broke into our position meetings. There was a role call for those who made the team, and some guys who were kept for the taxi squad." Everyone who had been cut was already on their way home.

Socially and politically, the 1960's, stand alone as a time of turbulence and change. During that period, authority was questioned and challenged. Paradoxically, Lombardi was held in high regard throughout America for his unquestioned control, adherence to rules and demand for player discipline, as he collected championships. He was, however, a psychologist, he read each person and intuitively knew how to handle them. He was and could be explosive, but his fertile mind and grasp of complex issues were fairness in action.

Given this set of circumstances in 1963, what would you do? During training camp, your all-pro center comes into your office reporting he saw a black, rookie eleventh round draft choice, sitting in a car with a white woman. Your all-pro center is not pleased. Marv explains the training camp incident, "She was a student from school, the University of Utah, where I went. The Caucasian lady's parents had taken me for dinner, they came and picked me up on a Sunday, and took me to dinner, so she brought me back to training camp. I said, 'Let me out a block away, please.' While Marv and the woman were sitting in the car talking, Jim Ringo went by, "Yea, he drove by in his car. He goes in and tells Lombardi I'm with a white girl.

# MARV FLEMING

"Lombardi calls me in and says, "Marvin, I realize you come from a background, the University of Utah, all white, and you have all white friends." He says, "Just be discreet, that's all.""

"OK, I can do that." I said, "Aren't you going to fire me, cut me?"

He said, "Why should I cut you, you're part of this team. You have a lot of potential to be a good football player and help this team. I'm gonna help you be a better player."

"So I was discreet, my association with Coach Lombardi was pure, it wasn't distant. I didn't have to go through someone else; my connection was directly to Lombardi because we had talks. With Lombardi, we had talks; in the time I was there, I would say we probably had four serious talks." The delicate issue was handled decisively by the general manager, a reminder of what Boyd Dowler said of Lombardi's management of the entire racial situation, "He couldn't have handled it any better."

Lombardi was high strung, however he had a talent for defusing sensitive situations as Marv explains, "I remember one time the 'N' word was brought up. Yes, the 'N' word—and he just went over the top. He says, "There are only three colors on this team,"—three colors in which I think, 'Three colors? What are the others? There's green and gold, and… then maybe black stripe or white stripe? And he says, "Green, gold and Italian." And I thought that was great, I totally agreed."

Marv was prepared more than most black players to adjust to the Caucasian population in Wisconsin because of his lifelong interaction with whites. He did not suffer culture shock, "I went to an all-white school— University of Utah—and I was familiarized with the white culture, so I had no problems at all. And the people of Green Bay, I had no problems with the people in Green Bay. The problem was the players who came from the South. How did I adjust to that? Well, I still remained myself. I still was Marv Fleming, but I did things low-key, you can say."

Veteran black players were well entrenched in the Packer locker room

243

to help the new wave of younger ones fit it. Marv was one of three bright, articulate and athletically gifted rookies to make the team in 1963. They did not rely heavily on the liaison that had been put in place by Lombardi, "Well, not really. We had players–Willie Davis was on the committee. Willie Wood was the one, I think, that was the guy that would tell you things to do, things not to do. He was open about that. Dave Robinson, Lionel Aldridge—we were the new kids that came in--we were the new group that came in with an attitude. We came in, we were winners and some of the guys hadn't met our type before. They had not dealt with our free personalities. There was a control, someone would tell me, "You can't say that." I said, 'What do you mean I can't say that?'

From early in life, Fleming had significant contact with lots of whites, therefore, "When people came to the practice field, Lombardi saw I had white friends, being from Los Angeles and going to school in Utah, and speaking English, and not being like the Southern guys. They come up from the South, and they really don't know how to talk to white people, they talk slow, you know what I'm saying. Then, you have people like Dave Robinson, Marv Fleming and Lionel Aldridge. "We were a different kind, a different breed. We all had Afro's, I even had cards made up, Muhammad Fleming." Lombardi's greatness touched the entire organization, but he was also touched by the greatness of those he selected to keep around him; those with intelligence, moxie, common sense, mental toughness and athletic talent. Marv Fleming was one of those.

A group of Marv's fans traveled to a 1963 preseason game to see him play. Marv explains, "Lombardi knew my friends, and most of them were white, especially when that bus with all those white people went to Cedar Rapids, Iowa. We played a game there and all these white people came and were hugging me and kissing me. I said, 'No, no, no, no, no, we got some crazy people on our team.'

Marv explains how Lombardi paid special attention to the tight end,

# MARV FLEMING

"He had to pass me to go to his locker room, and on Tuesdays, after Sunday games, he'd come out with that smile on his face. He would pat me on my back, and in a big booming voice, "Marvin." When he was pissed he didn't do that.

"Marvin."

"I knew we had a connection. I know Lombardi never did that to any other player, because I asked. I was on stage one time and turned around and asked the guys, 'Did Lombardi ever?' I was twenty years old when I got there; I was the youngest guy on the team. I'm glad Lombardi took that interest in me, if it hadn't been for that interest and that push……"

Before leaving for the Lions, Ron Kramer spent time with his protégé, to accelerate Fleming's adjustment to tight end. "Let me tell you, it's funny, during my rookie, year, Ron—I respected this man so much. I used to go in and watch him, watch his films, watch the way he caught the ball, the way he ran. I was so respectful of him, and even today when I see him I thank him as a leader—a guy who showed me how to do it right. I remember one time I was watching films, and he came in and he asks, "What are you doing?"

"I'm watching you play."

"And he sat down and we stayed there for a couple hours, and he is showing me what to do, and what not to. I guess at this point, he knew he was going to go somewhere else, and he kind of gave me the torch, so to speak. Ron, he has the biggest heart in the world."

Remember the joke about the two Boy Scouts arriving late to their meeting and being asked why they were late? They told the scout master they were determined to do their good deed for the day by helping an old lady across a street. They were delayed because she didn't want to go. Likewise, Fleming was a little too helpful pointing out his virtues to the general manager, "I had a great negotiation. I went in and I had a book of what I did the previous year—"Marv Fleming, Best Improved", "Marv Fleming is a great blocker", "Marv Fleming Wins Games," things like that. I had dates,

# The Lombardi Legacy

I had times, I had games, and all that, and he's looking through it. First of all, I wanted like a fifteen thousand-dollar raise, and he says, "You're no John Mackey."

"Sir, but John Mackey is not a Marv Fleming, and he doesn't play with the Green Bay Packers. Sir, would you look at this, please." And he looked at it, I said, 'Right there--'

Lombardi said, "I see it, I see it."

"The other page."

"I see it, I see it, too."

"You don't deserve it."

"Ooh, you should have gone for fifty thousand dollars," I thought.

From Marv's point of view there was little difference between general manager and Coach Lombardi, "I think he was the same--just a hard-assed Italian guy who wants to save a buck, and get the best out of the players."

Fleming was one of several players who left the Packers shortly after Lombardi put down the whistle, he played out his option, "I didn't feel I was getting paid enough and I wasn't getting any extras." With so many legitimate star players on the great Packer teams, there were not enough honors to go around; only so many Packers could be all-pros, MVP's, Rookies of the Year, and so on. For example, ten of Lombardi's players are in the Pro Football Hall of Fame, twelve if you count Lombardi and Emlen Tunnell. A team reaches a saturation point regarding post season and post career awards. As Marv says, "Like now, Robby should be in the Hall of Fame. Some of us were overlooked. I felt if I'd go somewhere else, I'd get a fresh start, which I did. When I got down to Miami I was a big cheese, huge cheese." Miami's new big cheese had jewelry unique to the area; three World Championship rings.

Miami built a powerful team in the early 1970's, and received a couple injections of talent during the first year of the decade, as Marv explains, "They needed two things, a tight end and a receiver. They got Paul Warfield and Marv Fleming. Paul was one third of our team, hear me, one third. If it wasn't for Paul, we never would have got it."

Forget pass receiving statistics for most tight ends, especially those who played in run oriented offenses like Green Bay's, and the one Fleming went to in Miami, with Larry Csonka, Jim Kiick, and Mercury Morris. "I got down there, I could block my ass off, and they threw me passes." Marv is not in either the Packer, or NFL Hall of Fame, and before his death, the great John Mackey clarified the role of tight end, "he said, "Marvin they utilize you differently, they take advantage of your blocking capabilities." With the Packers we had a balanced attack, we ran the ball, and did not rely on the passing game. Look at the Super Bowls; Bart passed twelve, or thirteen times. Lombardi believed in we keep the ball on the ground, it's our ball, and it's in our hands. Once it goes in the air, it's up for grabs.

"When I went to Miami, I don't think anybody with the Packers made as much money as I did, contract wise. My base contract was three times as large as it had been in Green Bay. I had a huge bonus, I had so many 'if's'; if I make the team, $20,000.00. *If I make the team?* Lombardi always said, "When you don't pay a man his worth, he cheats on you." So, I played my option out. A lot of teams wanted me, but the Packers wouldn't move."

So, Marv ended his career as a Dolphin, but his life was changed by Lombardi, "He was true to his word, I loved Lombardi, if it wasn't for Lombardi, I wouldn't be the man I am today. Coach Lombardi is one of the five people that gave character to my life. He said so many incredible things… One thing I can remember is, "When you win, you wallow in your victory, after you've played your heart out." I think about that, I see on television, when people win, I know they've sacrificed to be to that point; to wallow in your victory."

If given the chance to speak with him, Marv would say, "Wow. I'd say, 'Coach Lombardi, thank you for believing in me, thank you for making me into the person I am today, and I still live by your rules, and I remember you said, "Anybody can run the race, but you gotta run to win," and that's what

I try to do."

"Thank you Lombardi."

If you have a chance to meet Marv Fleming, do yourself a favor and take advantage of the opportunity, he is an entertaining part of football history.

# CHAPTER 22
# KEN BOWMAN:

*"I wasn't the kind of guy he wanted to sit down and have a cup of coffee with."*

# THE LOMBARDI LEGACY

A rugged warrior, Ken Bowman was Green Bay's center for 10 years after being drafted in the eighth round in 1964. Lombardi's offensive line was remarkably stable throughout the dynasty, with the exception of center. Jim Ringo, Ken Iman, and Bill Curry were in and out of the position for various reasons until "Bow" nailed it down in his rookie year.

The middle of Ken's forehead was raw during the season. It was gruesome to see the pulverized area where his helmet was repeatedly jammed into the front of his head by opposing defensive linemen. The nickname Frankenstein was perfect. Under his number 57 uniform, Bow's left arm was chained to his torso to keep his shoulder in the socket. Between the shoulder and elbow, he had a sheep skin padded leather strap connected to another just like the one wrapped around his chest. A section of chain connected the two straps. If his arm were raised above a 90 degree angle, he was at high risk to dislocate the shoulder. Both of his shoulders had been separated.

His passion for battle off the field manifested itself in union activities. Ken was the Packers player rep for five years. A union activist, he became vice president of the National Football League Players Association and was arrested in 1974 while leading a strike in Green Bay.

During his playing career, he attended law school during the off season, and became a partner in a successful law firm in DePere, Wisconsin. Ken and wife Rosann moved to Oro Valley, Arizona in 1994. These days he serves as a special magistrate for the city of Tucson.

Even though the AFL-NFL battle to sign college players was intense in 1964, Ken Bowman received little attention while at the University of Wisconsin. "Before I was drafted, I'm gonna say none. After I was drafted, Vern Lewellen came down to Madison and talked with me and basically tried to get me to sign a contract. I had been drafted by the Jets, actually the round earlier, so I got drafted by the Jets in the seventh round and the Packers in the eighth round. Back then, the game was to try to get them to work against each other to your benefit. But the Jets never contacted me. It was kind of funny, I got a hold of Weeb Ewbank years later, he was the general manager and coach of the New York Jets at the time and said, "We, what's wrong with you? Seventh round draft choice and you didn't even contact me, didn't even *call* me." He said, "We saw who drafted you in the NFL, you were a University of Wisconsin boy, at that time the Packers were the team of the decade. So we figured we were not going to be able to compete with 'em." I said, 'If you only knew, back then I didn't follow the Packers. I came from Chicago originally, if the Bears would have drafted me, you'd have had a problem.'

Bowman attempted to prod the two teams into a bidding contest for his services, "I tried to tell Vern Lewellen I had been drafted by the Jets and I was awaiting their initial offer. I think my first contract I got a giant $6,000 signing bonus and $12,000 for the first year. I became friends with various people who had been drafted when I went to all of the post collegiate games; East-West Game, Hula Bowl, and the College All-Star game down in Chicago. Most of those guys had signed contracts for twenty, twenty-five thousand bucks, and here I am sitting at twelve. I felt a little set upon until I got up to Green Bay and found that really there weren't that many people that were making any appreciable money."

When Ken got to Green Bay, there was a noticeable lack of centers on the roster. Jim Ringo had been dealt to Philadelphia and Ken Iman went to the Rams to complete the Zeke Bratkowski deal. Not a bad situation for rookie center, Bowman said, "When I got up there, they really were without a center. They tried Bob Skoronski at center; they put Norm Masters at left tackle. That was the year Jerry Kramer got hurt. We had to do some shuffling and move Forrest Gregg into right guard. It became a question of whether they put Norm Masters over at the right tackle position and put "Ski" back at left tackle and start me. Or, leave Skoronski at center and put Norm Masters at left tackle, and start Steve Wright (right tackle) who was a rookie in '64 from Alabama. Lombardi, I think, made the right choice, he started me and

I didn't ride the pines again unless I was hurt."

Some contract negotiations, for instance those of sixth round rookies, did not get Lombardi's personal attention, "My best recollection is Lewellen acted as the go-between for that first contract and I really didn't have any face-to-face with Lombardi. Back then, just about everybody signed a one year deal and you warranted in your contract that you were in top physical condition, you were in excellent physical shape, and you were basically capable of playing the game of football. So, if you got hurt, they had to pay you that one year, but after that you were done because obviously you breached your warranty. If you signed longer than one year, you signed one year deals. You hear about the deal, say a three year contract, well they had him under contract for three years, but he signed three one year deals. If you got hurt the first year, you breached your warranty in years two and three, so they didn't have to pay you."

Ken missed the majority of Packer training camp in 1964, "I got there late; I was in the College All-Star game. I didn't show up for the training camp part of it until August. The stuff over at Sensenbrenner Hall was pretty much over with by the time I got there. I had been down in Chicago and the coach down there was Otto Graham. It was more of a country club atmosphere. We came in and played the Bears in the All-Star Game about August 6th. Packer draft choices Lloyd Voss, Dennis Claridge, myself and I think, Tommy Joe Crutcher were down there in Chicago. The Packers were already into the exhibition season, the second week of the exhibition games were on that Saturday night, so we practiced just one practice a day."

Like so many others, Bow discovered that redoing a contract was not really a negotiation, "It really wasn't, he had a figure and you were gonna play for that, or that was it. I remember, I wasn't happy with the second year I got thirteen five. You go from twelve to thirteen five. But the second year, we got into the championship game. The third year we got seventy-five hundred. I think it was for the first Super Bowl. The nice thing about Lombardi, we

252

would get bonus money at the end of the year because we were always playing for championships. Everybody looked for that big bonus. Three of the four years he was there, I was there, we won the championship. It was kinda, 'Let's see, what am I gonna get if I go to Chicago and I might be able to up my salary five grand, the cost of living is gonna eat that up and rest assured I'm not gonna be in the Super Bowl.' He had some leverage due to the fact he was so successful.

"I can remember telling him I didn't think what he was offering was enough, the second year especially, I thought I was in for a pretty good pay day. Here I was, some college kid he was willing to pay a six grand signing bonus and twelve grand for the first year. I started the last eight games or something like that. You didn't really negotiate with him, I don't know too many people that did. Gale Gillingham *might* have, I know one year he played out his option, or tried to play out his option. Nobody was interested in talking to him so, he had to go back with his hat in his hand, and take whatever was on the table. That's kind of the way the owners worked though. While we didn't win anything that year, there were numerous other reasons why, I think that was the year after Paul (Hornung) was out with Pete Rozelle's suspension for betting on us. I can never understand that, you suspend a guy for a whole year for betting on his team. He's just confident we're gonna win, I mean, if I put some money on the Packers, I'm gonna go out and kill somebody to make sure I don't lose it. How is that detrimental to the game? Be that as it may, and I was kidding about killing somebody, there were any number of reasons why we didn't win in '64. You gotta understand these guys were used to winning. When I came into that I was kind of 'the kid,' I wasn't used to it. When I was here at the University of Wisconsin, we had one winning season.

"I can remember in '65 we were playing Cleveland up there in Green Bay for the championship, and Fuzzy's jumping around saying, "We're the champs again." I told him, here's me, a second year man, 'Hey, games not over yet.' Because I wasn't used to winning and a lot of fluky things can happen. I just wanted to be sure if we're gonna win this championship, we're gonna win this championship, we're gonna win it going away."

Union activities were and still are Bow's passion, he recalls what he saw in his rookie year, "I got there in '64, Skoronski was the alleged union rep and that was kind of funny because the reports we got back was they would have the owners meeting down in Miami. They would sit around the table and it would be like Bob Skoronski sitting next to Vince Lombardi and somebody else from, say the Cleveland Browns, sitting beside Art Modell, and somebody from the Giants sitting next to Wellington Mara. I can just imagine how much good faith negotiation went on around *that* table. After they were done negotiating the union contract, they would go out and play a round of golf or do something. It was more of a social club, at least that was the impression I got when we were in the early days, in '64. Then, Robby took it over in '66 and '68 we had a strike. I became player rep in '69 and I think I became the player rep because Robby has more intelligence than I. He realized this was the death knell of your career if you were a player. You either knuckled under and did whatever they wanted you to do, or if you stood up for your fellow players and your rights, you didn't last long. I can give you a couple examples, I know John Mackey in 1970 was voted the best tight end in the first 50 years of the National Football League, but he's also voted the President of the player's union the same year. He lost a step, gets traded to San Diego."

On the field, Ken Bowman was central to one of the most glamorized plays in history. Bart Starr's Ice Bowl sneak for the winning touchdown. The initial credit for the block went almost exclusively to Jerry Kramer, however, over the years it has become clear that Green Bay's center was in the thick of the play. Ken was asked if he has gotten his true credit over the years, "I don't know if I have or not. I know HBO did a supposed 'expose' how the other guy in the Ice Bowl blocked. The funny part about that is there are other people who had just a whale of a game in that game. I mean Lee Roy

Caffey, you talk to anybody on defense, he played about ten feet above his capabilities for that game. Boyd Dowler scored the second touchdown; there wouldn't have been any Ice Bowl block without him. We had the team and like I said, most of these guys were older guys and were used to winning. I guess by this time, it was the third championship that I was associated with, I was a believer, but it's awful easy to think this thing might slip away."

And Lombardi did not complement him on the block either, "No, no. Never." Getting approval from the Old Man was important to some, how about to Bowman, "Ah, I don't know, you know I was kind of outspoken. I think that's one of the reasons the guys wanted me to be their union rep, I was kind of outspoken and I would say what was on my mind. I didn't really think about what I'd say before I said it a lot of times. I remember one time we were watching films and I'll give the whole dialogue. Lombardi says, "Bowman."

"Yea."

"Bowman."

"Yea."

*"Bowman."*

"Yes sir"

"See yourself here?"

"Yes sir."

"You see that middle linebacker?"

"Yes sir."

"Can't you see that he's farther back on this play than he was?"

"I looked at him and if he was farther back he was maybe six inches farther back."

"Can't you see that?"

"I said, 'Coach, it was six of one and a half dozen of the other, I called it odd.' Back then the offensive line blocking was dictated on whether or not the center could get the middle linebacker. If he thought he could go out and get the middle linebacker, he'd call it where he got the middle linebacker. If you weren't gonna get him, you had to call somebody else out after him. So, six inches was ahhh, 'six of one and a half dozen of the other.'

"What?"

"Six of one a half dozen of the other coach."

"We had these blocking grades and that week he posted them up, you know. Forrest Gregg 90, on the pass, and 75 on the run and then "Bowman" 50-50. Forrest thought that was funnier than hell and said, "50-50. Bow, six of one, half a dozen of the other." So that's how I got to be player rep I think.

"As far as Lombardi and I ever sitting down and him saying, "Hey, I wanna talk to you-man-to man, or person-to-person." No. I don't know that I was his kind of player. I like to think I was. I like to think I played hurt a lot of times and I could suck it up and do it. I'm quite sure I wasn't the kind of guy he wanted to sit down and have a cup of coffee with."

# CHAPTER 23
# CARROLL DALE:

*"Thank God for the opportunity of
being in Green Bay."*

# THE LOMBARDI LEGACY

The Packers were World Champions in 1961 and '62, but missed the next two years. Between the 1964 and '65 seasons, General Manager Vince Lombardi made two significant trades. He fixed the kicking problem by acquiring Don Chandler from the New York Giants, and added a speed receiver through a trade with the Los Angeles Rams.

Carroll Dale, a small-town country boy from Virginia, came to Green Bay from LA, in exchange for linebacker Dan Currie. Not coincidentally, the Packers then captured three consecutive World Titles in 1965, '66 and '67. During those three years, Carroll caught 92 passes for 1,996 yards, 14 touchdowns, and an average gain of over 20 yards per reception. Lombardi got the speed receiver he needed and one of the finest human beings ever to wear a Packer uniform. Quarterback Bart Starr says of the acquisition of Dale, "He personified the approach Coach Lombardi took, because he was going after quality people. Those who did not want to, or who were reluctant to follow his guidelines and understand his principles of how it was always team first, they weren't around."

Carroll wore number 84 in Green Bay through the 1972 season before ending his career with the Vikings. He was a starting wide receiver for Minnesota, in Super Bowl VIII. Currie, the other half of the trade, played two years with the Rams before retiring in 1966.

A convincing case can be made that Carroll is one of the most important, yet under-publicized trades made by General Manager Lombardi. There is no doubt his addition to the Packers was a necessary ingredient in winning three straight World Championships from 1965-'67.

During his first five years in the league, 1960-'64 with Los Angeles, he and the Rams were winning about 30 percent of their games. When he was traded to the Packers in 1965, Carroll Dale knew what was going on in Lombardi Land, "Well, very much aware, because we were in the same conference--the Western Conference--and when we'd come to Green Bay, of course, we didn't have a lot of confidence. As a player, when Green Bay won the NFL Championship in '61 and '62, it was always on the news that Coach Lombardi bought the players' wives mink stoles and colored TVs, and so it makes your wife look at you kind of funny. We had a great deal of respect for Green Bay, and I guess fear of 'em, too. So when I found out I was traded to Green Bay in 1965, in the spring, I was overjoyed. It was like a Christmas present, because if I'd have had a wish for a team, not only because they were winning, because I'm a small-town boy and Green Bay was my kind of city to be playing in. Because in Los Angeles, you go somewhere and it takes you 30 minutes one time of day, and the next day, or it may take you two-and-a-half hours, so I was just thrilled to be part of Green Bay."

This man of Christian faith has an interesting story of coincidences or direct intersession by God, that led him to a college career worthy of a pro contract, and eventually to Vince Lombardi. As a freshman in college, it was improbable he would make the varsity. Carroll said, "I have often said I was very blessed. I can go back through my career going back to college when I made a decision to go to Virginia Tech, instead of the University of Tennessee. During the summer, there was one experienced receiver that had to pass one credit hour, he flunked. He went on to become a medical doctor. During training camp, an all-conference receiver breaks his ankle; career ending injury. All of a sudden, they had to call up a freshman, which happened to be me. The first game my freshman year the guy in front of me sprains an ankle, and I go on and start 39 straight games at Virginia Tech. That's when we played everything. They had that limited substitution, if you came out during a quarter you couldn't go back, so you had to play offense, defense, special teams; all of them.

"Then I go to the Rams, and I have a receiver coach named Tom Fears. We had five losing seasons. I had some tough moments out there. My first game as a rookie I catch five passes, one of them is a one handed catch for a 53 yard touchdown. The next morning I was up looking for the papers to read about the Rams new receiving star, and on Tuesday when we were working out, we're just loosening up and I pull a hamstring. So, back to humility, and it was a battle. Fears knew I was upset with the Rams and of course he had moved to Green Bay in 1964, as receiver coach. He thought a lot of me because he had a hand in trading Del Schofner to the New York Giants and keeping me at LA. I'm sure he had a great influence on Vince Lombardi to trade for me. Spiritually, what I do think of all those events? It's either a streak of good luck, or intervention, I don't know, but I have been blessed. I do know one thing, living a Christian life gives you the abundant life here on earth. I do know if we are truly trying continually to live a Christ like life, then we are going to reach our best potential as an athlete, as a father, grandfather, husband, or whatever. Of course, here I am at 71, and I'm still working on trying to improve in some areas. I'm a firm believer if we try to do what's right, we'll come closer to reaching our potential and being in the right place, at the right time, and those happenings I mentioned whether or not it was an intervention, or plain out luck, I don't know. But I was blessed, put it that way." So were the Packers, they got Carroll Dale.

Lombardi traded for a veteran and truly got a pro when he acquired number 84. The receiver was expected to hit the ground running in Green Bay, "Well, we didn't have any intros-I think his reputation preceded him. I think I got chewed out about twice from him, and then, I learned. First of all, if you dropped a pass, he'd holler at you, or tell you if you ran the pattern wrong; if you drifted downfield, always come back to the football-that kind of instruction. And then in meetings, there was only one answer to him, and that was, 'Yes, sir.' So, first time I was in a meeting, I think I tried to explain something and that didn't work. So, if you were trying to answer other than saying, 'Yes, sir,' while you were trying to give an excuse or something, and he'd just tell you, "Shut up and not give me any smart blank-blank answers." He was a guy you play your heart out for anytime. I felt that way then, and I still feel that way today."

Carroll found Lombardi to be, shall we say, efficient during contract negotiation sessions, "Well, they were pretty short." Lombardi was a devout Christian with a knack for the unexpected. Dale recalls a surprising contract resolution where two Christians emerged as winners. "One year, Coach Lombardi, being a very religious man, had to reach deep to try to give a little increase, so I told him I always tithe to my church. Green Bay wrote a check to my church for a certain amount; about 10 percent of my contract each year *for several years*. I got a little increase, but it didn't show up on my contract, see, so it helped him, helped me, too."

For those fortunate few who Lombardi traded for, invariably they were impressed by the man's character. He was a task master, tyrant and more, but Carroll noticed one compelling trait, "I think the greatest asset he had was he treated his players very fairly, and he did not jerk us around. I had played five years in L.A., which we talked about, and there, if you won, everything was hunky-dory, and if you lost, why then everybody went to pieces, with a lot of criticism and so forth. At Green Bay, Coach Lombardi did his coaching when we won. We were fortunate enough to win enough games, but when you won, why, he would chew butt, and if you won big, he'd chew harder. And if you lost, he'd still make corrections, but he wouldn't be nit-pickin', he'd make corrections and move on.

"I think we were playing the Baltimore Colts, or somebody, and I dropped a pass, and for some reason, he told me one of the reporters was trying to make something out of it and said, "How about Dale dropping that pass?" Coach said, "Well, he's caught a lot of good ones." And that was it. It's like everything else, he just stressed preparation, and I think that's a great asset—along with his coaching when we won. Human nature-wise, it's so easy to just be all smiles when you win, and not make corrections, and be hyper-critical when you lose, and that's human nature. Coach Lombardi with his experience, just knew how to handle players. If he was going to give somebody else another chance, he'd say, "Hey, I'm going to sit you down and give so-and-so a chance," and then he might come back and say, "Hey, you got your job back."

Carroll Dale was a football organizations dream. He was very skilled, devoid of ego, squeaky clean, and as solid a citizen as you could find. The buzz word today is "character," back then he was a good and descent man; still is. It is not surprising Carroll is humble and grateful to this day Lombardi wanted him. "Well, the trading for me was very meaningful, and just to be part of Green Bay and give me a chance to play, I'm very grateful for that. Somehow you knew he had confidence in you. I think he knew people from the standpoint of character and so forth. He tried to help build priorities in their lives, and of course, in my own life the spiritual has always been first and foremost. He taught that every year. He would tell us, "Hey, guys, there should only be three things on your mind: your church, God or religion, your families, and Green Bay Packer football, and nothing else." So every year, you got that speech, and I think it's a good idea to have that order; to have priorities and put first things first and realizing that football is very, very important, but still, it is just a game. So, to be part of championship teams and so forth, was just a wonderful experience and opportunity. Being a world champion, he gave me that opportunity. There's a lot of great football players who play in the NFL and never win a conference championship, let alone a world championship. To have that opportunity, not once, but three times is just very, very fortunate."

If given the chance to speak with Lombardi? "Well, I'd thank him very much for the opportunity, and for the job he did here in Green Bay, and pulling a variety of people together. He just made you feel like you were gonna win. And the story goes that when he came to Green Bay, he told the guys he'd never been associated with a loser and wasn't going to start, and if they didn't want to be winners, hit the road--the buses left Green Bay every hour, or something to that nature. I think basically everybody knew everything he did was to help us win. A lot of it was tough, but we knew it was to win, so that part you adapted to. So, I'd definitely give him a big hug and really a big thank you for the opportunity."

Does the credit go to God? "Yes, thank God for the opportunity of being in Green Bay."

If decency were a garment, it would fit Carroll Dale perfectly.

# CHAPTER 24
# DON CHANDLER:

*"You could hear him all over that county
up there just yelling at me."*

# THE LOMBARDI LEGACY

If Don Chandler would not have been with the Packers from 1965-'67, the team probably would not have won World Championships each of those seasons. The personable combination punter and place kicker was a real difference maker and only cost Green Bay a third round draft choice. General Manger Vince Lombardi acquired Chandler and Carroll Dale before the 1965 season, and those two were positively critical to winning three in a row. Beginning in 1963, when Paul Hornung was suspended, Green Bay's kicking game was a mess. One guy would punt, someone else would kick off, and somebody else handled placements. When Don was acquired, he tidied up the place by handling all of the kicking chores in '65 and '66, before Donny Anderson assumed the punting duties in '67.

Chandler had a remarkable 12 year career that saw him play in nine NFL Championship games and two Super Bowls. He played in the NFL's first two overtime games; as a punter and running back in the historic 1958 Giants loss to Baltimore, and as punter and kicker in the famous Packer-Colt playoff tilt in 1965. That was the game he hit a controversial 27-yard field goal with less than two minutes left that tied the game. To this day, some say the kick was good, some say it was not. The ball carried over the right upright of the goal post, no doubt it was close, but the posts were much shorter then, making the call difficult for officials. The following year, 1966, the league extended the height of the posts by ten feet, from twenty, to thirty feet above the crossbar. The extension has been referred to as "The Don Chandler Rule." Don hit the game winner in that contest, at 13 minutes, 39 seconds of overtime, from 25 yards, to send the Pack into the Championship game against Cleveland.

Chandler was with the Giants for nine years, including three seasons when Lombardi served, as what would be called offensive coordinator, in today's game. Because Don was a reserve running back, in addition to being the team's punter, Lombardi was his position coach and thus, Chandler had the unique distinction of seeing him operate as an assistant in New York, and

# DON CHANDLER

later as head coach in Green Bay.

Number 34 was selected as punter for the NFL 1960's All-Decade team and was inducted into the Green Bay Packer Hall of Fame in 1975. He is the only member of the Packer Hall to have played just three years in a Green Bay uniform, but what a three it was. In his short Packer career, he racked up 261 points, placing him ninth on the team scoring list when he retired. Don still holds the team record for longest punt at 90 yards. He scored five points in Super Bowl I, and 15 more in Super Bowl II, as the Packers finished off the threepeat.

Pat Chandler calls her husband Don, "The Miracle Man," not because of his athletic accomplishments; he has beaten cancer three times. Now that's a real hat trick. The Chandlers have been married for 51 years and reside in Tulsa, Oklahoma, where family, not football, occupies center stage of their lives. However, Pat is quick to add those football teams are family also.

Don Chandler nearly had no NFL career, because he walked out of the Giants training camp during his rookie year of 1956. An inaccurate story has made the rounds as to how and who fetched him back to camp. Don explains, "I think I'm the only one who made it to the airport, I don't know where I was going. I didn't have any money to get on a plane. Head Coach Jim Lee Howell came and got me; over the years the story changed from Jim Lee Howell to Coach Lombardi. I never tried to correct it, there wasn't any reason too." There have been accounts that say Lombardi retrieved both Chandler and Sam Huff from the airport, as Don says, "Well, that makes a good story."

Having played for Vince Lombardi in New York, Chandler describes how the assistant coach conducted himself in the Big Apple. "He was just like he was when he was the head coach; he was very demanding and very driven. He wouldn't accept anything but the best, which was part of his success, a big part of it. I think he was extremely loyal to his people until they did something that crossed him; they were gone."

# THE LOMBARDI LEGACY

The New York Giants of the 1950's, and early '60's, were a powerful team and Chandler went to the title game with them in 1956, '58, '59, '61, '62, and '63. However, the bottom fell out in '64, when the club slumped to 2-10-2, and the purge was on, according to Chandler. "They pretty well cleaned house. I think they sent Sam Huff away, Dick Modzelewski, I think Andy Robustelli retired, pretty much of a house cleaning. I was probably a bad actor. They did me a favor didn't they?" Yes sir, and Green Bay too. A lot of what was ailing the Packers got well when his talented foot arrived in Titletown.

Like Carroll Dale, Don Chandler was not a big city guy and he wanted to spend the week in Tulsa with his family and join the Giants to perform kicking duties on weekends. "That might have been one of the reasons they shuffled me off. They did me a favor, I'm not complaining. I was not a big fan of New York, of living up there the way we did in hotels. We were married, and had children, and ended up living in Connecticut in apartment houses with rented furniture and stuff like that." By 1965, Don had enjoyed all of New York he could stand and Lombardi gave him a ticket out.

Green Bay surrendered a third round draft choice for the answer to their kicking problems. "It seems to me like I got a call from either Vince, or Pat Peppler that they had made the trade. I didn't get one from the Giants I know that." Don was happy to get the boot out of Gotham City with, or without well wishes from his former team.

Given his druthers, he would have liked to have done more than kick. "At one time, I was an offensive back; I used to have to play every once in awhile in New York." He was not one of those specialists who would meander off in the corner of the practice field by himself; he was a football player and wanted to mix it up. "I would get in contract drills before Lombardi would know about it. When he found out, you know how he could yell; you could hear him all over that county up there just yelling at me. We used to run what they call the "nutcracker" drill and I'd get in there for nothing more than to spell the other guys, and I'd end up gettin' my butt chewed out."

The game became more sophisticated in the mid-1960's, and special teams were treated as an important part of the winning formula. Lombardi served as special teams coach.

"Sure, if anybody was thorough in their coaching, it was him. He covered all phases; we even had to view the special team's films. You know they used to break the films up into offense, defense and special teams." Lombardi paid attention to details that others around the league viewed as less important, and thus gained an advantage over the competition.

The 1965 playoff game with the Colts was a strange one. Both Baltimore quarterbacks, Johnny Unitas and Gary Cuozzo could not play due to injuries, Bart Starr was hurt on the first play from scrimmage, and only returned to hold for Chandler's kicks. The "Depleted Quarterback Bowl" had lots of pressure for the kicker as Don explains, "You put a guy out there under those circumstances, as I recall they were both fairly short field goals (27 and 25 yards), you're not supposed to miss those. If it would have been back 50 yards, why then, if you'd have missed it, people would have accepted it." Another source of pressure was the guy on the Packer sideline in the hat, "Absolutely, there's a lot of pressure in that. You bet you didn't want him giving you that look."

Despite tremendous success in the National Football League and his kicking skills in tact, Don knew when it was time to call it a career. "When I found out Lombardi was gonna retire. We kept our home in Tulsa, we lived up in Green Bay during the season. We had three school age children and you know, it was time. I played 12 years, and we'd just won three straight championships. My kids were all in school and what have ya, so it was time to quit. And be home year round."

"I did go up there and personally tell him I was retiring.

He said, "Well you didn't need to do that."

"Well I thought I did."

# THE LOMBARDI LEGACY

During his fine career, Don was selected for the Pro Bowl just once; following his final season of 1967. So, he could still get the job done when he hung it up.

Lombardi liked the familiar, therefore, it is reasonable to assume he would have liked to see number 34 trot out to kick for his new Washington Redskin team in 1969. Chandler is not one hundred percent certain, but thinks he got a call. "I'm trying to recall, I think somebody did make contact with me. I doubt seriously if it was him, he used to get other people to do his stuff pretty much." Lombardi loved those veterans and did coax linebacker Sam Huff out of retirement. So, Chandler was probably given a chance to kick in Washington. As further evidence, Lombardi changed kickers replacing soccer styled Pete Gogolak with the conventional Curt Knight, during his one year with the 'Skins. Don was a "straight on" kicker and the Old Man might have felt more comfortable with that.

Seventy-five years old, and living a contented life, Don Chandler leaves no doubt about his loyalty to his former coach and general manager. "Let me tell you something and I'll stand by it 'till the day I die. The success of the Green Bay Packers was a guy named Lombardi; nobody else. I'm not trying to downgrade Starr, or Hornung, or anybody else, they were all *exceptional* football players, but the guy that made the clock tick was the coach.

"You know, I had the opportunity to have a very, very nice career, in two places, the biggest market and the littlest market. I'm very proud of that."

Packer fans can be proud of this big time kicker with the little ego who helped secure the Lombardi Dynasty.

# Chapter 25
# Chuck Lane:

*"I figured it was cheaper than a casket."*

# THE LOMBARDI LEGACY

Chuck Lane was Director of Public Relations for the Green Bay Packers beginning in 1966. Like many in the Lombardi administration, Chuck was young, bright, observant, confident, teachable, meticulous, humorous, dedicated, and very well liked by the media. He dealt with the press very well, whereas, Lombardi viewed the Wisconsin media with disdain. Chuck lights up when talking about his former boss and readily confesses that meeting Lombardi so early in life, had one disadvantage, no one else ever came close to matching his impact.

Lane had two stints with the Packers, choosing to resign following the 1974 season due to a growing philosophical difference with Dan Devine. He returned to the organization as Publicity Director, when Bart Starr was named head coach and general manager in 1975. Despite having been Starr's biggest supporter to land the head coaching job, under pressure from the Packer Board of Directors, Bart dismissed Lane in 1980.

In the ensuing five years, Lane struggled for occupational stability, but in true Lombardi fashion he persevered. In 1985, he joined Employer's Health Insurance/Firemen's Fund. The company, now known as Humana, has been Chuck's employer for 25 years.

A Minnesota native, Lane grew up without a true "home team" to follow. Wisconsin had the Packers in football, and Milwaukee Braves in baseball, long before the Gopher State had a franchise in either professional sport, and Chuck was an avid and knowledgeable fan of both teams. When he was following sports as a kid, there were dynastys in all four major sports and the allure of excellence settled comfortably into his mind. Many times Chuck has said, "Give me those winners, the Montreal Canadians, Boston Celtics, New York Yankees, and Green Bay Packers." In 1966, at age 23, this Minnesota kid was allowed to step into his dream with one of those teams.

Chuck Lane reflects on good fortune. "I pinch myself every time I think about it because I was just plain lucky. I was in the right place, at the right time. I had a try out with the Minnesota Twins baseball team in Minneapolis, the curve ball got between me and a contract. I was living in the Minneapolis area just fiddlin' around, didn't know what I wanted to do, and my mom got me an interview with the president of the Minnesota Vikings. Come to find out, they were looking for someone with experience. Obviously, but he said I could work for him if I wished, promoting Harlem Globetrotter basketball throughout the upper Midwest, and Canada. I was working weekends with the Vikings, did that for three years, and unbeknown to me, there was a NFL league meeting going on and Jim Finks, General Manager of the Minnesota Vikings, met with Lombardi. Lombardi said he was looking for a young, single PR guy he could mold. Did Jim have any ideas? He said, "We got a guy right here, I'd hire him." So Lombardi told Public Relations Director Tom Miller to talk to me. I was lucky enough, I was in Green Bay, needed a cup of coffee, probably couldn't afford one, so I stopped by the Packer office to have a cup of coffee with Tom Miller. By the time that conversation ended, he virtually offered me the job, and asked if I'd be interested. What do you think? You know I'm out in the carnival life, trompin' around Canada, and the North Dakota prairies, you betcha I was interested."

Despite Lombardi's micromanagement style, he allowed Miller to hire an unproven Chuck Lane without meeting him. "I was there for about two days before I met the man. I was in the kitchenette one day and he was in there and I stuck my hand out and said, "Coach, I'm Chuck Lane, as long as I'm working for you, I oughta meet ya." He laughed and that's the way it started."

Imagine being twenty-three years old and having this living legend as your boss, how would you address him? Chuck says, "In fact, that was my first conversation with him. I said, "Mr. Lombardi, how would you like me to refer to you, what would you like me to call you Coach Lombardi, Mr. Lombardi, how do you like it?" He said, "Whatever you'd like, "Coach" would be fine too." Since then, a lot of people call him Vince, I never did in the years I knew him. Lombardi had an image in my mind of excellence.

# THE LOMBARDI LEGACY

I was a Packer fan, I was a pro football fan, I played college football; he was the epitome. I got here and it only improved from there, I mean a fabulous, fabulous human being. Very inspirational, frankly he had his warts that everybody's talked about, but I'll tell you what, to me, he was the absolute top drawer all the way."

Immediately, Chuck was aware Lombardi had an aura and a huge national appeal. "Did he ever. He could walk into a room and dominate. I saw him in a room with Hollywood stars, politicians, what not; they were in awe of him. That's where he stood. In fact, I brought it up to him once, I said, 'Coach, I really think you should get into motivational films, you've got a great message, I really think you should do that sort of thing.' He told me no. Shortly after that, he went off and signed a contract with Dartnell Corporation out of Chicago on a motivational movie and the theme of it was, do not take "no" for an answer. They say he made a million dollars, Dartnell made a million dollars and I got a $125.00 actors minimum for walking on the set and saying, "Coach, got a minute?" But yes, I do think he got a perspective of where he was going, his speaking engagements started to pick up, a lot of things fell in place and I think he saw he had a more prominent national stage than just Green Bay, Wisconsin."

According to Lane, Lombardi's administrative managerial style was like his coaching, basic. "It was a lean operation he ran there. I think he looked at the corporate expenditure as his own; he obviously didn't have a percentage or anything of that sort. He was one of those people who was so much in control he wanted to keep everything as lean as he possibly could. He got into such micromanagement, which was amazing; he was very effective at it. When you worked for him, you knew he knew every detail, every little minute detail he had in mind, he could see it, he would comment on it. So, therefore, he pushed you to a level of production and attention to detail that was second to none. He had total control and he worked hard at it. Was Lombardi difficult to work with? Not at all, there's one way to do it, if you did it his way, everything worked out fine."

The fit with Lombardi and the Packers seems so uncomplicated in retrospect. It was a franchise in need of a radical make over and in the relative isolation of Green Bay his dictatorial approach of total control worked magnificently. According to Lane, there was not a dimension of the organization, or person in it he did not control. "Absolutely none, absolutely none. I find it interesting, a lot of people say they weren't intimidated by Coach Lombardi, we were all intimidated. He could do things in Green Bay he probably could not have gotten away with in New York, and other larger metropolitan areas. Lombardi basically told the Executive Committee in person, "If you don't agree with me, I'll take away your "yes" vote." He had control here, it was a perfect match.

"He had six coaches; I think there were about six of us in the front office, which is amazing. Now they have 20 some coaches, and they have a hundred and ninety some, people on their payroll.

"I was probably 15, 20 yards away from his office. I remember, Coach Lombardi used to come down in my office, put his hands in his back pockets, look out the window, and he'd talk out loud. It was absolutely *fantastic*. He would just come down there and let his hair down and just discuss things, looking out the window.

"I remember one day being near the teletype machine when the AFL-NFL merger had come across. Another one, when the NFL had taken away his drafting of "junior eligibles." There was a system in existence, where you could draft junior eligible players, if they had already been in college four years. You could draft them in their junior year and they could continue their eligibility in college for one more year. We picked up people like Donny Anderson and Bill Curry. That was how Lombardi felt he could maintain his dynasty. When the league voted against that, he was absolutely livid. He predicted that would be the end of the Green Bay Packer Dynasty."

Packer President Dominic Olejniczak, helped screw that up. Ole, went to an NFL meeting with specific instructions from Lombardi to vote in favor of retaining the junior eligible rule and ended up voting the wrong way. Chuck said, "He did. You've done your homework. The Packers voted against Lombardi's proposal to maintain junior eligible drafting. Yes indeed, I was there the day it occurred. He was not happy and when he was not happy, nobody around him could be happy."

So, did Lombardi and Ole tangle upon the president's return? "I'm sure they did, but I was not there for it. The league has a policy that you can send two representatives to league meetings, but only one of them can vote. The other person had to leave the room when things came to a vote. Coach Lombardi was not there for that meeting because it was during the football season. What really rankled him was the fact that he could attend, he could represent the Green Bay Packers, but when it came to a vote, he had to leave the room. That just really got his goat."

Even though Lombardi brought unprecedented success to Green Bay, Chuck explains there were those on the Packer Board unhappy with their loss of power to him. "The seven man board was divided. There were probably the people who were not too happy with Coach Lombardi, then the people like Tony Canadeo and Richard Bourguignon who were close social friends of his as well. For whatever reason, in Packer history it's been a power struggle. When you have a strong coach, the Executive Committee is weakened, when you have a strong Executive Committee, the coach was weakened. You either have one, or the other, and it's been a constant struggle; it's been an antagonistic relationship between the two."

Young, but not dumb, on an advance publicity trip to the west coast in '67, Chuck found himself in a precarious situation where he could have caught the Old Man's wrath. With a strong sense of self preservation, he bought up all the newspapers in the Packer hotel to keep sensitive information away from his boss. "I did, I figured it was cheaper than a casket. I was out in San Francisco and they were trying to do an exposé on the Paul Hornungs, the

Max McGees, and the Donny Andersons. The single guys in Green Bay had a pretty good reputation in those times of being very social. I'm trying to play it down, I'm saying, "Well, really it's not a big deal because it's just a small city, single guys are out and about and everybody knows your business." And I said, 'I'm a single guy, I'm out and about, everybody knows our business, by and large you're seeing many of the same gals and you're hearing all the same stories, etc.' Well, the story broke in the paper and suddenly I'm one of the Hornung, McGee, Donny Anderson types and it sounds like we were a big social fraternity, rather than a football team. I thought, '*Oh my God*, this is not what I want Coach Lombardi to see the first thing he arrives in San Francisco.' So I bought up all the newspapers in the hotel. He would find out about it, but by that time hopefully, he won't go off. I don't know if he did or not, he never brought it up to me. It was not exactly the message I wanted. I thought I was gonna deflect a lot of this attention from the players, but it didn't seem to work out that way."

Little recognized is the remarkable intelligence of Vince Lombardi. As a coach at St. Cecelia High School in Englewood, New Jersey, he had teaching duties in addition to coaching. He taught chemistry, Latin, and physics at the high school level. Many very bright people are not highly emotional, but that did not apply to Lombardi and Chuck recalls being on the receiving end of one of his explosions. "He must have also studied gun powder. One day, a fella by the name of Bob Brockman, who worked for one of the San Francisco newspapers came to town. Bob's an old time writer and he expressed to me that he was a good friend of Lombardi's and had known him for years and years and years. I took him at his word.

"He had to leave town, but he wanted to see Lombardi. Coach had the team on the practice field, so I checked my watch, and said, "OK they should be off in about 15 minutes." I waited about 10 and took Bob down to the practice field to say hello to Coach Lombardi. Well, I'm walking onto the practice field when Boyd Dowler is coming back from a fly route and he said, "Watch your ass, the Old Man is really PO'd at you." I'm thinking, 'What in hell, I'm just bringing his friend out here to say hello to him at the end of practice.' Oh my God. But here again, Lombardi was putting on a performance for the players and he *chewed me out* and chewed his buddy, the writer, out. Later, he gave me hell again for bringing a spy into practice; he couldn't win with a spy at his practices. I tried to explain to him Brockman billed himself as a friend of his, that's why I delayed the arrival 'till a time when practice was supposedly over. Besides, I said, 'Bob doesn't know if the ball is pumped up or stuffed, he doesn't know what you're doing out here.' It didn't make much difference; he was performing for the players."

Lombardi had a huge ego and was reluctant to share credit for the team's success. Green Bay's defense under Phil Bengtson's direction was always among the leagues elite. When Chuck tried to give credit to the defensive coordinator, Lombardi set the PR Director straight. "Oh, I'm still healing up. I used to write the game programs and the news releases. The game program had a story on the upcoming opponent, the news releases gave the guys in the media some tid bits they could build upon for the promotion of that upcoming game. Our defenses in those days were pretty doggone good. I happened to make the mistake of writing in there that Phil Bengtson's defense was ranked number one in various categories. Of course, I had to clear the news release every week with Coach Lombardi. Well, he got down to the part where it was Coach Bengtson's defense; he corrected me that in no uncertain terms that wasn't Coach Bengtson's defense.

"That is *my* defense."

Chuck Lane is and was a straight shooter; members of the media could trust information that came from him either written or spoken. He, more than anyone, knows what Vice Lombardi's interactions were with the press and describes it. "I think in retrospect he had two standards: one for the local media and one for the national media. He was far more comfortable with those who he knew from his days at West Point and the Giants, and gave them far better treatment than he did to those here in Green Bay. I felt terribly sorry for Green Bay Press Gazette writers Art Daley and Lee Remmel here in Green Bay, who often felt his wrath. As was typical of the era, NFL teams seemed to think the media should be an extension of the team's PR Department and when and if they wrote anything deemed "negative" God help them.

The Coach got into it with all of them at one time or another, and one of the most uncomfortable 'dust ups' occurred when Coach Lombardi accused CBS broadcaster Ray Scott of saying something about Jim Taylor's situation (playing out his option). Actually I think it was Hal Scott, Ray's brother who worked for a TV station in Minneapolis, who made the supposition Taylor was going to New Orleans. Coach thought it was Ray who said it, or had leaked it to his brother, and that put me into a real firefight between Ray, who was himself pretty feisty, and Coach Lombardi, who wrote the book on volcanic behavior.

"He felt the media was something to be tolerated, and I'm not sure he was comfortable around them. He had gotten so badly treated by an Esquire writer named Leonard Schecter, who absolutely abused Lombardi's hospitality and time spent together at training camp in the summer of '67. I believe from that time on, no one was above suspicion. As it turned out, the national media rallied to the coaches defense after the hatchet job written by Schecter, who characterized Mr. Lombardi as some sort of Bavarian Madman, not unlike Count Dracula. It was about as bad a piece as I have ever read, and Coach had every right to be upset. He was betrayed, and that always hurts when you attempt to do something correctly and it gets turned against you."

Chuck said, "Being in the crossfire between these two forces was something, but I always understood whose name appeared at the bottom of my paycheck, plus I had such respect for the coach. It was easy for me to defend him, and there was so much positive and inspirational about him, that it was always an easy sell. Then, there were people like Tex Maule of Sports

# THE LOMBARDI LEGACY

Illustrated, Jim Murray of the LA Times, and countless others who had such respect for Coach, it made my job very easy. The players on his teams were always articulate gentlemen who were courteous, fun and had something to say. Tex Maule used to say, "Every team is a reflection of the coach," and the Packers under Lombardi were all he wanted them to be: professional in every sense."

Chuck saw the complex and contradictory side of Lombardi. Famous is Lombardi's dictum that God, family and the Green Bay Packers were to be priorities in the lives of those in the organization. God and the Packers received Lombardi's dedicated attention, in reality his family was somewhere down the list. "He had a son my age, Vince Junior. I worked for him in the United States Football League and I've hired him as a speaker in my present job with Humana. We've gotten, I think, to be fairly close friends. Coach Lombardi had two kids my age, Susan and Vince Junior. I have said this on many occasions, I hope it's taken in the right context, I think I had a better relationship with him than his own children. He didn't treat them very well, he really didn't, and it was a shame, because it took them a long, long time to come to grips with their father's treatment of them. He was so focused on football, the success of the Green Bay Packers and the control of that operation he put his children and family, unfortunately, in a secondary position. So, I had a privileged seat being one of the six people who worked for him in the front office."

According to Lane, there was an event in late 1967, which signaled trouble was looming for Lombardi. "He had physical problems going into that Ice Bowl game in that final year. I've heard since, on good authority, he'd passed out in the locker room during the week. Apparently, he had something at that time; extreme exhaustion, brooding colon cancer issue, it was debilitating, whatever it was it manifested itself in his later stages at Green Bay and it scared him to death.

"The players used to say, "Our injuries never bothered him," and there was some truth to that. I used to get a kick out of this, because he was a bit of a hypochondriac. Like an ingrown toe nail, he used to go into the training room and the trainers would remove it, or do whatever they had to do, and he would just bellow like a wild creature. He wasn't very good with his own pain and he was oblivious to others. But, I think he knew there was something wrong, and he ignored it for so long, thinking that he had such strength he could overcome it. He was a man of contrasts without a doubt and that's one of the things that's a contrast and tough to explain."

The tyrant, dictator image *is* Lombardi; however, he was a father figure with a soft side according to Lane. "Yea, very much so. I'll tell you what; he was absolutely wonderful in so many ways. I lost my dad when I was young. I was seeking a father figure and he was it for me. I was 23 years old, I was working with this guy I had the utmost respect for and I think he cared for me a certain way which was very nice. We just shared a *great* relationship. Yes, he did have a soft side. When he left Green Bay for Washington, he had a little fatherly chat with me. I'm driving him to the airport, we had a two seater Corvette with his golf clubs, he and I in it; he was giving me some excellent advice about my future. He was spot on; he called the shot right away. He told me people had been close to him would be an endangered species with the Packers, so be very guarded because of my association with him. I would probably have a shortened career."

Following the trip to Austin Straubel Field, Chuck returned to the Packers offices and ran smack dab into the reality of the emptiness. "It was almost like a death and then unfortunately we experienced that as well. I wrote a piece for the game program, the summation of my emotions about the coach. I accessed a bunch of Vern Biever's photography and we ran a two page spread in the game program with various shots of him, showing the fact he was inspirational, hard working, driving, demanding, de da, de da. It was kind of my tribute to him and then the last picture I remember was a picture Vern shot of the empty office, and I finished it up with, "And now he is gone." It was pretty traumatic, still is."

Those touched by the Lombardi greatness usually experience a certain lifelong emptiness, for the rest of their existence, no one matches up. "Never. Everything after that is second place, I can truly say that. I've had some great experiences in my life, I've met some fantastic people, I've traveled the world, but everything is second place. Any time you do anything, are you gonna deliver a hundred percent effort, or are you gonna give it a half assed effort? I keep thinking, Coach Lombardi would be so disappointed to think I had done something that wasn't my best, delivered a product that wasn't up to his standards. His standards were the highest. He got you to go excel, to go that extra step or two for excellence; everything was the pursuit of excellence, and he was very, very effective. You see pictures of him in the locker room after the Ice Bowl, tusslin' the hair of the players, and putting his arm around 'em. That, I'm sure had an effect better than the checks, better than the rings. The appreciation from the great leader was more than anything. Having that relationship, having those memories, that means more than anything."

Older now, than Vince Lombardi was when he died, and with 40 years of reflection, Chuck Lane would say this if he could talk with Vince Lombardi, "I would start off with "thank you," and try to tell him just exactly what he meant; I probably couldn't adequately do that. I would tell him one of my greatest memories was sitting in the press box with him watching the Packer, Redskins game. That was the weekend he apparently struck the deal with Edward Bennett Williams to go run the Redskin organization. I think that is one of the memories that will stick with me forever; sitting in a press box watching a football game next to the greatest coach to ever be associated with the game of football. Sitting in there like two guys at the bar discussing a football game with each other. *It was just a memory of a lifetime.*

"But what was amazing, talk about naivety on my part; *I'm giving him my opinions.* I played college football and I'm a fan of the game, but I'm telling him what I think is going on, on the field. He would say, "Yeah, but yeah......" We were just back and forth and talking almost as equals and that was what made me feel darn good."

To paraphrase something said after his death, don't feel sorry for Vince Lombardi, feel sorry for those who were not touched by him. Chuck Lane is among the fortunate who were touched by greatness and carried it forward.

# CHAPTER 26
# TOM BROWN:

*"I still was a baseball guy and I really loved baseball."*

# THE LOMBARDI LEGACY

A versatile and gifted athlete, Tom Brown had his choice of playing major league baseball or professional football. He did both. Vince Lombardi thought enough of Tom to spend a second round draft choice to land him in 1962. He was first team All-American in baseball at the University of Maryland, as well as, an All-Atlantic Coast Conference selection in football. He opened the 1963 season on the Washington Senator's roster as a switch hitting outfielder, but finished the year in the minors. He became the first man to play Major League Baseball and participate in two Super Bowls. With so many stars on the Lombardi era teams, it's easy to overlook Tom Brown. Similarly, with the attention placed on the Ice Bowl, it's easy to forget Tom's interception in the '66 NFL Championship game that put Green Bay in Super Bowl I. Wearing number 40, he played safety for Green Bay from 1964-'67.

While he is proud of his football accomplishments, Tom takes at least as much satisfaction from his work with youngsters over the past 35 years near his home in Salisbury, Maryland. Since 1974, Tom Brown's Rookie League has been dedicated to teaching youth sports in a positive sports atmosphere. Students in the Rookie League learn to play as a group with instruction in a relaxed, positive fashion. The kids learn a love for the game from a man who cares about them and the game. Tom and Nancy Brown have poured their hearts into America's youth by helping introduce young people to athletics.

Tom Brown explains why he chose the Senators over Green Bay.

"Well, because I grew up playing baseball—my whole career, ever since I was 10 years old, I played baseball. In the summertime, when I was in college, I went to South Dakota and played two years there. I was a baseball player in a football sense, because football, you got a scholarship. In college, there was no scholarship money for baseball. But you only have the hammer one time in your life—when you're being recruited, and that's the time when they say, "We'd like for you to come to the University of Maryland." And I had the best agent in the world, my father. He said, "Let me handle this."

# TOM BROWN

So he told University of Maryland football Coach Tommy Nugent, "My son will come to Maryland if you let him play baseball in the spring." Nugent said, "Spring. That's spring football practice."

Dad said, "Yeah, I'm aware of that, but he's not gonna come to spring football practice, he's gonna play baseball. If you want him, those are the terms."

So Nugent said, "I tell you what we'll do, freshmen are not eligible to play varsity sports so, he only has to play one year of spring football practice--that's his freshmen year." So, that's what I did. The rest of the time I didn't have to go to spring football practice. That's a terrible time. Football players hate spring practice, 'cause there's nothing to look forward to—just a big head-whoopin."

Tom had a chance to join the Packers when they were at their best. In 1962, everything came together, the talent stock piled by Jack Vainisi and the trades and drafts consummated by Lombardi, put the roster in great shape. It was year four under Lombardi's whip and the combination of player's age and experience was ideal. It was a golden time for the green and gold. Brown decided not to join the NFL World Champions for the '63 campaign. "Well, I still was a baseball guy and I really loved baseball. I went up to Yankee Stadium in 1962 for the NFL championship game. It was a cold, windy, frozen day and I'm in the locker room with the players, and I said, "These guys are so big, I'm gonna go play baseball." I missed the whole '63 football season. In December, at Christmas time, Lombardi calls me up and he says, "We're still interested in you for football, but you can't miss another year."

I told him, 'Well, there's nothing happening in football until July. I'm going to play baseball until July 1st, and then I'll make up my mind.' It's the worst thing I ever did, because it always gave me an out. If I was 0 for 3 or 0 for 4 in the minor leagues, I could tell myself, I could always go play football. So it was bad."

When Tom made his decision to play baseball, Lombardi did not beg, plead or blow up. "No, I don't think he did. He probably knew I wasn't going to do very good in baseball. But I think I could have. I think I could have been a journeyman player. I was a switch-hitter, I could run good. I was a good baseball player, not a particularly strong home run-hitter, but I was an overachiever. And that's the kind of guys that really do good under Lombardi."

After a year and a half between the major league Washington Senators and their top minor league affiliate, Tom made the switch to football, without talking with Lombardi. "Actually, he never talked to me after that. Lewis Anderson, he worked in the Pentagon—he was the contact on the east coast for all the draftees— he arranged everything. He told me how much they were going to pay me. I only talked to Lombardi that one time—at Christmas time, and then I went up there about July 6th, when I reported to the Packer training camp."

There were actually three professional choices for Brown because the AFL had strong interest. "Yes, yes. I was drafted number two by Buffalo. I went up to Buffalo, and they played in old War Memorial Stadium. I got letter after letter. I must have gotten a thousand letters from the Buffalo Bills, but when you have an opportunity to play for the World Champion Packers, no, I would have never gone to Buffalo, but baseball—I really did love baseball."

During the 1966 NFL Championship game against the Dallas Cowboys, Tom Brown was directly involved with the biggest, most under publicized play in Green Bay Packer history. The Pack held a rather comfortable 34-20 lead in the fourth quarter, when Dallas' tight end Frank Clarke got behind Tom for a 68-yard scoring pass, pulling the Cowboys within a touchdown. On the very next Dallas possession, Clarke ran the same pattern and was about to break clear for what would have been the tying score, when Brown grabbed him and drew an interference call, putting the ball on the two. The penalty saved a touchdown. Following a Cowboys off-side and three more plays, quarterback Don Meredith faced a fourth and goal from the two. Then, came *the* play. Blitzing linebacker Dave Robinson got to Meredith, forcing him to throw off balance and early, allowing Tom to intercept the looping pass, seal the victory, and send Green Bay to Super Bowl I.

Tom was not completely impressed with himself. "It wasn't so great. No, no, I caused them to go down there. I interfered with him and put the ball on the two-yard line." If the interference would not have been called? "He would have caught a touchdown pass. Yeah. Yeah. Dave Robinson was the guy who made the play. Obviously you have to be at the right place—and we had a certain defense called with Herb Adderley and myself—but Dave made the play. He was the one who forced Don Meredith to throw the ball up in the air--it was fourth down. If it was less than fourth down, he would've probably taken the sack.

"Dave made the play—he acted instinctively and--listen, if there's any man who should be in the Hall of Fame, it's gotta be Dave Robinson. It's a crime that he is not in the Hall of Fame. He was the smartest linebacker, outside linebacker. I can't imagine anybody smarter than he was. He knew his responsibility, he knew the responsibility of his guys behind him and he knew the guys in the back counted on him to be in a certain spot, and that's what made the Packer defense so good. If we knew where our help was coming from, we could compensate, because a lot of times, they wouldn't throw into coverage because somebody was there. We weren't playing for individual glory; for an interception."

When Lombardi graded the play, he gave Dave a minus two. Tom thinks he received a zero. When Brown was asked if the Packer Coach said anything to him after the game, Tom simply said, "No."

There is one sad dimension to the 1966 Championship game against Dallas; it was overshadowed, obliterated by the Ice Bowl a year later. Those games were so similar and featured the mental discipline and toughness of the Lombardi teams. According to Tom, "I just think it's a matter of pride in your performance, being ready to make the big play, do your assignment first, and then good things might happen to you. Two bad things happened to the Cowboys—fourth down in 1966 Meredith throws an interception—fourth down, Starr in the Ice Bowl goes for the touchdown. We made the plays; they didn't make the plays. But then, they made the plays later on; the next year, and the next year. They weren't ready to win those in '66 and '67." Regarding football per se, Tom and his defensive mates had limited interaction with the head coach, "We never, ever saw him in a defensive meeting on Tuesday when the films came out. He never came into the defensive meetings. He didn't do anything on the field with defense. All he would do is get after us if we didn't hustle during the week, or we didn't make the play he thought we should make. He never, to my knowledge, came out on the field. Now, he hollered at us on Sunday, "What the hell is going on out there?"

When Lombardi moved to the Washington Redskins in 1969, three of his former players, Bob Long, Chuck Mercein and Tom Brown tried to make the squad. Only Long actually played in regular season games for both teams, but Brown had a strong desire to play in the nation's capital. "I called him when I found out he was coming to Washington, and I asked, 'Is there any way you could trade for me, I'd love to play in Washington?'

He said, "Well, I'll see what I can do." About three weeks later, I get a call from Joe Blair, who was their public relations guy--he was at Maryland when I was at Maryland—he says, "Guess what? You're now a Redskin."

So Lombardi just said, "I'll see what I can do." He never guaranteed me anything. I wanted to play free safety—I never played free safety in Green Bay, I was always the left safety. Willie Wood was the right safety—and I wanted to get an opportunity to play free safety because, see, I was a centerfielder in baseball. Centerfielder in baseball is a lot like a free safety in football. I wanted to get an opportunity to do that, and I just loved playing for him because he was mentally tough. He made me play better than I ever thought I was capable of doing, it was just a great experience.

# TOM BROWN

"I'm a Washington boy, Silver Spring, Maryland, and the Redskins weren't very good at that time, and I knew he was gonna bring a Super Bowl there—there was no doubt in my mind, and I guess I was looking at it from a standpoint of selfishness. I wanted to be there when they were going to win a Super Bowl, because the town would be going crazy. Unfortunately, it didn't work out. Number one, I had a bad shoulder—Jackie Smith fell on my shoulder and dislocated it in, like 1966, and the trainer in Washington didn't know how to tape it. Packer's trainer Bud Jorgensen could tape my shoulder where it would never pop out. But up in Washington, I had two dislocations during the exhibition season, because I was just an arm tackler. My job was to make sure that nobody caught passes deep, and Lombardi said, "Just get 'em down. Just hold on to 'em until somebody helps you." In Washington, I dislocated it twice, and he said, "Listen, we're not going to win this year. But I think we have a good chance next year. Get yourself operated on, get it fixed, and we'll be much better next year." He died before that next year came."

When Lombardi accepted the Green Bay job in 1959, he took veteran defensive back Emlen Tunnell with him from the New York Giants. Tunnell served several roles in addition to playing. He was a solid professional and strong leader who knew Lombardi's ways and could convey that to his new team. Ten years later, Lombardi made Tom Brown the Washington version of Emlen Tunnell, even though Tom did not realize it at the time. "I think he just brought me there thinking I could tell those guys--and you were the first one to say he brought in Emlen Tunnell—I probably was, yes. But I didn't play that year. I played the first half of the New Orleans preseason game; I didn't play the rest of the season. As the year was going on, he probably would have come to me and said, "You've got to do some things now, because I'm comparing you to Emlen Tunnell." But he never came out with that, but that's a good comparison. Yeah, they always came to me and said, "what's gonna happen next?"

"But you know what? He wasn't as tough that first year as he was in Green Bay, especially in the grass drills. But, I think he also felt sick. He had cancer; he might have had some part of cancer, he didn't get it checked, and when he finally got it checked, it was the worst cancer—black cancer—just closed him up. In Washington, I think he was feeling pain. I remember somebody saying he was taking a lot of aspirin.

"I think it really was affecting him, his energy, and all that. He put so much energy in that last year in Green Bay. He said, "You guys have a chance to create history." You know, it's unbelievable that nobody gives us credit for winning three in a row—it's like, "Well, you won the first two Super Bowls-- when the AFL came in, but that was wrong. We won in '65 and *then* they came in; we won three in a row. Nobody's ever won three championships in a row, and he drove us that year harder than he ever drove us the years before. It could have been worse his first two years in there, but it certainly was the hardest year I had, as far as mentally and physically, him driving us to perfection."

Lombardi's lessons are engrained in Tom Brown like stain in wood. Tom said Lombardi told him, "I want you to do your best. When those fans leave the stands, they'll say I just saw the best safety man I ever saw. You're not gonna be an All Pro, but I want you to be the best that you can be, and I want you to practice hard every day, because you're going to play the game on Sunday exactly the way you practice during the week."

"You know, the Detroit Lions, Chicago Bears, everybody had the same physical ability as we had—they were just as fast. But they didn't have the mental toughness, and they didn't understand what Lombardi told us— "Three plays are going to make the difference in the outcome of the game. And you never know when those three plays are gonna come." It could come in the first quarter, the third quarter, or the last two minutes of the game. That's why you have to give 100 percent—120 percent—on every play. You could watch the films of some of the Bears, some of the Lions. When they played the Packers, they played 100 percent on every play. The next week or the week before that, they didn't play 100 percent."

Tom and Nancy Brown have spent the better part of a lifetime helping youngsters fall in love with sports. The former safety is confident Lombardi would like Tom Brown's Rookie League, "I think he would be proud of what I did in my life after football. He said, "Just do the best you can after your playing days are over. Whatever you're gonna do, do it to the best of your ability." And if Lombardi were to come to me and say, "You really did a great job the last 35 years of your life. You did something that you like to do, you found a niche and you were able to develop that niche where you really worked and developed something for little kids and made them understand what sports is all about. So you made a contribution in your community." That would be very, very important to me.

"I have this little camp—I've been doing it for 35 years—and I just try to tell the boys a little bit of the experience I had with Lombardi--but they don't even know who Lombardi was—their parents do. I just tell 'em that Lombardi would have never coached the youth kids as he coached professional athletes. Unfortunately, all the youth coaches are coaching the way Lombardi did."

When Vince Lombardi died at 6:30 on the morning of September 3, 1970, Tom experienced it in a very personal manner. "I was with the Minnesota Vikings; I got cut by the Washington Redskins after Lombardi died. They had a new coach, Bill Austin and he cut me. I was in Minnesota, where Jerry Burns picked me up. At 6:30, I woke up and I found out that morning Lombardi died around 6:30. I swear to God, I woke up right then. When I woke up, and went to breakfast they said, "Did you hear what happened to your old coach?" They said, "He died this morning." I couldn't believe it."

# CHAPTER 27
# DONNY ANDERSON:

*"He put his arm around me and said, "Today, you became a man."*

# THE LOMBARDI LEGACY

Donny Anderson probably had a better career than you thought. He accumulated 8,225 all purpose yards and averaged 12.2 yards per catch on 209 receptions out of the back field. For many years now, every punter is evaluated on "hang time." That's the amount of time the punt is in the air allowing the coverage team to get down field in order to restrict return yardage. Donny Anderson originated the concept of "hang time." According to Wikipedia.org, in 1967, Anderson punted 63 times and opponents returned only 13 of them for a total of 22 yards. That's about one third of a yard per return.

He was a running back and punter for Green Bay from 1966-'71, and handled the same duties for the St. Louis Cardinals from '72-'74. This proud Green Bay Packer was inducted into the team's Hall of Fame in 1983.

Donny, and fullback Jim Grabowski were known as the "Gold Dust Twins" or "Million Dollar Babies," because of the huge contracts they signed during the height of the AFL-NFL bidding war. Donny's contract was the largest in pro football history to that point, and to some degree it overshadowed his playing career.

The NFL had a rule that players were eligible to be drafted if their original class had graduated, even if the player had not. Donny fell into that category because he was red shirted his freshman year. In an attempt to replace an injured and aging Paul Hornung, Anderson was drafted as a "future" by General Manager Lombardi in 1964. Due to the Packer's strong and deep roster, the team could afford to wait a year before Anderson graduated from Texas Tech. Donny was a consensus All-American as a junior, and senior, as well as Sporting News Co-Player of the Year in his final season. Therefore, he was the pick of litter for Lombardi. With his pride on he line, Green Bay's general manager was going to do what he could to sign his future halfback.

The AFL-NFL war reached its peak in 1966. Of the 111 players drafted in '66, by both leagues, 79 signed with the NFL, 28 with the AFL. Four did not sign. The NFL and Green Bay Packers needed to sign Donny Anderson

# DONNY ANDERSON

for image if nothing else.

Wining three consecutive championships was a goal of Lombardi's and he nearly did it twice. From 1965-'67, Green Bay accomplished the feat and it stands as a singular three-peat in the modern NFL era. The epic Ice Bowl battle was a shinning moment for Anderson. In normal conditions, his 18 carries for 35 yards and four receptions for 44 would be ho-hum. That day, at Lambeau Field, was far from normal. He came up big in the historic Packer win.

During retirement, he has been very involved in Packer Alumni functions as well as efforts to help fellow retired NFL players who have encountered difficult times. He cares about the Packers and the people who have played the game. Green Bay's number 44 has earned the ultimate player complement; Donny Anderson was a good teammate.

His story reveals the obstacles he overcame to leave his native Texas in order to join Lombardi's Dynasty, contribute to winning three consecutive World Championships, and gain his coach's approval.

Donny Anderson describes his reaction to being chosen by Green Bay: "Surprise more than anything else. I had not had anybody call me or anything, being a junior, but being eligible for the draft. The Cowboys had talked to me a little bit about drafting me, but that was it. Thanksgiving 1964, Lombardi called and said, "We just drafted you in the first round." I was working on having a baseball career, that's really what I loved to do is play baseball. That was my dream. The fact the NFL and AFL were negotiating at that time, fighting against each other, and the Houston Oilers drafted me in the first round. So, for some reason, I chose to play my senior year. I was drafted by the Packers and by the Oilers, because I was a red shirt in '62, which my class graduated in '64. That was Joe Namath's year. The year I was a junior, he was a senior. Most of the salaries doubled, so from that stand point, it eliminated baseball."

Anderson took a chance by playing his senior year at Texas Tech. He

297

avoided injury, racked up All-American honors and saw professional football salaries sky rocket as the AFL and NFL opened the money vaults. He gave us a glimpse of his character by playing his final year, rather than grabbing the cash.

"Obviously, from that stand point it would have been a big contract if I would have signed. I'd have probably got three, four-hundred thousand. Oilers owner Bud Adams had a lot of money, and being a Texan, that was one of the things that shined like a star for me. But, I always felt the Packers were the Yankees of football, and Lombardi at that time had already won three championships. So, I knew there were quality people, with all the makings of having championship written all over it again. The Houston Oilers did not have that offensive line, didn't have all the things. I don't think you play well in football if you don't have a good offensive line, I just don't think it works."

Funny how it went, he had a dream to play baseball, a club willing to give him a contract and he didn't sign, "The New York Mets offered me a pretty good contract at that time in '65, actually about $35,000, which was pretty good money. My life was just timing, it was strictly timing. I think Pete Rozelle told Lombardi and the other NFL teams they better sign people, or they're gonna lose them all. Lamar Hunt, Kansas City Chiefs owner, told me this story years ago. AFL owners copied the NFL verbatim. The absolute best NFL franchises in the world, right? His daddy, H. L. Hunt had taught him that, "If you want to be the best, copy the best, and if you can't copy the best, go to work for 'em." They had more money than the NFL owners, the AFL did, so they were gonna sign people, and they did, they signed a lot of people. They finally said, "We're giving away money here." They merged the leagues and that was the end of the big money. Two years there, '64, '65."

There are two ways to spell Bud Adams. 1). B-u-d A-d-a-m-s. 2). Phillips Petroleum Company. The second version complicated Anderson's decision, "Well, my father worked for Phillips Petroleum Company. My dad was a cowboy, rodeo type performing guy that roped forever, 'till he was 50 years old. His personality was such that he would just say, "Well Son, go ahead and get it over with, you know, sign with the Oilers and let's move on. You've got three uncles who live down in the Houston area working for Phillips." So that was a very difficult time. At 21 years old, I had to tell my dad I was not going to sign with the Houston Oilers. Bud Adams jacked up the price, way up higher than the Packers, as far as overall money. Actually, he got in the nine hundred thousand range. I just felt it was better for me to try to be a Packer and it turned out well."

Adams had lots of assets, but it came down to real dollars. "He didn't offer me a lot of money; it was more like service stations. Phillips 66 service station leases for twenty years, that type of thing. But the Packers had very little to offer, other than money. When you figure cash, cash is king. Then Bobby Layne, the old famous NFL player Bobby Layne said, "Just take cash, take money, all the rest of it doesn't matter." He told me that three, or four times. The Packers were cash king at that time, where Bud was more, "I'll give you a house." I remember a little bit about a house that had 21 rooms in it, seven bathrooms, and a swimming pool worth $35,000.00. It was three hundred grand, or something, remember that? That doesn't impress anybody probably, unless your 40 years old and it's paid for. It would be a nice asset, but we never got into that. So, the cash was not nearly what the Packers offered."

The first face-to-face meeting between Lombardi and Anderson occurred December 12, 1965 following a 42-27 Packer win over the Colts. Donny remembers the encounter with crystal clarity. "Well I went to Baltimore. I recall because it was a foggy day and Hornung scored five touchdowns. I went up to see the game. I met with Lombardi, and Lombardi had very few words. He just looked at me and said, "Are you gonna play for the Green Bay Packers, can we sign you?"

"Well we're working at it."

"What's it gonna take?"

"Right now I'm working with my agents, my lawyers to get a contract."

I was looking at a TV screen, and he didn't have any time, and he hollered at Pat Peppler and said, "Turn that TV off; I can't even get this kid to pay any attention to me." He turned the TV off, and I looked him right in the eye and said, 'Well, if we're gonna get it done.'

"Well do you wanna play for the Green Bay Packers?"

"I'd like to."

"Fine." Shook my hand, we got up and he left.

"Pat Peppler was the guy that went in and negotiated all the contracts for Vince Lombardi. He spent a lot of time with me. He'd say, "Well, are we gonna sign you?"

"I don't think so, Houston just keeps coming. I got a car for my mom, a car for my brother.'

"Lombardi would get mad, "What does this kid need three cars for?" Peppler said told him, "The kid's a country cowboy, he's gonna give one to his mother, one to his brother."

Lombardi said, "Oh, he's a good boy."

So, once he figured all that out, that it wasn't just for me, we went on down the line. Vince made a decision to sign Grabowski and I, and Gale Gillingham, which was the three number ones he had drafted."

There has been speculation all these years every NFL team had to pony up money to pay Donny's contract. Pat Peppler doesn't think so and Anderson says, "I don't know the answer to that. I would doubt that, but I do not know that."

Even Lombardi's rules took a hit during the AFL-NFL bidding war. Under normal circumstances, he would not pay rookies more than veterans. According to Donny, "I think when Pete Rozelle came and told George Halas and Vince Lombardi they better sign some kids, that went out the door. I think Vince's biggest deal was he knew they had to sign, or the AFL would eventually have more power than the NFL in negotiations and mergers.

# DONNY ANDERSON

"The biggest thing with Lombardi and rookies, you just didn't play football, you played special teams. You were not counted on, because through his experience, rookies just made too many mistakes. Grabo and I didn't play unless somebody was hurt, and Gillingham didn't play much, we were on special teams. The next year we were thrown in there with a year of experience, but it was not playing experience. I wish I would have played a lot more my rookie year. I punted a few times. He didn't really say, "Go watch this or do that." Your players teach you a lot. Lee Roy Caffey and Dave Robinson taught me how to run certain patterns and how to pick up linebackers; things like that. You learn more from your teammates."

Speaking of teammates, how were the two rookies received by the veterans?

"Actually, they were warm and considerate. I don't know if Lombardi talked to the team about it, saying, "We're bringing these kids in, they got a lot of money, and we know you guys are not making that." Everybody was fine, and I don't think Grabo and I were pressured kind of guys. He actually met with Jimmy and I, and had us come into his office and tell us, "Hey, you guys are on the team, don't worry about it, don't be pressurized, don't get nervous, you're on the team. Just go out and practice, learn the system, learn how to play and don't be nervous. Don't put it all on your shoulders that your gonna start and play and do all these things." He didn't tell us we wasn't gonna play that much; that was the disappointing thing. We didn't get to play much. I think I carried the ball 25 times the first year.

"We were probably humbled more than anything else to be with the Green Bay Packers. The World Champions. Our athletic skills were strong enough we could make the team and be part of it as number one draft choices. Obviously, your gonna play if your number one, your gonna get a chance to play. I think Ray Nitschke was probably the only one that growled, more than anybody else, but he growled everyday anyway. It was difficult at first, but once they learned our personalities and they put all that together, it was about the Green Bay Packers and playing football, we moved on. We got bonus monies and insurance deals, making more money than most all the guys, but Bart Starr made more money than Jimmy and I did the first year. There were guys in the 20's, and I just barely got over thirty thousand my first year. So, it was not lopsided from that stand point. Then, the Super Bowls became very important because everybody doubled their salaries with the playoff games, as well as the Super Bowl money. That fifteen thousand meant a lot to guys. That was very important to us as players, to win and get the money."

Anderson and his historically large contract could have been an easy target for Lombardi in a fit of anger during practice, or games, but he kept the player-coach relationship clean: "Never. Never mentioned it, never in the times I was with the Packers and the three years he was around, never mentioned it." The temptation must have been there, especially in practice.

"Guys like Bob Skoronski and Zeke Bratkowski, all those guys have said practice was harder than the games. During practice you would make mistakes, because of the plays, and things you were trying to learn for the game plan. So, you would make mistakes and Vince would just, oh, he'd just wear you out. He had his special guys he wore out and the guys he didn't talk to. He had that carrot thing and the whip. I always called it the mule deal, with the whip and the carrot. He was a good physiologist, he knew guys to beat on, and he knew guys not to beat on. First meeting I was in, he chewed Hornung out so bad, and it was all because of me. It was my first meeting after the College All-Star game. Jimmy Taylor, he never chewed on, and never chewed on Grabowski. They had similar personalities, you know."

Lombardi drove his players to avoid mistakes and in one area Donny was terrific. In 387 punting attempts, he had just one blocked and it sticks in his mind, because mental mistakes were not tolerated. "Oh yeah, I remember it well. We were in LA in the season of Super Bowl II, which would have been '67, Super Bowl of '68. We had a down block and Tommy Joe Crutcher was the full back. He called "down" and lineman Steve Wright called it off. The guy came right up the middle. Steve went right. Everybody else went left, and nobody blocked the guy. It was a big punt block because the Rams ended up winning 28-27, something like that. We flew back on the plane, and everybody that was on that punt team, were as nervous as could be because it was blocked. I didn't see the guy, I caught the ball, and he was just open so quickly. Normally, I could run, or move around and get the ball off without having the punt blocked, but I had no way to do that. We finally found out what happened---the film doesn't lie."

The week previous, Green Bay played the Bears and Donny was accidentally kicked in the head sometime in the first quarter. The mild concussion affected his reaction time and provided Lombardi an ideal platform to whip his Golden Palomino. Donny explains what happened when he got in Lombardi's gun sights, "I played, which you can 'play on your feet.' I was just slow, and I was one of the faster guys on the team at that time. So, I would get off the ball slow. I remember the first quarter. I scored a touchdown and we were ahead, and then late in the fourth quarter, I'm back in the game. The rest of it's just foggy. Lord, Lord, he beat up on me the next week. He started the film with the offensive team: "Anderson, where are you?"

"Right here coach."

Lombardi said, "I'm gonna tell you something." And he could get up and holler. "I figured it out, you are mentally incompetent. Why in Heaven's name did we draft you in the first round and not realize that you were mentally incompetent as a player—as a person?"

" I'm sittin' there, and my old heads just down, as far as it could go. He said, "But, I figured it out." Now that's mild compared to what he hollered at people. He said, "Every time I say something to you I want you to have a pen and a piece of paper in your hand, 'cause I'm gonna make sure you write it down." He said, "You hear me?"

"Yes sir."

"Now I want you to have pen and paper every time we go to a meeting, every time we start the film, every time." He's screamin'.

Well, you know after awhile everybody in that room had been in that barrel. I used to call it, you were in the barrel. And he said, "Do you understand me?"

"Yes sir." Well I said "yes sir" about six times, which is what I was taught to say.

Finally he was so mad he said, "Well don't you know anything besides "yes sir?"

"No sir." Everybody just died laughing, they started laughing, and it was over. OK? But, those are the things Vince would do to get your attention."

"We broke the meeting. There were three doors in the old Packer deal where, to go to the locker room, you turn right, and you turn left to go to the weight room, so a lot of crowded area there. Vince is coming out and he hollers at Red Cochran, "Get me some coffee with some sugar." Jerry Kramer was coming around the corner and I was coming. I had my notebook for the meeting and Jerry said, "Did you get that down? Coffee with sugar." Lombardi died laughin'. It wasn't funny to me because I had been chewed out so bad."

Lombardi was a teacher by training, and as Willie Davis said, "he never missed an opportunity to make a difference." Donny only had Lombardi as coach for two years, but it was ample time to catch his fury and principles for life after football. "Vince would say, "Now you guys aren't going to be playing football forever, so pay attention here. This is what you guys are gonna be doing, life is so precious, this is about life and about what your gonna do when it's over."

"When we were playing, we didn't realize how fast our life was gonna be over in football. I remember so much about Lombardi talking about life after football; how you would become a citizen in America and blend in. To become a family man, to raise your kids, to have a job, do what American people do. He taught that way, he didn't teach just "X's" and "O's."

"He would take certain guys, he would beat you up *so* mentally, just wear you out where you just were as low as you could get. You never could understand why he would continually beat on you; beat on you to be better mentally. It wasn't about physical, it was about mental things.

"It's nice to go through the door and the coach pats you on the butt and say, "Man, I need a hundred yards from you today." Vince wasn't that kind of guy. But, you grow and you get mentally better. I carried that flag all my life. Most people I've run into in my life, in the last 40 something years, after being around Lombardi, I find people are not mentally tough like he taught us to be. They haven't been in the arena to be taught that. So, once I figured out they hadn't been in the arena to be mentally tough, then I learned to deal with it a lot easier. What I mean is, 'give me a break, don't be so hard on me,' all those things are a turn off to me. Because if someone in their life would get 'em over that hump they would be much stronger, and they would perform much better, and that's all we do in life I think. What are you gonna perform, what do you do in your life, what are you gonna be? That was the adjustment I found, but it was also a gift that Lombardi had given all of us."

Remember chemistry class? The teacher gives the theory then, it's off to lab to see if you really do get smoke when liquid from beaker "A" is poured into beaker "B"? Nine years of the former Chemistry teacher's theory was put to the ultimate test on a definitive stage under brutal conditions in The Ice Bowl. Theory became championship reality due in large part, to mental toughness, and discipline, when Lombardi's players and team applied his theory flawlessly down the stretch. Second year student Anderson said, "Well, I think Lombardi has to have a credit factor there. I think going back in his life with General Douglas MacArthur and his coach Red Blaik, all those people. He believed the mental side of it was how you win in the fourth quarter. You're in better shape and mentally you're tougher. So, did we win the Ice Bowl because of that? I think that was what Lombardi was all about. That's what he taught us. When we got in the huddle, and we had to go 68 yards for a touchdown, there wasn't anybody talking except Bart. It was about execution, execution, mentally execute, don't make mistakes."

There is a twinge of sadness in Donny's story. Two important men in his life seldom if ever, complemented him on his athletic accomplishments. Ironically, Lombardi's warmest comments to Anderson came after the team's coldest game. Donny says, "Well, he didn't say a lot of good things. I would say the turning point with my personal relationship with Vince Lombardi was the Ice Bowl. I played something like forty something games and Vince never gave me a complement, never. I was around my dad for 26 years, and he never gave me one either. I think by nature you would like someone to give you a complement, I think that would be nice. "Hey, you played good." My dad used to say, "You had a really good game, but I've seen you play better." It was kinda both ways. Vince was kinda that way, but he never did come up and say, "Hey, boy that was an unbelievable punt, or that was a great catch." Or something like that, or, "Good run on third down." He just very seldom ever got into that with the guys, I don't think that was his makeup, and I think it came from the military. I think it came from the hard nose of his life being in West Point, and that's what you do, it's hard, everyday it's hard. Right? You're teaching young boys to be men."

"But the one that hung with me, that carried on for my life, was after the Ice Bowl. He came up to me, sat down, which he only did that twice, he put his arm around me and said, "Today, you became a man. I'm proud of ya." Well, that's all you needed. I mean, my chest puffed up and I never forgot about it. I played football the rest of my career with a lot of enthusiasm and a lot of using my gift, instead of having doubts, or negatives that I couldn't do it, or wouldn't do it, or whatever. From that point on I played really well. So, I would say that was a pretty big complement."

The next year, 1968, Lombardi was general manager only. He had gotten his Donny Anderson complement out of the way and rode number 44's back some more. "Yea, he chewed me out all the time. If he'd catch me off by myself he'd say, "You ever gonna learn how to run that 47B, or you just gonna do it wrong?" He'd just chew me out. Obviously, he made me a better player because he was on my butt all the time. He picked (drafted) me and I was gonna be a player, so he didn't ever give up 'til, I guess the last day he left Green Bay to go to Washington."

Bottom line, Donny Anderson is grateful to have been touched by greatness and if given the chance to talk with Lombardi would say, "Well, I'd probably say something like, "Thank you for the gift to expand my life as a mentor." I think about Lombardi from time to time and I wonder would he be proud of me? You know, am I doin' OK? It's kind of a tough question you ask, but you think about Vince, and he oughta be really proud of a lot of guys. He helped us and helped us mature in a way that most people do not have that opportunity."

# Chapter 28
# Bob Jeter:

*"He offered me ten thousand more than what I was gonna ask for."*

# THE LOMBARDI LEGACY

Several of Vince Lombardi's outstanding defensive players were converted from offense. Willie Davis played offensive tackle for the Cleveland Browns, but defensive end in Green Bay. Linebacker Dave Robinson was a college All-American tight end and defensive end at Penn State. Three of Lombardi's defensive backs, two NFL Hall of Famers and one All-Pro, were outstanding offensive collegians. Free safety Willie Wood was a quarterback at Southern California, cornerback Herb Adderley played running back and corner at Michigan State. Lombardi put Bob Jeter from the University of Iowa, on the other corner. Bob was an outstanding college running back who rushed for a Rose Bowl record 194 yards, on just nine carries in 1959. Originally tried as a wide receiver in Green Bay, Jeter found himself deep on the depth chart behind Boyd Dowler, Max McGee and Bob Long. There was no room at halfback with Paul Hornung, Tom Moore and Elijah Pitts, so Lombardi moved him to right corner where he flourished.

NFL Films, in their "Greatest" series, selected the tandem of Bob Jeter and Herb Adderley as the fourth-best set of cornerbacks in NFL history. Both were moved from offense to defense by Lombardi, who evaluated talent with the eye of a jeweler.

Jeter was selected All-Pro in 1967, and inducted into the Green Bay Packer Hall of Fame in 1985. While patrolling the right corner for Green Bay, he recorded 23 interceptions and scored two touchdowns. From 1964-'68, the Packer defense led the league in fewest passing yards allowed and from 1965-'67 Green Bay sat atop the pro football world.

Bob Jeter explains his long trip from the University of Iowa to Green Bay, Wisconsin. "Well, I went to Canada because I didn't think I was gonna get drafted by Green Bay. I signed a three-year contract to go play ball up there, in Vancouver, British Columbia. Then, I find out the Packers drafted me in the second round, and they kept sending these guys down there, askin' me to sign. Back then you didn't have no agents. Shit, I didn't know nothin' about no doggone contracts or agents, I didn't want to talk to anybody. I said, "I already signed a contact to play football."

"Where? Where?"

"Up in Canada?"

"Well, why are you goin' up there?"

"I don't know; to see. I signed a three-year contract."

"I got up there and they had me playin' both ways. I said, "Wait a minute." I was on all the kicking teams--kickoffs, ran back kickoffs, ran back punts, I was on the punting team, I was a defensive back and I was a running back. I found out my running mate Willie Fleming, he was makin' about twenty grand more than I was making. All he did was just run the ball, and I said, "Oh, no. Hell no." I didn't have no doggone agent, but hell, I know I can count. I know the difference between dollar signs, so yeah, I demanded more money after my second year and they didn't want to hear it. I told them I was going to leave. They ended up trading me to the Hamilton Tiger-Cats.

"I was over there during their training camp, and I kept telling them, "I want more money." Oh, didn't nobody want to hear, so I left. 'Cause I'd found out that Pittsburgh was interested in me, and Pittsburgh was near my hometown. So I got down there and Coach Buddy Parker told me, "Well, Jeter,"--I never did practice with the Steelers—he said, "We can't do nothing with you."

"Why?"

"Well, Green Bay's still got your draft rights." He said, "Why don't you call Coach Lombardi—don't tell him where you are—just ask him what should you do?" Blah, blah, blah."

Lombardi was not going to let good talent slip away, so he pounced on the chance to get Jeter.

"I called Coach Lombardi--first thing came out of his mouth, *"What the hell you doin' in Pittsburgh?"* I didn't think he knew where I was. And he said, "Well, I'll tell you what. There'll be a plane ticket waiting for you at Pittsburgh airport," the next day. So I went to Green Bay and Willie Wood met me at the airport. He said, *"what the hell were you doin' in Pittsburgh?"* I said, 'How in the hell did *you* know?' That's when I met Wood, and I told Willie what had happened and Coach Lombardi signed me to a three-year contract."

There was no caller ID in 1963, so how *did* Lombardi know he was there?

"I have no idea to this day. Nobody told me anything."

Consistently, Packer players encountered basically the same thing racially with Vince Lombardi, no issue.

"Yeah, you know, I had no problem with Coach Lombardi. He was fair. He treated everybody the same way. He had no preferences, whether you were black, white, or whatever--none. And that's one thing I noticed about him when I first went there. I think that's why he was successful, there in Green Bay, 'cause there wasn't too much in Green Bay at that time, you know."

Jeter's athletic ability, combined with Green Bay's glut of talent at wide receiver, and running back, offered Lombardi options. Bob tells how he became an NFL cornerback, "I played both ways in college. Played both ways up in Canada, and Coach Lombardi had me as a running back, my first year down, 'cause I had to sit out a year, because I was still under contract up in Canada. But when I got finished with the offense in practice, I went over there on defense, and played on the corner, played behind Jess Whittenton and those guys. I guess he thought, "Well, Jesse Whittenton's going to retire, we'll put him in back, there in the cornerback, and that's what happened, that's how I ended up. I was a wide receiver, I played behind Boyd Dowler and Max McGee. I would go on defense, and cover the same guys I was playing with on offense, it wasn't no big thing to me, all I wanted to do is just play football. He happened to see the talent I had."

Not all contract negotiations were high drama, bullet sweating events involving Lombardi. They were a breeze for Bob Jeter, "I never had any

# BOB JETER

problems with him. I said, "Well, this is what I'm going to ask for." Because like I said, I didn't have no agent, or nothin' like that. I went in there and got ready to sit down, and I thought, 'Oh, shit, I'm probably gonna have a problem.' He offered me *ten thousand* more than what I was gonna ask for, per year. I went on and signed the contract to play. I guess he knew I could play both ways if he ever needed me. My first two years with the Packers, I was a wide out--wide receiver. Like I said, I played with Dowler, McGee and Carroll Dale, so playing behind those guys and running offensive plays, I had a feeling when he put me on defense, what to look for, how to react, look at certain situations and stuff like that. So, it was no big thing."

If Bob would not have played in Canada, and if he would have been put at cornerback right away in Green Bay, he may have had a shot at being enshrined in the big Hall of Fame in Canton, Ohio.

# CHAPTER 29
## BOB LONG:

*"I'm the only guy to play actively in both places."*

# THE LOMBARDI LEGACY

Tall and fast with "basketball hands," Bob Long joined the Packers in 1964, following a very good basketball ball career at Wichita State. In Bob's senior year of 1963, the Wichita Shockers defeated two-time and defending NCAA champion Cincinnati, to end the number one ranked Bearcat's 37 game winning streak.

His Green Bay experience was the epitome of good news/bad news. Good news: Having played just one year of college football he joined the powerful Packers who would win three World Championships, in his four years. He was with Green Bay from 1964-1967. Off the field, Bob was one of the first, and most successful Pizza Hut owners. His initial franchise was located about a mile from Lambeau Field, on Highland Avenue, later renamed Lombardi Avenue.

Bad news: Boyd Dowler, Max McGee and beginning in 1965, Carroll Dale were Lombardi's trusted veteran receivers making it difficult for Bob to get playing time.

Following his trade from the Packers, he was enjoying an outstanding season with the Atlanta Falcons in 1968 when a head on traffic accident nearly ended his life and career. Despite serious injuries, Bob returned to football playing for Lombardi and the Redskins in '69 before ending his career with the Rams in 1970.

Only one person played in regular season games for Vince Lombardi in both Green Bay and Washington; Bob Long. He made a terrific comeback by catching 48 passes with those basketball hands.

Following a successful business career, Bob enjoys retirement in Brookfield, Wisconsin with his wife Joan.

Bob Long's introduction to football was curious to say the least, "I played intramural football at Wichita. I still hold the record - kind of funny – of scoring seven touchdown passes in one game of intramural football. I guess one of the football coaches was watching that game. 1963, I was asked by an assistant coach at Wichita to come out for the football team; they needed a split end. They didn't want me to get hurt learning and they said, "Long, we don't want you to block." At Wichita, I never blocked. They said, "We don't want you to get hurt. Run an experimental pattern where you don't hit anybody and nobody can hit you, and you won't get hurt."

"Yeah, I like this deal. This is almost like flag football."

Despite playing just one year of collegiate ball, he drew interest from the pros, "There were two leagues and all at once I was drafted number nine by the San Diego Chargers of the AFL. I went out to San Diego; that's when they had Sid Gilman as coach. I went out to practice one day; I'm sitting there with a friend of mine on the bleachers. I'm watching this receiver from the San Diego Chargers bouncing all over like a deer, and I said, 'That kid's pretty good, how old is he?' And the guy beside me said, "Oh, that's our new receiver, Lance Alworth, 24 years old."

I said, "Really? It might be difficult to beat out Lance Alworth"

So, I came back to Wichita, I called up Pat Peppler of the Packers, I said, "Pat, send me a program." He asked, "A program? Why do you want a program?"

"I'll tell you later."

"I got the program a few days later. I wanted to see the ages of the receivers, right? I see, Max McGee, 30, Boyd Dowler, 29, I said, 'That's the place for me, and if I'm not gonna make it, at least I can tell my grandkids I went to Vince Lombardi's training camp.' So, a week before the Green Bay training camp in '64, when I was a rookie, I went in to see my college football coach and asked, "Coach, I have an interesting question – am I going to have to block in Green Bay?" Because I didn't know how to block – I didn't block at Wichita. He looked up at me and he says, "Ray Nitschke is waitin' for ya." I said, "Uh-oh. I'm in deep trouble."

"Lombardi had a famous drill called the 'Nutcracker drill.' He'd go up in the top tower and they'd film it. The offensive guys had to block the defensive guys. And in our case, the offensive receivers had to block the linebackers.

# THE LOMBARDI LEGACY

Here I am with Max McGee and Boyd Dowler, they didn't like to block. I'm sure they could block better than I could. One day, I'm a rookie standing in line, and Max McGee's in front of me, and Max McGee's pretty funny; he started counting off, "Dave Robinson, Lee Roy Caffey, Ray Nitschke." He says, "I'm number three, I'm gonna have to face Nitschke. Well, I don't want to block Nitschke, he's gonna kill me." He reached back and he grabbed me by shirt and says, "Rookie, get up here." He wanted me to block Nitschke. Well, I got absolutely killed. I got killed trying, but I found out later, Lombardi knew that his wide receivers couldn't block very well. But, he just wanted to know that you had some courage that you'd put your head in there, which I did; I almost got my teeth knocked out. But that's what I discovered later, it was a test of courage, according to what Vince Lombardi wanted. He really wasn't too worried about technique, and how well you could block, he just wanted to see if you could withstand a blow to the head and had a little courage."

Bob did not have a solid indication who, if anybody, would draft him. "The night before the NFL draft, I'm in my apartment at Wichita, Kansas, I get a long distance phone call. Guess what? I picked up the phone, and the person on the other side of the line said, "Bob Long, this is Coach Vince Lombardi from the Green Bay Packers." Now you can imagine what that did for a young kid, 21 years old. I'm thinking to myself, "Vince Lombardi – why is he calling me?"

He said to me, "We're thinking about drafting you tomorrow," which was a shocker, because no one had even talked to me about the Packers. And he says, "If we draft you tomorrow, would you sign with us?"

I said, "Sure, coach, I'll sign with you. I'll sign with you tomorrow, don't worry about it."

The next day I was in a classroom - I was dating this girl, and the door was open to the classroom, she was waving outside the classroom door, asking me to come out of the classroom. I walked out and she said, "The Green

Bay Packers just drafted you fourth." No one expected it to happen. There hadn't been any rumors, nothing. The Dallas Cowboys were scouting me; the Cowboys, the Rams. In those days, they would take a player to a motel and hide 'em. They'd hide you in a room so that someone else wouldn't get to you. I was 'hid out' by the Cowboys and the Rams, during the draft, but they didn't draft me, Green Bay drafted me before they could. That's how it all came together."

The AFL-NFL bidding war hadn't driven up salaries by 1963, at least not for fourth round draft choices out of Wichita State. "I made eleven-five. One-year contract - wasn't guaranteed, of course. They did give me a three thousand dollar bonus, which was a lot for a college kid from Wichita, and I bought a car with it – my first car ever - so I could drive to Green Bay, and feel like an adult.

"If I had come to the Packers in '64, and someone would have told me, "Bob, we have a brand new team, a brand new stadium and we're not financially stable right now, so we can pay your rent, your expenses, your food, your utilities, but we can't pay you a salary," I'd have said, (rising from his seat) "Where's the contract?" I mean I'd have played for nothing. I think other guys would have played for nothing. Can you imagine the thrill which happened to me in '65, of being in the starting backfield with three Hall of Famers: Bart Starr, Jimmy Taylor, Paul Hornung and myself? I mean, it doesn't get any better than that.

"You had to negotiate with Lombardi by yourself; you didn't dare bring any agents, of course, and negotiating a contract with Vince Lombardi was kind of intimidating. He could growl and frown at you and things like that. You knew he wasn't very happy; he wasn't going to give you more money. And he always used to tell you in negotiations, "Around here, we count the playoffs in your salary. You made fifteen thousand from the Super Bowl." I doubled my salary. If I made ($13,500), or ($14,500), or whatever with the Packers, he made me count the playoff money as part of your remuneration;

the total amount. And that was part of the way he negotiated.

"My big year was in 1965, that was when Boyd Dowler was hurt a lot. If you remember, we won the NFL Championship. I went in to negotiate my '66 salary with Lombardi and he said to me, "Well young fellow, what kind of year did you have?"

"Coach, every game I started—every game in '65 – guess what, I scored a touchdown. Coach, every game I started, we won. Every game I started. That's pretty good, right? And guess what, Coach, we won the NFL Championship. So, I think I was really an asset to the team."

"Well, quit dancing around the issue. How much of a raise do you think you deserve?"

"Coach, considering I think I was underpaid a little bit at ($11,500), I think I deserved at least a two thousand dollar raise to $13,500." I swear this is the truth. He looked at me with a scowl on his face, "Well, young guys make mistakes."

"Coach, if I'd made mistakes, I wouldn't be here. You don't keep guys who make mistakes."

"Well, most young guys make mistakes," or something like that. He says, "How much of a raise do you think you deserve?"

"Considering I only made eleven-five, I think I deserve a two thousands-dollar raise to thirteen-five."

"Well, I'm gonna give you a one thousand dollars raise. However, if you want a two thousand dollar raise, I think New Orleans will pay it to you on Monday." In other words, if you don't accept, I'm going to trade you on Monday. I said, 'Well, considering everything, I think I'll keep the one thousand.' That's how it was; that's how he negotiated."

Bob was on a collision course with fame in Super Bowl I when Lombardi's philosophy got in the way, "Well one thing about Coach Lombardi; he loved his veterans – he loved them. I was playing behind Boyd Dowler. Boyd got hurt in that first series of plays. I was thinking, (rubbing hands together and

# BOB LONG

grinning) "All right, here's my chance to go in and replace Boyd Dowler, and my buddies in Pennsylvania can see me play on national TV, and I might turn into a superstar, playing in the first Super Bowl game of all time." In typical Lombardi style, he called out, "McGee!" Well, McGee wasn't playing all year; wasn't supposed to play in this game, he had been out all night chasing girls, or whatever they were doing, his eyes were bloodshot, he had forgot his helmet in the locker room, so when Lombardi yelled out, "Mc Gee, replace Dowler," I was shattered.

"I said, "Oh, man, how could he?" I played behind Boyd Dowler, how could he pick out McGee? What I'm saying is he loved his veterans, he had this thing about, veterans don't make mistakes, and young guys do. I was younger then, and he thought maybe I'd make mistakes, or for whatever reason, he called for McGee to go in. Max couldn't find his helmet. He had left it in the locker room. So I said, "McGee, take my helmet." So when they show all these pictures of Max McGee scoring – catching that touchdown pass, he had my helmet on."

In the mid '60's, professional sports teams encouraged their players to enlist in the National Guard in order to serve a six month hitch, rather than be drafted for the Viet Nam War, and serve a minimum of two years. Long explains, "The Packers were like everybody else; they got us in the National Guard. Three of us, Jim Grabowski, Phil Vandersea and myself, they put us in the Green Bay National Guard, and Donny Anderson, they put him in the Oshkosh National Guard. When you're in the National Guard you still had to do basic training, one meeting a month, two weeks active duty in the summer time at Camp McCoy here in Wisconsin, but before anything, you had to do six months of basic training. They sent Jim Grabowski, Phil and I to Fort Leonard Wood, Missouri. Fort Leonard Wood was not a pretty place. Grabowski, Vandersea and I were down there and we're trying to get through the six months, because we couldn't make any money, it was drudgery work. Lombardi's training camp was a lot worse than this training camp; it was almost boring because we were in pretty good physical shape from playing pro football. We were down there from February to July."

"When they released us from Fort Leonard Wood, I think the Packers flew a plane in. They flew us directly to the Packers training camp at St. Norbert's in Green Bay. Essentially, the entire years of '66 and '67, I spent in basic training, and playing football for Lombardi. I didn't have much of a vacation."

Several longtime players retired following the '67 season, when the club won its final championship, and Lombardi retired as head coach. The departure of Max McGee seemingly opened more playing time for Long. "Phil Bengtson traded me to Atlanta in '68, not Lombardi, Phil Bengtson traded me. Pat Peppler gave me the news in Green Bay, it was on Labor Day, Peppler called me up and he says, "Bob, come to Lambeau Field and bring your playbook." Well, when they tell you to bring your playbook, you're gone; you know you've been traded. I walked into the office, I said, "Pat, where am I going?" He says, "Atlanta.""

I said, "I don't want to go to Atlanta, I've never been there. I like it up here, I've had a great four years, I have friends up here. I'm starting my Pizza Hut business down the street, how am I gonna run the Pizza Hut from Atlanta?"

"I don't know, that's your problem," he said.

Bob did not have the problem of getting to know the Falcons, head coach. "Unbeknown to me, the coach of the Atlanta Falcons was Norb Hecker, who had been the defensive backfield coach in Green Bay. If anybody knew me at Green Bay, how I did against his defensive backs, it was Norb Hecker. I was probably one of the greatest practice players they ever had. It was hard for me to get into the game because Lombardi loved his veterans, but Norb Hecker knew I was a fairly good player. About six or eight games into the season, Norb Hecker gets fired. Guess who replaces Norb Hecker? 'Stormin' Norman' Van Brocklin. He could curse with the best of them. I was Van Brocklin's best player in Atlanta, by far. Norm Van Brocklin had been the head coach with the Minnesota Vikings and Minnesota would play Green Bay in the early '60's, the Packers would always beat 'em. Lombardi would always beat'em. I scored a touchdown one year against them when Van Brocklin was coach, so anybody who played for Green Bay, Van Brocklin hated. He hated Lombardi 'cause Lombardi used to beat him all the time. So, even though I was Van Brocklin's best player, we had kind of a tentative relationship. I didn't like cursing, which he did all the time. I didn't like the things he said. I just didn't respect him very much and I guess it was a two way street.

"For example, in the first week he was down there as coach, I ran a pass pattern in practice against Ken Reeves the great cornerback for the Atlanta Falcons. I blew off Ken Reeves, I caught the ball, I was wide open. Here comes Van Brocklin out there yelling at me, shaking his finger, cursing at me. He was hollering, "Your Lombardi's pet, your Lombardi's pet." I'm stunned, I've never been called Lombardi's pet before. That's the nickname he gave me. The only thing I could think to say was, "Thank you Coach, that's a complement."

"Well, you don't say that to Norm Van Brocklin. He threw me out of practice for four days, "Get off this field, get out of practice, I don't want you to come back for four days." This was like Tuesday, I wasn't allowed on the practice field until Saturday, but he wanted me back before the game on Sunday 'cause I was his best player. Can you imagine that?

"I wrote a letter to Vince Lombardi on Atlanta Falcon stationary, and told him I didn't like Van Brocklin and his cursing and drinking, he used to drink a lot too. After you play for Vince Lombardi for four years, you don't want to put up with that stuff.

So I wrote him a letter and a couple weeks later I have my car wreck in Atlanta. The other guy was killed, he hit me head on. I broke my back, lost a kidney and a whole bunch of other stuff. So, I was gonna retire. I had just started to build Pizza Huts in Northern Wisconsin; I knew I could make more money from pizza than I could playing pro football. I was hurting a lot, I still had a lot of pain and I couldn't run as fast.

"I went to training camp with the Atlanta Falcons in 1969 at East Johnson City, Tennessee. We were in camp and Van Brocklin was all over me. He had no empathy or sympathy at all. Van Brocklin was that type of person, he didn't care.

"In the middle of training camp, a friend of mine who had been my Pizza Hut manager in Green Bay, called me and said, "Bob, they discovered a big tumor in my stomach. They don't give me long to live." He was at a hospital in Philadelphia. He said, "I'd like to see you one time before.

"So, I went to see Norm Van Brocklin and I said, "Coach, my very good friend from college, he runs my Pizza Hut, he may have terminal cancer. I'd like to get three days off and fly up to Philadelphia to see him one last time." In typical Van Brocklin style he said, "absolutely not, I'm not gonna let you leave our training camp." A day later I walked in and said, "Coach, I'm leaving, I'm retiring." I walked out of training camp in '69 with the Atlanta Falcons."

Lombardi was in Washington at that time molding the Redskins into his vision of excellence. Just because Van Brocklin didn't like Lombardi didn't mean he wouldn't do business with him. Norm "The Dutchman" had called Washington to let them know Long was available. Bob said, "By the time I drove from East Johnson City, Tennessee down to Atlanta, I had a call.

"Bob Long?"

"Yes."

"This is Coach Vince Lombardi."

"Hi Coach, how ya doing?"

"Well, I'm calling to see how your doing."

"Well, I'm OK Coach, I mean I can still run, but I can't run as fast as I used to in Green Bay, I lost a little speed in my car wreck. I've decided to retire because I don't want to get beat up any more. When I catch a pass now it really hurts when someone hits me in the back, I had a broken back, it has healed, but it still hurts. I would never play for Van Brocklin again.

Lombardi told Long, "Bob, I need a flanker. Bobby Mitchell's retiring; I need a flanker to replace Bobby Mitchell."

"Coach I can't run as fast, I don't have the quickness I had in Green Bay."

"You still have those basketball hands don't you?"

"Yeah, I still got the basketball hands, I didn't lose the hands."

"You still know my system don't ya?"

"I still know your system."

"That's all I want, I don't need speed anymore, we've got Charlie Taylor, our great split end, and he has great speed. We have Jerry Smith at tight end. I need someone who can catch the ball; I want you to be my starting flanker."

"I said back to him, "Coach, listen, when I was in Green Bay we had four great receivers, Max McGee, Boyd Dowler, Carroll Dale and myself. Every time I played, I did pretty well; I did great, I'd score a touchdown, we'd win or whatever, and you'd still go back to the other guys. It was hard for me to sit on the bench. When I came to Atlanta, they started me every game. I'm a starter; I did pretty well in Atlanta. I was averaging over 22 yards a catch with the Atlanta Falcons; that's pretty good Coach." I said, "I don't want to sit on your bench anymore. I had four years of it, I was willing to do that for the team concept, to win the Super Bowls and stuff like that, I fit in perfectly, I was a good asset. I could replace Boyd Dowler, or whoever. If I don't start, I'm not gonna play, I'm gonna retire. If I come to Washington for you and you sit me on your bench, I'm leaving."

"Well, your not gonna sit, your gonna be my starting flanker."

"Coach, as long as we know if you sit me on the bench, I'm retiring immediately, I'm gone. I'm going back to Wisconsin and run my business."

"Bob, I promise you, you won't sit, you'll be my starting flanker."

In 1963, when Gary Knafelc wanted Lombardi to guarantee he would play him in three games, the coach blew up. He was changing with the times according to Long, "He knew what I could do; he knew I didn't make mental mistakes. I played for Lombardi both in Green Bay and Washington. I'm the only guy ever to be active, Chuck Mercein and Tom Brown were on the injured reserve, or taxie squad, but I'm the only guy to play actively in both places, I'm kinda proud of that."

Bob had a good year in Washington, catching 48 balls, one more than he had in his previous five years in the NFL. "Thank you, that's because I wasn't getting the chance to catch more in Green Bay, it was tough to get playing time."

Bob Long is a very nice man, but apparently even nice guys like revenge, "To tell you about Lombardi, the '69 Redskins played the Atlanta Falcons, my old team. I remember specifically, that day I caught 10 passes, the most passes I had ever caught. That was a lot of passes in the '60's. I caught 10 in one day; in fact they gave me the game ball. We beat the Falcons, 27-20. I caught 8 of the 10 right in front of Van Brocklin. It was like Lombardi had told quarterback Sonny Jorgensen, "Throw 10 quick outs to the Atlanta Falcon's sideline so Bob can catch the passes in front of Van Brocklin." I don't know if that's what happened or not; I've heard people suggest that to me, but who knows."

What the Redskins would have done under Lombardi is open to speculation, but he was a gigantic figure in the nation's capital as Bob explains, "I remember in '69, Lombardi was coming down one side of the street in the Georgetown District; it was like he had an entourage, hundreds of people following Lombardi down the street. President Nixon was on the other side of the street, there was hardly anybody. Lombardi was more popular than President Nixon. This is a fact, I mean, that's how popular he was."

From a football standpoint, Long saw some differences in his coach, "What I noticed, he wasn't quite as tough in D.C., as he was in Green Bay. Jerry Smith, our All-Pro tight end had long hair. He would never have put up with long hair in Green Bay, never. His rules were a little different and little easier in D.C. I think he realized it was a bigger city than Green Bay, it was East Coast. However, what he did do, he told the same kind of stories he told in Green Bay." Bob refers to the hallmark of Vince Lombardi, motivational speeches. Long said, "He asked me before the season started, "You won't get tired of my stories will you?" I said, "Of course I won't." I was closer to him in D.C. than I was in Green Bay."

According to Long, Lombardi delegated more coaching assignments in Washington. "He did more coaching in Green Bay, he didn't do much of that at all in Washington, he left that up to the assistants. In my opinion, he was so happy to get back into coaching. I think the year he sat out he missed it, he realized he missed it." Long believes that Lombardi's long time dream of being part owner of a team made a difference, "That's what he wanted, he got that, I think that kind of settled him down. I know Marie was very happy out there; first of all she was closer to New Jersey where she's from. That's a pretty good guess on my part." It's the old adage, if the wife is happy the Head Coach, General Manager, and part owner is happy.

As former Publicity Director, Chuck Lane, mentioned in chapter 25 of this book, Lombardi rode rough shod over the Wisconsin press corps. Long saw a difference in the nation's capital, "I think he was more cautious out there, I did not see him be real amenable to the media at all." It's important to remember the stinging experience the Old Man experienced with Esquire magazine writer Leonard Schecter in 1967."

As general manager in Washington, he was doing a great job of putting players where they needed to be. Bob gives his observations, "He was rebuilding the team, and they hadn't won in 14 years. Lombardi went 7-5-2 in his first and only year." How eerie, his first Packer team was 7-5. "That will tell you, he did the same stuff for both teams. He had this innate ability to put personnel in the right position. Let me tell you about the Redskins and Mike Bass. Mike had been in the Packer camp, but with the tremendous talent, he could not crack the roster. Lombardi had so many great players on that team; it was tough to make that team, he might keep two or three new players a year. Mike Bass in Green Bay was let go in the final cut. Lombardi cut him, it killed him, he said at that time, "Mike Bass is gonna play some place in the NFL." Two years later, Mike Bass is playing cornerback for the Washington Redskins. Little Pat Fischer became an All-Pro cornerback for him."

"How about Brig Owens the great safety for the Washington Redskins? He was a quarterback at the University of Cincinnati. Two college quarterbacks, Willie Wood and Brig Owens, and he turned them both into safeties. He had that ability, if I were to say who is the greatest judge of talent I've been around, he was for sure."

The most famous personnel incident in Washington involved marginal running back Larry Brown who was selected in the eighth round of the 1969 draft. He had good ability, but got off the ball slow. Lombardi, the master of details, had Brown's hearing checked and discovered he was virtually deaf in one ear. With special permission from the league, a hearing aid was installed in Brown's helmet, allowing him to move on the quarterback's signals, rather than looking for movement before starting the play. Larry Brown became an All-Pro and league MVP.

In late June of 1970, Lombardi was diagnosed with a very aggressive form of colon cancer, but word was kept relatively quite. One of his former Green Bay players, Lew Carpenter was an assistant coach on the Washington staff and explains how the news was broken to him and his colleagues, "We didn't have any idea until he called us out to his house the day before we went to training camp. He said, "Well I'm not going to be going with you, but you go ahead and get things started; I'll be out there later." At that time he looked good, but he really went down quick. About a month later, just before the first preseason game, I saw him again and he really lost a lot of weight from the time we saw him thirty days (prior)." Vince Lombardi drew his final breath on September 3, 1970.

# CHAPTER 30
# GERALD "DAD" BRAISHER:

*Whenever you see the Green Bay Packer logo, the "G" on the helmet, you're looking at Dad.*

# THE LOMBARDI LEGACY

If a vote would have been taken to select the most liked person within the Packer organization during the "Glory Years," Equipment Manager Gerald "Dad" Braisher would have won it hands down. He had the demeanor you would want in your father, best friend or school teacher. He was one of the very few people Lombardi never yelled at. Paul Hornung said, "He was loved; there isn't one player that didn't like Dad. He just took care of everybody. You needed something, you got it."

Lombardi was superstitious and found comfort in the familiar. He was a New York Giants assistant coach for five years and saw the team logo of "NY" on the helmets. After two years in Green Bay, apparently he wanted something for his Packers, and rumor has it he wanted a "GB." It is not totally known if it was Dad's decision, or Lombardi asked him to design a logo. Based on indictors, General Manager Lombardi wanted something on his team's helmets. It was in his room at the Union Hotel that Dad Braisher gave birth to the famous Packer "G."

The Union Hotel is a landmark in De Pere, Wisconsin. It is famous, quaint and old with an atmosphere that engulfs patrons with a sense of well being upon entry. Originally purchased by the Boyd family in 1918, it remains owned and operated by the descendants.

McKim Boyd, one of the family members explains Braisher's relationship with the facility: "He lived in an apartment in De Pere that was destroyed by fire. Dad needed a place to live so he took a room here at the Union Hotel." He checked out of room number 17 forty years later.

Braisher was the same person every day. He was always happy, mild, stable and comforting. He and the Union Hotel had a lot in common. Boyd says, "Braisher would just be sitting up in his room tinkering around, trying to design this thing. He must have had something in his head. My dad locked up the hotel six nights a week and 'Brais' would come down, have a drink and just visit at the bar a little bit. He would bring this down and ask my dad what he thought. My dad said, "What was I supposed to say? Yeah, it looks great, whatever you're trying to do." Dad Braisher told him he was trying to fit a 'G' inside a football, which is what the shape is, the shape of a football.

"My dad, Jim Boyd, was concerned that Braisher wasn't given proper credit for the design, so my dad actually had it placed on Braisher's tombstone."

Dad had an outstanding high school and college athletic career, in which he was State of Wisconsin champion in the 100 yard dash. As a football player he wore number 5. Hornung, says, "He was the original number 5, he wore number 5 in high school and college. I think that's why he liked me and I tried to take care of Dad." Many players would stop by the Union Hotel to see Dad long after their playing days were over. Whenever you see the Green Bay Packer logo, the "G" on the helmet, you're looking at Dad.

Some Packer players who participated in both the Ice Bowl and the 1962 Championship game in New York say the '62 game was more brutal from a weather stand point. A cruel wind off the ocean made for miserable conditions at Yankee Stadium. Those were the days before a 'wind chill index' was developed, so players didn't scientifically know how miserable they felt.

The field's texture was that of broken glass because of the icy covering. Dad Braisher anticipated extremely poor footing for the game and took the initiative to address the problem. Using a small sharp tool, like a pin knife, he stayed up most of the night before the game cutting channels in the rippled shoes to be worn by the Packers. Not only did the shoes prove beneficial in the game, they are a prominent part of Packer history and on display in the team's Hall of Fame.

The unassuming Braisher had a personality as consistent and predictable as Lombardi's winning. Following practice one day in the Packer locker room, some players were talking about investments they had in the stock market. According to Dave Robinson, "Dad said, "I bought some stock years ago in a little mining company. I wonder if it's worth anything?"

Robby recalls, "Fuzzy Thurston had his broker check on the stock. Come to find out, Dad had been a ground floor investor in a company known as

# The Lombardi Legacy

Minnesota Mining and Manufacturing; better known as 3M."

Dad Braisher remained the same guy in the same room at the Union Hotel after becoming a millionaire.

# CONCLUSION

# THE LOMBARDI LEGACY

When colon cancer cut Vince Lombardi's life short at age 57, he was molding the Washington Redskins into a replica of his Packer organization. As general manager he was doing the same things he had done in Green Bay, with the same results. He was a superstitious creature of habit; therefore if something worked he did it until it failed. As he said, "I've never been associated with a loser and I don't intend to start now." He went to his grave as the NFL's ultimate winner.

His first year in Green Bay was 1959, in Washington, 1969. His first year records were virtually the same. His Packers went 7-5, the Redskins 7-5-2. Image changes for his new club were being made; he replaced the Native American logo with an "R" on each side of the Redskins helmets, similar to the "G" in Green Bay, similar to the "NY" that was the helmet emblem for the Giants when he was an assistant coach in New York. He made Washington's uniforms mirror those of the Packers. Gold piping on uniform sleeves and socks, a letter on the helmet, and numerals that matched those of Green Bay made the two teams attire nearly identical except for color.

His great football mind was putting better players in those uniforms and getting more out of the ones he inherited, just as he had done Green Bay. Lombardi was turning the Redskins into a winner as they finished second in their division in his first and only season at the helm of the football operation. It was Lombardi's foundation that helped George Allan succeed during the 1970's when he took over the 'Skins in 1971. Unfortunately Vince Lombardi was taken from us on September 3, 1970.

He is remembered as a coach but also as a national treasure who was not afraid to win and say winning was *the* goal. He was the only general manager in modern time to win three consecutive NFL championships, but was also an ethical social reformer especially in the area of advancement for blacks. Professional sports, perhaps our entire nation, has not seen the likes of Vince Lombardi and probably will not. We can only cherish the memories and live his lessons as proud Americans, as winning Americans. If only he could

# CONCLUSION

coach our politicians.

Following the only championship game his teams did not win, 1960 against the Philadelphia Eagles, Lombardi said his Packers did not lose, they just ran out of time. While in our nation's capital attempting to resurrect another football franchise he just ran out of time and we all lost.

# AFTERWARD
## BY BOB HARLAN

# THE LOMBARDI LEGACY

The Green Bay Packers were a franchise in terrible shape when Vince Lombardi took over in 1959. I was a student at Marquette University in the 1950's and when the Packers won in those days, it was a shock. So, he had a *huge rebuilding job* when he got to town and he did it so fast. He had some good material, but he made players who were here much, much better.

It was probably the most remarkable turn around in the history of *any* sport; to go out a win five championships. He really put Green Bay back on the map.

He was a huge influence on the National Football League, which is evidenced by the fact the Super Bowl Trophy is named after Vince Lombardi. I think it shows the impact he had not only on the NFL, but on the country as a whole. He was a winner and people admired the way he won.

He created a great image for the State of Wisconsin, the City of Green Bay and the Packers. I think that was a huge contribution.

When I had the good fortune to be named President and CEO of the Packers in 1989, we were coming off some terrible years, similar to what the franchise experienced thirty years prior. The 1970's and '80's had not been very kind to the Green Bay Packers. We only had four winning years and two playoff appearances in those decades. Our number one priority was to find a way to win again. I kept hearing from fans, and they still loved us, but they were losing hope. I actually had some fans tell me, "We will never win another championship. The last great era this franchise is ever going to have is the Lombardi era."

I wanted to get the franchise back among the elite teams in the league and I thought we needed to do what the Packers had done in 1959. Lombardi demanded full authority over the football operation when he got here. The organization gave it to him and the rest is history.

When I started as President in 1989, I decided if we were going to get back to the glory days, I needed to find a very strong football person, give him total authority over the football operation and get out of his way and let

# AFTERWARD

him do his job. The perfect person turned out to be Ron Wolf. The method we used was similar to what the organization had done by giving Vince full authority in 1959. I gave Ron Wolf full authority in 1991.

In the next twenty years we had sixteen winning seasons, won the division seven times, went to the playoffs eleven times and went back to two Super Bowls. We won a Super Bowl and brought the Vince Lombardi Trophy back to the State of Wisconsin for the first time in 29 years.

Ron Wolf was a tough, tough football person who demanded the best. I think there were similarities in the personalities between him and Lombardi and the way they ran their football operation. I could not have gotten Ron if I had not promised him full authority.

The history and tradition of this franchise has great appeal. The Green Bay Packer organization holds a fascination that both Vince Lombardi and Curly Lambeau helped create by making winning an expectation. Ron Wolf used to make the statement, "If I walked a player down the ramp onto the field, and he looked at names on the bowl of the stadium; if he didn't get goose bumps, he shouldn't be a Green Bay Packer."

The story of the Green Bay Packers is the greatest story in sports. When you really think about it, there are not many good-will stories in this world today. I think the story of the Green Bay Packers is an exception. It's wonderful and it's true.

Congratulations to Dave Robinson and Royce Boyles for writing *The Lombardi Legacy*. It is a tremendous look at Vince Lombardi and many of those who were "Touched by Greatness."

**Bob Harlan**
**Chairman Emeritus, Green Bay Packers**

# *To those few who were fortunate to be touched by greatness:*

....and if by chance

Random are those things and events that have no reason and many times no organization or purpose. Most things however, are designed with reason, organization and for purpose. For both the daring and timid, those events produce opportunities.

Design, of both the tangible and intangible, is God's direct involvement in our daily lives. This silent, invisible labor on our behalf is many times credited to coincidence.

Is it by chance that a star stays in its assigned place? The delicate balance of our existence continues? The eye, mostly water, can some how take light and image through tissue and cords to give accurate images we understand. That is random?

Meetings, encounters and relationships. Random?

And if by chance He offered a gift, it was not by chance at all. Reason and purpose may be unknown. If by choice this gift is cherished and tended, its meaning will be discovered and its designer revealed.

If by choice this gift is neglected, the designer remains and the recipients lesser by default.

And if by chance you choose to nurture this gift, your heart will embrace and explore while giving thanks for the treasure.

**Royce Boyles**